HIZZY

THE AUTOBIOGRAPHY OF
STEVE HISLOP 1962–2003

HIZZY

with STUART BARKER

CollinsWillow

An Imprint of HarperCollins*Publishers*

First published in Great Britain in 2003
by CollinsWillow
an imprint of HarperCollins*Publishers* London

This paperback edition first published in 2004

The HarperCollins website address is:
www.harpercollins.co.uk

ISBN 0-00-715641-3

Typeset by Rowland Phototypesetting Ltd,
Bury St Edmunds, Suffolk
Printed and bound in Great Britain
by Clays Ltd, St Ives plc

PICTURE ACKNOWLEDGEMENTS

All photographs supplied by the author with the exception of the
following: **Belfast Telegraph** p.3 (centre); **DPPI** p.13 (bottom); **EMAP
Automotive** p.5 (centre), p.9 (bottom); p.12 (centre), p.14 (centre), p.15
(bottom); **Gold & Goose** p.9 (centre); **Island Photographic** p.6 (top);
Tim Keeton Photography p.4 (top); **G.V. Kneale** p.2 (centre left);
Mac McDiarmid p.8 (top); **Don Morley** p.3 (bottom), p.4 (bottom), p.6
(centre), p.7 (all); **Original Double Red Ltd** p.6 (bottom), p.8 (bottom),
p.9 (top), p.10 top and centre), p.11 (top and centre), p.12 (top and bottom),
p.13 (top and centre), p.14 (top and bottom), p.15 (top), p.16 (top);
Pacemaker p.4 (centre), p.5 (bottom); **Pacemaker/Stephen Davison** p.15
(center); **Val Watt** p.16 (bottom left).

**For Aaron and Connor Hislop –
sons of a very special dad**

Contents

Acknowledgements

I can't thank my mum and dad enough for bringing me into this world and my only regret is that my dad didn't stay in it long enough.

Alexander or 'Sandy' Hislop, as he was known, died when I was just 17 and at a period in my life when I desperately needed someone strong to guide me and advise me. What he left in me was a love of motorcycles which has given me a career and a lifestyle I would never have known had it not been for him and I'd love to thank him for that.

Since dad died, my mum, Margaret, has been a constant source of love, support and encouragement and I admire her more than anyone else on earth. She's endured all kinds of pain and heartache with bravery and dignity and has always been there for me no matter what. I've never known a stronger woman.

I have to thank Kelly Bailey for giving me the two most gorgeous little boys any father could ask for. Aaron and Connor are the most important people in my world and I can't imagine life without them now. I love them to bits.

Career-wise, a big thank-you must go to Honda and in particular to Bob McMillan of Honda UK who spotted my talents and plucked me from obscurity by offering me the factory Honda contract that really kick-started my racing career.

I'd like to thank Stuart Barker for helping me to tell my life's story in a way I feel reflects my true emotions and opinions and I'm also grateful to all at Harper-Collins *Publishers* for making this book possible.

So many people have helped me in so many ways over my long career that it's just not possible to thank them all here, no matter how much I'd like to. But I have appreciated everything they've done for me.

The final thank you goes to all the motorcycle racing fans who have supported me over the years either at race meetings or just while watching at home on television. A huge thanks to each and every one of you. Without your support, none of what you are about to read would ever have been possible.

* * * * *

Author's Note

Steve Hislop and I were looking forward to sitting down at the end of 2003, cracking open a few beers, and writing the final instalment of his book for this paperback edition. Due to the tragic events of 30 July 2003, this sadly never happened and it fell to me alone to finish the story of Steve's often tragic, equally triumphant, but never anything other than incredible life.

It was with a heavy heart that I undertook the task because I knew I'd miss Hizzy's guiding hand, his criticisms and his impeccable memory for detail when it came to recalling races, lap by lap, turn by turn, making me feel as if I was there on the bike with him. But most of all I'll miss the laughs. It's no easy task recalling every last detail of your life as Steve found out but it's hell of a lot of fun trying and fun was what made this book worthwhile. Sifting through Steve's considerable collection of old press cuttings and photographs not only jogged distant memories and created heaps of laughter at old fashions, hair-cuts and bikes but also led to some of the most vivid storytelling sessions I ever had the pleasure to listen to.

When Steve Hislop was on form, he was the best storyteller in the world and I would sit completely enthralled as he told me in minute detail of how he beat Carl Fogarty in that 1992 Senior TT or how he managed to hustle his customer Ducati round Doning-ton Park faster than Valentino Rossi could manage on his priceless Honda MotoGP bike.

In late summer of 2002, Steve and I sat down at a blank computer screen and set off on a journey to tell the story of his life. The result was the first edition hardback version of *Hizzy: The Autobiography of Steve Hislop*, launched at the Isle of Man TT in June 2003 – scene of some of Steve's greatest victories.

Hizzy was delighted with the book and even more delighted with the feedback he received from it. He really felt he had achieved what he set out to do which was to write from the heart and explain himself to all those who'd misunderstood him – and there were quite a few.

Unbelievably, the very next month, Steve was killed in a helicopter crash when he was on the verge of retiring from the dangerous sport of motorcycle racing after more than 20 years of competing.

To fulfil my commitments to my publishers and, more importantly, to Steve himself, I have undertaken to finish his story as best I can as a lasting memorial to a great man and a good friend. I only hope I can do Steve justice in adding the final chapters to his incredible, and ultimately tragic, tale.

I know that nothing in the world meant more to Steve than his sons Aaron and Connor so I'd like to dedicate my final efforts to them so that they will always have a complete record of their father's outstanding bravery and achievements.

Author's acknowledgements

I'd like to thank the following (in alphabetical order) for their help in compiling the final chapters of this book: Andrew Brodie, Jim Davidson, Tim Douglas, Stuart Easton, Ally Greenwood, Margaret Hislop, Niall Mackenzie, Peter Maher, Gary Mason, Rob McElnea, Jim Moodie and Ian Simpson.

Thanks also to Jim and Josie Barker, Donna

Costello, Neil, Angela and Emily Hewitson and Chris Moss for their emotional support through what was a very difficult period following Steve's death.

Stuart Barker
Kettering, Northants
2003

1 Day Number One, Life Number Two

'I'd been trying to race bikes for a month with a broken neck.'

Everyone thought I was dead – except me because I wasn't thinking at all.

I lay unconscious in the gravel trap at Brands Hatch with my neck broken in two places, my spinal cord twisted into an 'S' shape and with a fragment of bone impregnated in the main nerve to my left arm. It was one of the most horrendous-looking crashes anyone had ever witnessed – and there were more than 100,000 people at the race that day. Even the national newspapers hailed it as the worst crash ever seen on TV.

World Superbike riders Neil Hodgson, Colin Edwards and Noriyuki Haga all got tangled up at about 120mph going into the fearsome Paddock Hill bend at Brands Hatch during the year 2000 WSB meeting. Neil had clipped the kerb because he couldn't see where he was going as all the other riders were so tightly bunched. His bike bounced back onto the track and started a chain reaction and I got caught up in the mêlée as Haga rammed my back wheel and Edwards took my front wheel away. The result was total carnage: there were bikes and riders tumbling everywhere, bits and pieces flying off the machinery and scything through the air and sparks showering down the track as metal collided with tarmac.

As my bike was rammed, I was thrown 15 feet in the air and started cartwheeling towards the gravel trap. My bike was spinning end over end and it slammed into my head twice – all 350lb of it – sending me tumbling even more spectacularly. It's a good job it did too because, ironically, that's probably what saved my life. The first smack it gave me knocked me out so I was unconscious as I tumbled and that meant my body was limp and relaxed. Had I been conscious and tensed up, I would probably have done even more damage to myself.

After doing four full-body cartwheels, I landed square on the top of my head with my feet pointing straight up in the air, as if I'd been planted in the ground by the celebrity gardener, Alan Titchmarsh. Then finally I tumbled over, came to a halt and slumped into the gravel, knocked out cold and lifeless as the dust began to settle and the bike finally came to a stop. The race was stopped immediately and the huge crowd that had been screaming and cheering just seconds before then, fell completely silent. Joey Dunlop had been killed in a race just one month previously and no one wanted to witness more tragedy at what should have been a fun day out. I don't know what the millions of armchair fans watching on TV around the world thought but what did annoy me afterwards was that it took such a horrific crash to get bike racing onto the main news. Usually the sport is never considered important enough to be mentioned on TV news bulletins unlike football, cricket, golf, Formula One or tennis. It was only when I had such a horrendous smash that almost every country in the world ran a story on it. What a way to get famous.

But if it weren't for the TV coverage, I wouldn't be able to describe the crash in detail because I can't remember it. The last thing I remember was feeling a thump when I was banking hard into Paddock Hill bend and that must have been when Haga hit me. Because the crash looked so bad and because I had landed on my head and wasn't moving, everyone who witnessed it presumed I was dead. My girlfriend Kelly, who was watching on TV back home, was in hysterics and couldn't get through to anyone in my team when she tried to call to find out if I was alive or dead. The Virgin Yamaha team wasn't taking calls because they were too busy trying to find out if they still had a rider. Kelly had to wait for about two hours before she got through to someone who told her I was OK. At first she didn't believe it and thought I must at least be in a coma, but someone finally convinced her that I was conscious and moving.

The first thing I remember through a foggy, dizzy haze was hearing a paramedic's voice shouting, 'there's a good vein, stick it in there,' as they immediately tried to stabilize me by hooking me up to an IV drip and an oxygen mask. Apart from that, everything was completely silent as the crowd looked on numbed and fearing the worst. There were paramedics swarming all over me and thankfully they knew to remove my helmet carefully with the aid of a neck brace because there was a risk of spinal injuries.

As I was stretchered off to the nearest hospital I started coming round a little and that's when I felt a pain in my chest and thought I might have broken my back. I was also getting a prickly feeling every time a medic touched me but it turned out that I was just covered in thousands of scratches from the gravel as I tumbled through it.

Anyone who thinks motorcycle racing is glamorous only needs to experience one big crash to realize it's not. The frequent injuries are bad enough to deal with but the undignified hospital procedures are just as bad. On this occasion, I was still feeling groggy when a doctor wearing rubber gloves approached me and that can mean only one thing. Sure enough, I jolted as he inserted a finger straight up my backside and had a prod around but at least he was kind enough to explain the theory he was putting into practice. Apparently, men have a kind of ultra-sensitive G-spot up there and if you hit the ceiling when the doctor touches it, you've got a broken back. I'd have thought most blokes would hit the ceiling anyway when a doctor shoves a finger up their arse, broken back or not but apparently I didn't flinch too violently so the prognosis was good even if the examination wasn't.

I was then x-rayed and pushed into a little cubicle

and left on my own for what seemed like an eternity as I still hadn't a clue what was happening to me. Coming round from concussion is not a nice experience and even though I'd been knocked out several times before, it doesn't get any easier because you're starting from scratch every time it happens as you've got no memories to draw upon.

I was really scared lying in there trying to piece my world together bit by bit. Where am I? What day is it? What year is it? The answer to every question was the same – I didn't know. I could only lie there like a newborn baby staring at the curtains round my bed, my brain completely devoid of any memory, any sense of belonging or any history; any sense of anything in fact. It really was like being born again – I didn't have a bloody clue what was going on.

Eventually, with a huge effort, I remembered I'd been at Brands Hatch but I still couldn't remember what year it was. I became convinced it was 1999 and only realized it was the year 2000 because I remembered which front suspension system I'd been using on the bike and that I'd been swapping between 1999 and 2000-spec forks that season. It's the most horrible, helpless feeling there is but for bike racers, it comes with the territory and you've just got to get on with it.

Some time later, my team boss, Rob McElnea, came in to see me and started asking me questions. As a former racer himself, he knew the routine for concussion as well as anyone and when I could tell him who I was, where I was and what year it was he reckoned I was all right and tried to get me to sign myself out.

The doctors had checked all the x-rays and said the only thing that concerned them was a cloudy area around the C5 and C6 vertebrae in my neck. I told them I'd had a prolapsed disc in 1995 at that very spot which seemed to explain the cloudy area. I hate hospitals and when I looked around and saw an old woman who had choked on a sandwich and another old girl who hadn't been able to shit for a month I thought, 'I hate these places – I need to get out of here.' So I signed myself out, even though the doctors wanted to keep me in overnight for observation, and I went back to the hotel that night. The following morning I drove my hire car to the airport and was back home on the Isle of Man a couple of hours after that.

When I saw a video of the crash on ITN news I realized how close to death or paralysis I had come. It looked much worse than triple world champion Wayne Rainey's crash at Misano in 1993 did and he's now wheelchair-bound for life because of that incident. Being paralysed or maimed scares me more than anything else in the world so I'd readily have chosen death over being stuck in a wheelchair. But then that's a choice we never get to make – fate decides it for us.

But I wasn't paralysed, I was just in pain all over. My head hit the inside of my helmet so hard that the mesh lining was imprinted on my forehead, and my forehead itself was so badly swollen that I looked like a Neanderthal. I had a black eye, my face was covered in cuts from where my helmet visor had come off allowing gravel to scratch my forehead and even my eyebrows were sore, although I can't think how that happened. I felt as if I'd been put through a full cycle in a washing machine. However everything seemed to be in working order and I figured I'd be fully fit again in a few days, so that, as far as I was concerned, was the end of my Brands Hatch crash. I couldn't have been more wrong.

Just four days later I set off for a round of the British Superbike championship at Knockhill in Scotland. Everyone in the paddock was amazed to see me on my feet and most people, I think, were glad to see me alive. I managed to qualify for the races but felt really weak and couldn't hold myself up on the bike properly. I figured I must have come back too early and since there were two weeks to recuperate before the next round at Cadwell Park, I decided to sit out the Knockhill meeting just to be on the safe side.

During those two weeks I had some physiotherapy and tried to lift some light weights but I still felt really weak down my left hand side. Then a really peculiar thing started to happen – I started walking into doors. I would put my left hand out to push open a door but my arm just buckled under the slightest strain so I'd end up slamming my face into the door. I wasn't in any pain (apart from the fact that I kept banging my nose), but I just had no strength or feeling in my left arm. It was weird.

Anyway, I went to Cadwell as planned but in the first few laps of practice it was apparent that something wasn't right. When you brake for a corner on a motorcycle you lift your body up out of the racing crouch to act as a windbreak which helps slow you down. This involves locking your arms against the handlebars as you lift up but every time I tried it I almost fell off the left-hand side of the bike. My left arm was just folding under pressure and it was way too dangerous to continue. I tried taking the strain on my knees against the fuel tank or with just my right arm on the bar but nothing seemed to work, so after six laps I pulled into the pits.

Everyone asked me what was wrong and I said I had no idea. I wasn't in pain, I just couldn't ride the bloody bike. Rob McElnea got really mad because he thought I was cracking up. I've been blamed a lot over the years for being fragile or temperamental when it comes to racing a bike because my results have not always been consistent and Rob probably thought that I just couldn't be bothered to ride or that I'd lost my bottle for some reason.

You've got to realize that in motorcycle sport, it's very common for riders to compete with freshly broken bones, torn ligaments or any other number of painful injuries. A trackside doctor is always on hand to administer painkilling injections to numb the pain for the duration of the race if required and riders often have special lightweight casts made to hold broken bones in place while they race. Basically, they will try anything just to go out and score some points so for me to explain that I was not in pain but just couldn't ride the bike must have sounded a bit odd to say the least.

Anyway, there was no way I could race but I hung

around Cadwell anyway and at one point bumped into a neurosurgeon I knew called Ian Sabin. He was a bike-racing fan and came to meetings when time permitted. I explained my problem so he carried out a few tests in the mobile clinic that attends all race meetings. He asked me to push against his hands as he held them out and I nearly pushed him over with my right hand but couldn't apply any pressure at all with my left hand. After another couple of simple tests he told me I had nerve damage and needed to get an MRI scan as soon as possible.

I went to London for a scan and had to pay the £600 fee out of my own pocket but it was the best £600 I've ever spent as it probably saved my life (and I eventually claimed it back through my insurance anyway). Ian looked at the results and I could immediately tell he was worried. He didn't tell me what he saw at that point but called another department and told them I needed an ECG test immediately. It was only then that he turned to me and said, 'Steven, you have a broken neck. What's more, you have been walking around and trying to race bikes for the last four weeks with a broken neck.'

Fuck! I couldn't believe what I was hearing. How could I possibly have a broken neck and not notice? How did the hospital not diagnose it straight after the race? How do you fix a broken neck? Would I be able to ride again? All of these thoughts were rushing through my head as Ian explained that the C5 and C6 vertebra in my neck were broken and badly crushed as well. As a result of that my spinal column was twisted into an 'S' shape and to further complicate matters, a piece of sheared bone was chafing against the main nerve which controlled my left arm and was threatening to cut through it. No wonder I had no strength in it.

Ian said that I'd been incredibly lucky over the previous month because my head was, quite literally, hanging on by a bunch of fibres with no support from my spine. If I'd been slapped in the face or had knocked my head in any way, then that would have been the end of it – I'd have been dead, or even worse in my book, paralysed from the neck down. I thought back to all the daft things I'd done over the last month like going out on the piss when I could easily have fallen over. If I'd fallen off the bike at Knockhill or Cadwell, even if I'd slept on my neck in a funny position the results could have been catastrophic for me. The odds of not damaging the injury further in that month were incredible but somehow I'd beaten them. You could call it luck but I prefer to think of it as destiny: it simply wasn't my time to die.

During the ECG test, they stuck needles in almost every muscle of my body and eventually found out that it was the nerve to my tricep muscle, in the rear of my left arm that had the most damage. It was deteriorating more with every passing day as the stray piece of bone gradually sawed its way through, and so I was scheduled for an operation as soon as possible.

Whilst I waited for the operation, I re-evaluated my entire life. I thought about everything I had done, pondered on everything I still wanted to do, and gradually realized how amazingly lucky I was to be getting a second chance at life when by all accounts, I should have been dead. I never once thought of quitting racing.

I'd never really believed there was a God and the crash didn't change my mind. If there was a God, why would he have allowed my father to die in my arms when I was just 17? Why would he have allowed my kid brother to be killed racing a bike when he was only 19? Why, after my mother had lost her husband and son within three years of each other, would he then pair her off with an abusive second husband who battered her regularly? Why would he have allowed a good friend of mine to be beaten to death outside a chip shop because he refused to give his chicken and chips to a gang of thugs? No, I was pretty sure God didn't exist or if He did, I didn't like His way of doing things.

I also thought of how many of my friends and racing colleagues had been killed in racing accidents over the years while my own life had been spared so miraculously. The list makes for grim and depressive reading: names such as Joey Dunlop, Phil Mellor, Steve Henshaw, Ray Swann, Kenny Irons, Sam McClements, Simon Beck, Lee Pullan, Colin Gable, Gene McDonnell, Mark Farmer, Robert Holden, Klaus Klein, Donny Robinson, Neil Robinson, Steve Ward and Mick Lofthouse. I could go on but it's not something I like to dwell on. We're all going to die if we live long enough and I became more hardened to death than most people after losing my father and brother, so racing deaths never bothered me as much as they might have done.

But each and every one of those riders chose to dedicate his life to the sport of motorcycle racing because he loved it. It's a sport that delivers thrills like no other but also one that punishes mistakes more harshly and more violently than any other. The risks are multiplied 10-fold when a rider also decides to race on closed public road tracks like the notorious Isle of Man TT. It is undoubtedly the most dangerous racing event in the world, but it's also the event where I made my name and where I enjoyed so many great victories.

Since its inception in 1907, over 170 riders have been killed at the TT and the list is added to almost every year. Some years, as many as five riders are killed in the two-week event. Yet I won there 11 times at speeds which no one had ever witnessed before. Racing between walls and houses at over 190mph and averaging over 120mph for a lap was an awesome rush even if it was highly dangerous. But I cheated death on the world's most unforgiving racetrack for 10 years and was never even hurt once while racing there. Ironically, it was a so-called 'safe', purpose-built short circuit that nearly claimed my life and almost left my mother with no sons at all.

I pondered on all these things as I awaited my operation and repeatedly questioned why I still wanted to race motorbikes more than anything else in my life. It certainly wasn't for the financial rewards since I haven't made any serious money from racing even though I've raced for more than 20 years. The truth is that when I retire I'll have to get a normal job like everybody else because I have no savings worth talking about. Some racers, like my former team-mate, Carl Fogarty, have become millionaires from the sport but I've been financially naive throughout my career and consequently never got the rewards I feel I deserve.

Having said that, racing at least gives me some sort of wage to live on from day to day, so I suppose money was one of the reasons I had to get back on a bike again. After all, I have two small sons to support with no other obvious means of earning cash to feed and clothe them. But more than anything I wanted to get back on a bike again because I desperately wanted to win the British Superbike championship – the toughest domestic race series in the world.

Throughout my career people have always thought I could only win on dangerous street circuits and couldn't adapt my style to the short sprint, purpose-built tracks, which require a different and more aggressive riding style. Even when I won the 250cc British championship in 1990 on short circuits people said I just got lucky, so the 'road racer' tag still weighed heavily round my neck.

In 1995 I won the British Superbike series but this time pundits said it was only because my arch-rival Jamie Whitham developed cancer midway through the season. It seemed as if nothing I did was enough to convince people that I was a world class short-circuit rider who could hold his own against the best in the world.

After winning that title in '95 I had seven years of bad luck in the BSB series. Two of my teams folded mid-season through lack of funds, two other teams sacked me for 'under performing' and I didn't complete three seasons because of injury. So, more than anything, I wanted to come back from my injuries this time and win the British title so convincingly that no one could ever have any more doubts about my ability on a motorcycle.

I don't mind admitting that I was absolutely shitting myself going into that operation. Motorcycle racing may be dangerous but at least I was always the one in control: I could back off the throttle or slam on the brakes if things got too hot or I could even pull off the track and quit if I was totally unhappy about something. There was at least some sense of being in charge even if it was only a delusion. But being knocked out and having someone, however well qualified, operating on your spine? That's really scary.

Lower spine operations are quite common and generally successful but the neck is a different matter. From the chest upwards, it's like a bloody telephone exchange inside your body with all those nerves crisscrossing each other and that's where things can go wrong. As I've said, my biggest fear is being paralysed so if the surgeons were going to mess up, I'd rather they just put me to sleep for good.

You'd think that for an operation on your neck, the surgeons would go in from the back, but in my case at least, they didn't. Instead, they cut open my throat, pushed my windpipe aside and went to work from there. They picked out all the shattered pieces of bone and generally cleaned up the mess, then they cut open my hip and chipped a disc of bone from my pelvis to graft into my neck. I swear they must have used a bloody sledgehammer to chip that bone off because the pain in my pelvis when I woke up was like nothing on earth and I've had my share of serious injuries so I'm well accustomed to pain.

As you'd expect, I was also pretty groggy when I woke up and I remember wondering why the fuck there was a red Christmas tree bulb hanging out of my pelvis and one hanging out of my neck too. As I came a bit more to my senses I realized they were blood drains – little suction pumps that suck out any surplus blood so it doesn't start congealing. My neck and throat felt OK but that bloody hip was unbelievable and when Ian wanted me on my feet the morning after the operation I was horrified. Man that hurt.

Anyway, normally that procedure would have been enough and any other patient would be told to take it easy for a while until the bone healed itself. But because my surgeon knew I wanted to go racing again as soon as possible, he strengthened my neck by screwing in a titanium plate which I still have in there – and always will have as a matter of fact.

A CT scan showed the operation had gone well and my neck was stable and I was on my way home two days later, but I'd been told there was no guarantee that I'd ever get any feeling or strength back in my left arm. Ian said it might return in six weeks, six months, one year or perhaps never at all. I had almost torn that nerve clean out of the spinal column as my body was twisted in the crash and no one could tell if my arm would ever be anything more than the relatively lifeless object that was dangling by my side. I was at nature's mercy.

Every day for weeks – even though I don't believe in God – I prayed for some feeling to come back, but every day for weeks it didn't. I tried to build up strength in it but could only lift light weights and I was starting to get really depressed thinking my career was over and that I was going to be left with a useless arm. I couldn't even try to set up a deal for the following season because I didn't know if I'd be able to ride a bike or not.

Then one day, about two months after the crash, it started happening. I felt a slight sensation on the back of my hand and then in my index finger. It wasn't much but it was definitely something. I thought, 'Yes! Here we go, I'm back in business.' I felt totally elated but not as elated as I was when, near Christmas time, I was finally able to lock my left arm out fully. That was the best Christmas present I'd had since my first son was born on Christmas Day in 1997. I was over the moon.

It was game on after that and I started training slowly and gently to rebuild some muscle in my wasted arm. That was day number one of life number two as far as I was concerned and I never stopped thinking about racing after that. There were still some months until the start of the new season so I had time to try and organize a ride for the year, even though I'd burned my bridges with most teams over the last few years. But I didn't care – I'd been given a second chance at life and I wasn't about to waste it. Somehow I would find a bike to race even if it meant remortgaging my house and buying one myself. The way I saw it, I had nothing to lose because I should have been dead anyway.

Steve Hislop was back – and he was going to win the British Superbike championship come hell or high water.

2 Shooting Crows

'My real name's actually Robert Hislop but my dad made a mistake when he registered me.'

The Isle of Man TT is a totally unique event and probably attracts more controversy than any other sporting fixture on the calendar.

It's held on the world famous 'Mountain' circuit that runs over 37.74 miles of everyday public roads on the Isle of Man. The roads are, naturally, closed for the races but they're still lined with hazards such as houses, walls, lamp-posts, hedges and everything else you would expect to find on normal country roads.

Because of the dangers and the number of competitors who have been killed there, the event lost its world championship status in 1976 when top riders like Barry Sheene, Phil Read and Giacomo Agostini refused to race there any longer. When you consider that the current, fastest *average* lap speed is held by David Jefferies at 127.29mph and bikes have been speed-trapped at 194mph between brick walls, it's easy to understand the dangers of the place, as there's no run-off space when things go wrong. But the thrill of riding there is unique and that's what keeps so many riders coming back year after year.

Riders don't all start together at the TT – they set off singly at 10-second intervals in a bid to improve safety although mass starts have occurred in the past. That means the competitors are racing against the clock and the longest races last for six laps which equates to 226 miles and about two hours in the saddle at very high speeds and on very bumpy roads. It's an endurance test as much as anything else and you can't afford to lose concentration for a split second or you are quite literally taking your own life in your hands. It is an event like no other on earth.

The TT (which stands for Tourist Trophy) fortnight is traditionally held in the last week of May and the first week of June and the Manx Grand Prix is traditionally held on the same course in September. The latter event is purely amateur with no prize money and it exists as a way for riders to learn the daunting 37.74 mile course before tackling the TT proper. The name should not be confused with the world championship Moto Grand Prix series because the two have nothing in common.

Both the Manx Grand Prix and the TT races have played a huge part in my life, which is why I'm describing them in detail now. Without them I simply wouldn't be where I am today, or even writing this book, and a basic understanding of the nature of both events is crucial to understanding my later career.

I first visited the Manx GP as a child, then later on

spent 10 years racing on the Mountain course, both at the Manx and the TT. I grew to love the Isle of Man so much over the years that I moved there in 1991 and it's where I still live to this day.

It was my father Alexander, or 'Sandy' as he was known, who got me interested in the TT and the Manx GP in the first place as he raced at the Manx back in the 1950s. I went on to have incredible success at the TT and that's really where I made my name in the world of motorcycling. But believe it or not, the Steve Hislop who won 11 TT races (only two men in history have won more) isn't actually called Steve at all thanks to one of the daftest blunders anyone's dad ever made.

I may be known as Steve Hislop throughout the bike-racing world but on every piece of documentation that proves who I am, the name given is actually Robert. I still don't know exactly how it happened but it was definitely my dad's doing. Both he and my mum, Margaret, had decided on calling me Steven Robert Hislop and that's the name I was christened under, but my dad messed up big time. For reasons known only to him, he registered me as Robert Steven Hislop and to this day even my passport carries that name.

Robert was my grandfather's name, but he died when he was just 30 after he fell from the attic in his dad's blacksmith's workshop. His was the first in a series of tragic early deaths in my family.

I was born at 7.55pm on 11 January 1962 at the Haig Maternity Hospital in Hawick in the Scottish Borders.

But although I was born in a Hawick hospital, I'm not actually from the town itself despite what all those race programmes, TV commentators and magazine articles have said over the years. I'm actually from the little village of Chesters in a parish called Southdean, a few miles south east of Hawick. My mum was only 16 when she had me, while my dad was a good bit older at 26 – a bit of a cradle snatcher was the old boy!

Money was tight so we all lived with my widowed granny for the first few months of my life. Mum worked in the knitwear mills; knitwear is a big trade in the Borders and my dad was a joiner who worked for a small country joinery firm in Chesters village before eventually buying the business when the owner died.

My younger brother, Garry Alexander Hislop, was born in the same hospital as me on 28 July 1963, just 17 months after I was and we were very close right from the start. I loved having a brother.

Dad loved his bikes and was very friendly with the late, great Bob McIntyre, another Scottish bike racer and the first man ever to lap the Isle of Man TT course at 100mph. Dad raced between 1956 and 1961 on a BSA Gold Star and a 350cc Manx Norton. He travelled to all the little Scottish courses that don't exist any more, such as Charter Hall, Errol, Crimond and Beveridge Park, including some circuits in the north of England such as Silloth – a track which would later have tragic consequences for my family.

He was a pretty handy racer in the Scottish championships but never really had the money to do it properly. He used to ride to meetings on his bike with a racing exhaust strapped to his back, fit it to the bike for the race then change back to the standard one and ride home again! That was proper clubman's racing. As I mentioned earlier, my dad also raced at the Manx Grand Prix a few times usually finishing midfield but when mum became pregnant with me he packed in the racing game to support the family.

As a kid, I went to Hobkirk primary school. I remember being absolutely shit-scared, waiting for the bus on my first day of school because I was a very shy child and hadn't mixed much with other kids since most of the time I just played with my little brother. Shyness is something I have mostly grown out of now but it was definitely a problem for me in the early days of my career.

I can't remember much about primary school except that I always seemed to be sticking up for Garry in fights, particularly with a kid called Magoo who was always picking on him. My other outstanding memory of primary school was of Mr Thompson, the head teacher, who had a wooden leg, though I never found out why. Instead of giving us the belt when we were bad, he pulled our hair repeatedly! I clearly remember him telling me off and yanking the tuft of hair at the front of my head in time with his rantings. No wonder I've got no bloody hair left!

My secondary school was Jedburgh Grammar, but I was never interested in going there because I was a real out-door type, thanks to my dad's uncles, Jim and John Wallace, having a farm. Almost every weekend I would cycle down to that farm and have the time of my life. I fed the sheep and the cows, picked the turnips and generally mucked in with the chores, then after that it was back to the house for a big farm breakfast and in the afternoons John and I would go shooting.

At that point, all I wanted to be when I grew up was a gamekeeper. I was like a little old man with my deerstalker hat with the 'Deputy Dawg' flap-down ear covers and a bloody big shotgun cocked over my arm. I used to feed up all the birds and ducks and make little hideouts round the ponds then come the shooting season I blew the hell out of everything that could fly – and some things that couldn't.

I know that sounds cruel now but that was the norm in the country, especially back then, and boys will be boys after all. Having said that, I was a bit of a nasty little fucker when it came to things like that. I shot baby crows that had left the nest with my .22 rifle and kept the shotgun for the bigger birds and the nests themselves. I'm not particularly proud of it now but as I said before, it felt normal at the time.

On Sunday evenings I would cycle home again as late as I could get away with and dreaded going back to school the next day. I had pushbikes from a very early age but they were always hand-me-downs and were far too big for me. I never had any stabilizers either so I had lots of crashes because I was too small to reach the ground. My folks would hold on to me to get me going then seconds after they let me go there would be a big crashing noise, a yelp and a puff of dust as I hit the deck again. But I loved two-wheelers from the start, even when they were too big for me.

The first time I ever got a new bike was when my nana bought Garry and I brand new Raleigh Choppers for Christmas but they were just as dangerous as the too-big hand-me-downs. Choppers may have looked cool but they certainly weren't designed for riding – they were bloody lethal. Garry once smashed his face to hell one night when he crashed cycling down a hill and he squealed in pain all the way home – the poor little bugger. We used to get into high-speed wobbles because the front wheels were so small and the high bars provided so much leverage that they made the effect worse.

Even back then we pretended we were riding motorbikes and like most kids at the time, we gripped playing cards onto the fork legs with clothes pegs so they ran through the spokes and made a noise like a motorbike. But showing an early aptitude for setting up machinery, I eventually found that cut-up bottles of washing-up liquid lasted longer than playing cards and made a better noise too!

Before we even had pushbikes, my mum says that Garry and I would sit in the house and pretend to be bike racers. We would be at opposite ends of the sofa over the armrests in a racing crouch, our little legs dangling over the side, and cushions under our chests acting as petrol tanks.

Apparently we fought over which racer we were pretending to be too and it was always Jimmie Guthrie or Geordie Buchan. Jimmie Guthrie was Hawick's most famous son and one of the greatest names in pre-war motorcycle racing. He was born in 1897 and went on to win six Isle of Man TTs and was European champion three times when that title was the equivalent of today's world championships. His admirers included none other than a certain Adolf Hitler who on one occasion even presented him with a trophy!

Jimmie was killed in a 500cc race at the Sachsenring in Germany in 1937 at 40 years of age and there's still a statue of him in Hawick, as well as the famous Guthrie's memorial on the TT course. Like I said before, Garry and I would argue over who was going to be Jimmy Guthrie and who was going to be Geordie Buchan, who was the Scottish champion at the time and also a friend of my dad. So in a sense, my first ever race was on a sofa and I think it finished in a dead heat with Garry!

Rugby is the big sport in the Scottish Borders and although I played it at school, I was never a big fan. In fact, I never liked football or tennis either and as for cricket – what the fuck is that all about? I'll never understand the fascination with that game. It's just grown men playing bloody rounders if you ask me. I was more into hunting and shooting things. My old Uncle John also taught me the art of fly fishing and I loved that too. I don't do it any more but I suppose I'll have to relearn it now to teach my own kids, Connor and Aaron.

However, I hope they never have to go through the experience I once had when I went sea fishing with my dad and Garry. Dad owned a little boat that we used to tow to the coast for a spot of line-and-rod fishing. On one occasion we took it to the Isle of Whithorn in Galloway and were anchored over some rocks on the Solway Firth doing a spot of rod fishing. It was a lovely hot, calm day so we didn't have any life jackets on and everything was just perfect, the sun on our backs and the water lapping gently at the hull of the boat. But all of a sudden the peace was shattered by my dad screaming, 'Get your bloody life jackets on boys, NOW! And get your rods in. QUICKLY.' I turned to see what the hell could be causing all this panic and was startled to spot a huge dorsal fin heading directly for the boat. Bloody hell, I shat myself; it was a huge basking shark, more than twice the size of the boat (which was 16 feet long) and it was coming straight for us!

Although I didn't know it then, basking sharks are harmless plankton feeders but they look just like great white sharks and are much, much bigger, growing to well over 30 feet. That's pretty damned big when you're a scrawny little four-foot kid. This all happened just two years before the movie *Jaws* came out and I'm pretty glad I hadn't seen that film beforehand because I'd probably have been even more terrified and I was scared enough as it was. The shark went under the boat and I remember seeing its head emerging on the other side before its tail had even gone under – that's how big it was. It just continued swimming away and that's the last we saw of it, but it was a pretty scary experience – even though it was good to brag about later.

Garry and I were very close and I suppose we

had to be really because there were very few other kids to play with. Obviously, we fought a bit as all boys do but we were the best of pals most of the time. We built tree houses and hammocks, messed about in the woods and by the rivers and had a real boys' own childhood. We did used to pal around with a guy called David Cook, or 'Cookie' as we called him, who went on to become a 250cc Scottish bike racing champion, but he was about the only other kid we were close to.

Way before we ever got motorbikes, Cookie, Garry and I used to hone our racing skills in 45-litre oil drums. Two of us would squeeze into a drum and the third person would push it down a massive hill. It was brilliant fun to be in the drum but just as much of a laugh watching the other two getting beaten up as they bounced and rattled their way downhill, bones clattering all the way. Eventually we came up with a new addition to the game – a tractor tyre! This thing was bigger than all three of us but we managed to wheel it up the hill then I'd spend ages trying to squeeze my way inside it as if I was an inner tube. Once I was in, the lads would give me a mighty shove and off I went, bouncing and bouncing for what seemed like ages as the heavy tyre picked up speed on its way down the hill. That bit was all right – it was the slowing down followed by the inevitable crash that caused the many injuries. I'd get thrown out at the end as the momentum died out and I was usually really dizzy and disorientated from being spun round like a hamster in a wheel, so invariably I fell on my backside as soon as I tried to stand up.

One time I actually fell out of the tyre while it was still bouncing down the hill at speed and I crashed face first into a grassy knoll and bust my nose. It was bleeding and swollen and in a hell of a mess. I don't know if it was actually broken, but to this day I've still got a kink in my nose and it was all because of that bloody tractor tyre.

As kids, our other passion was for bogeys, or fun karts, as people call them now. You know the type, a wooden base with four pram wheels and a rope for steering. We got really good at building them and even made one with a cab once. There was a steep downhill corner in the field next to our house which was good for learning to slide the bogeys on but we decided a bit of mud would help make it even slipperier. I don't know why we didn't just soak it with water but instead we had the bright idea of pissing on that corner for all we were worth to make it muddy so we could get better slides! If we didn't need to pee, we'd simply drink bottles and bottles of juice until we did – the more piss the better as far as we were concerned. We would eventually get the corner so wet that we had out of control slides and Garry once had a huge crash and ended up lying in that huge puddle of piss with several broken fingers.

It was a happy time for Garry and I, and it may have seemed idealistic at the time but in later years I realized the more negative effects my upbringing had on me. Because I was so isolated, I was very shy with other people. I still am today, to a certain extent, so I'm trying to encourage my kids to be confident and to mix freely with people so that they're better equipped to deal with the big bad world than I was. Even now, I hate calling travel agents and bank managers or dealing with any 'official' phone calls like that, so if I can, I ask someone else to do it for me! I know that sounds pathetic, but it's just the way I am.

There was another couple of kids, called Alistair and Norman Glendinning, with whom Garry and I sometimes played. They lived on a nearby farm called Doorpool. At the time, we were renting a cottage within the farm grounds which cost seven shillings a week (35 pence in today's money), if my mum agreed to top up the water trough for the cows every day, which she did.

Once I remember having a big argument with Alistair Glendinning and I ended up throwing a garden rake at him. It split his face open and cut his head – he was in a right mess. I got a terrible bollocking for that but a few days later we were all playing happily together again. Kids don't hold grudges, shame adults aren't the same.

When I was nine years old, in 1973, my dad, as a former competitor, was invited to the Golden Jubilee of the Manx Grand Prix. When he got there he met up with Jim Oliver who owned Thomas B. Oliver's garage in Denholm, just a few miles from where we lived. Jim was partly sponsoring a rider called Wullie Simson, who also lived near our home and my dad got to know him on that trip. It turned out that Wullie was a joiner like my dad but he'd quit his job when his boss wouldn't give him time off to go to the Manx! My dad was getting a lot of work in so he offered Wullie a job, which was gladly accepted. Garry and I helped out at my dad's workshop for pocket money and we liked Wullie straight away when he started there and we were always asking him about the racing.

Some two weeks after Wullie started his job at the workshop, my dad asked Garry and I if we'd like to go and watch some bike racing at Silloth, an airfield circuit just south of Carlisle. Too right we did! We were so excited at the prospect that we could hardly sleep. When Garry and I had been about five or six years old, we went with our nana and papa to stay in a caravan at Silloth. I remember hearing motorbikes howling away in the background and my grandma explained it was the bike racing over on the airfield. I ranted and begged her for so long to take us to see them that the poor woman ended up trudging with us for about six miles on the round trip to the airfield just so we could watch the bikes. There was a big delay in the racing because a rider was killed and my nana wanted to take Garry and I away from the track at that point, but I was having none of it. Apparently, I refused to leave the circuit until I'd seen the last bike in the last race go past. I obviously loved bike racing even way back then. That must have been in the late 1960s.

But I was 11 and old enough to really appreciate it properly by the time dad took me back to Silloth to watch another race and my most vivid memory of that

meeting is of a guy in purple leathers, because everyone else was wearing black. Every lap he came out of
the hairpin and pulled a big wheelie and I thought
he was amazing. He was called Steve Machin and I'm
now very friendly with his brother Jack though sadly
later, Steve himself was killed on a race bike.

It was great to watch my dad's mate Wullie Simson
racing and he must have enjoyed our support because
soon after that race, he turned up at our house in
his van and pulled out a Honda ST50. It must have
been an MOT failure or something because the engine
was in pieces but my dad soon put it back together,
got it fired up and that was it. From that moment on,
Garry and I spent every spare moment riding that bike
in the field surrounding the house. My motorcycling
career had begun.

3 Off the Rails

'All I seemed to do was get pissed and crash cars.'

Getting a little motorbike changed everything for Garry and I – it became the most important thing in our lives. We couldn't even concentrate at school any more because all we wanted to do was get home and ride that bike.

Around the same time as we got the ST50 my dad finally got back into racing, now that he had provided a solid backing for his family. He bought a 350cc Aermacchi and started racing it in single-cylinder events, which today would be called classic races. He was pretty good and won a couple of races here and there but it was more like a hobby to him rather than his whole life. So with dad racing again and Garry and I riding too, bikes were suddenly everywhere and were the main topic of conversation in the Hislop household. Looking back, it's really no surprise I turned out to be a racer.

There was corn growing in the fields around our

house in the summer and at other times there were horses grazing there too so Garry and I had to make sure we rode round everything but that certainly never stopped us. Pretty soon, the little Honda was joined by a Suzuki A50 with a five-speed gearbox and a clutch (the Honda was a three-speed semi-automatic). It was a great bit of kit and it was allocated to Garry while I got the Honda, which I felt was fair enough, because it meant we could finally race each other.

About this time, my nana took ill and the doctors soon discovered she was riddled with cancer. She lasted another year-and-a-half but died in October 1975. I was very close to my nana and missed her terribly but I was to lose even more close family members before too long. To take my mind off my sadness I just rode round and round those fields, day in day out, rain, sun or shine. It was my only release. When I was on that little bike I didn't think about anything else. I just wanted to learn how to go faster, how to control my slides better, how to ride more smoothly. I was totally self-contained; all I needed was my bike and my brother. Mum would call us in for tea and we'd scrub up a bit, wolf down our food and head straight back out into the field to ride again. Those were such happy times for me.

Cookie – who was the third 'amigo' in our little gang – got hold of his dad's old Triumph Tiger Cub round about this time and started riding with us. The whole village used to complain about the noise we made from morning to night but we didn't care.

We had mock races for hours on end and at the end of the day, we all looked like we'd fallen down somebody's chimney. All you could see were our little white eyes peering out of dirty, dusty faces like something from *The Black and White Minstrel Show*. We got filthy beyond belief but we didn't fall off much and if we did we fixed the bikes ourselves.

When we got bored with the field we pushed the bikes into the village where there was a spare bit of common land and rode round there until we'd messed the whole place up. In fact, we sometimes rode the bikes down the road, which was totally illegal but my dad never got to hear about that!

When we weren't racing each other, we'd try to imitate Evel Knievel whom we'd seen on TV. We made ramps out of old doors or whatever we found in my dad's joiner's yard. One day, I propped a panelled door up on two straw bales to act as a ramp. But when I hit it with the bike my front wheel went straight through the door and dug into the bales and I was sent flying over the handlebars in true Knievel style. Didn't clear any buses though.

Although Garry and I had bikes, there was never any spare money in the family. The bikes were just wrecks that we rebuilt so they didn't really cost anything. Even from an early age we worked at the joiner's yard for our pocket money, but having no money to get the bikes fixed up by a garage was a good thing because it taught me so much about basic mechanics.

By the time I was 14 and Garry was 13, I got a

SL125 Honda trail bike and he got a cracking little trials bike because we couldn't find another trail bike locally. It was a British-built Wassel with a 125cc Sachs engine, a seven-speed gearbox and it was all covered in chrome. We weren't into trials riding (negotiating obstacles like rocks, tree trunks and old barrels) because it was too slow, so we just raced those two bikes everywhere over the moors and through the forestry roads.

I never told my dad about those forestry roads because they were farther away than we would have been allowed and we shouldn't have had bikes on them anyway. Flat-out speed was always our thing rather than motocrossing over jumps so we nailed our little bikes over those bumpy forest roads at about 70mph which felt as fast then as the Isle of Man TT did in later years, even though that was more like 190mph.

My dad must have realized Garry and I would want to go road racing eventually because in the winter of that year, he asked us if we wanted to try schoolboy motocross. It was a shrewd move because he knew it would give us crucial racing experience away from the dangers of road racing. Falling off on grass is a bit safer than on tarmac, although you can still do some serious damage. But the idea was that by the time we were old enough to go road racing we would know all about wheel-to-wheel contact and sliding bikes around so we'd be better prepared for it. We sold both our bikes and dad bought me a new Honda CR125 while Garry got a Yamaha YZ100. He was to race in the intermediate group while I was old enough to be in the seniors.

We got all the riding gear sorted out and by March 1977 we were off in the van to Tow Law in County Durham for our first ever race. The course was on the slope of a boggy hill and there was sleet falling pretty hard. I was absolutely shitting myself with nerves and kept asking my dad, 'What do I do, dad? What do I do?' He sorted everything out, got us signed on, briefed us for practice and I ended up really enjoying the practice session and was looking forward to the race.

As soon as the starting tape went up, I dropped the clutch, pinned the throttle and arrived at the first corner at the head of the pack! I thought, 'Shit, what do I do now? Go faster? Slow down?' I didn't have a clue but I did what I could and I think I finished my first race in about fourth place, which wasn't too bad.

I can't remember how Garry got on that day but I know we both enjoyed it. When we got home we had to wash the bikes and get them ready for the next meeting. After that, we weren't allowed to ride them at home as often since they were meant for racing and we had to help fund our efforts as much as possible by working for my dad.

Towards the end of my first year of motocross racing, when I was 15, I got my first road bike – a Suzuki AP50. It was only meant to be a project bike to work on because I was too young to ride on the roads but I had other ideas. I got it for £90 instead of the £360 original price because it was salvage and I remember sending away for all the parts I needed from breakers so I could fix it up. It felt really fast at the time and I used to sneak it out of the garage when mum and dad were out and raced all over the roads with Cookie on his Yamaha FS1E.

My dad was out quite a lot because he played the accordion in a band so I always sneaked out on my bike when he was gigging. Incidentally, I was forced (and I mean forced) to play the accordion for seven years myself and even now I can still knock out a tune or two if I have to. But I realized by the time I went to secondary school that it was an old-fashioned instrument so I taught myself to play guitar, which I still strum now and again, mostly playing folk music.

Anyway, Cookie and I were very evenly matched on our new bikes and we were both complete nutters on them. To be classed as a moped in those days bikes had to have pedals like a normal pushbike. They acted as foot-rests when you weren't using them as pedals but they could be changed over by way of a little lever. I used to lean my bike over so far that I always scraped the pedals off in a shower of sparks and I'd constantly have to replace them. When they were intact though, we used to have pedalling races down the main street in the village for a laugh.

It's ironic that my first big crash didn't come about because I was riding like a nutter but because of someone else's carelessness. It happened in 1978 when a car driver pulled out in front of me and did me some serious damage. My mum and dad were at a wedding and Garry and I had been told to stay at home and watch television. No way! Garry wanted to go to Jedburgh to meet some mates and I wanted to ride my bike so we set off two-up on the bike and Garry didn't even have a helmet on which was the norm when he rode pillion.

Just outside Jedburgh, I dropped him off to walk into town so the police wouldn't see him on the bike without a helmet. I then was cruising through the centre of town at about 25mph when I saw a car sitting at a junction indicating right. I obviously had the right of way but just as I was riding past the car, it pulled out in front of me. Same old story. I broke my arm as I hit the car, then flew through the air and landed on a workman's metal post and sliced my leg on it, shattering my kneecap in the process. To top it all, I was knocked unconscious for the first of many times in my life.

Garry freaked out because he saw the whole thing as he was hanging out in the square with his mates. The ambulance took me away and the police called Jim Oliver's garage to come and take the bike away. Who should turn up to collect the bike but my dad's mate, Wullie Simson. He had been helping out at the garage that day and got the call from the police. Wullie recognized the bike so he took Garry back to Denholm and my mum and dad were informed. They gave me such a bollocking when they arrived at the hospital!

That was the first time I ever broke a bone and I was kept in hospital for a couple of weeks. The doctor told me I would never ride a bike again (I've since heard that one a few times) and even said I'd be lucky to walk properly again which shows he was talking out of a hole in his arse. I decided to quit motocross racing because it was a little more strenuous on the legs but as soon as I got home from hospital I started fixing up my road bike again. I wasn't going to let one poxy crash put me off.

I left school around that time too with four O levels, which are similar to English GCSEs, and decided I wanted to be an engineer. My dad said the best apprenticeships were with the armed forces so I applied to join the navy as a trainee marine engineer and actually passed all the tests and the medical. But as I was waiting to hear if I'd been accepted, I realized the chances of being able to ride a bike when I was stuck on a bloody boat in the middle of the Atlantic Ocean were pretty slim so I went off the idea immediately.

I attended a couple of job interviews locally but failed them both then I finally got a Youth Opportunity Scheme job with a local engineering firm for £19.50 a week. It was a company that made archery equipment such as sights and weights and that sort of stuff and I thought, 'Fuckin' great – that'll do me,' but I was soon to be disillusioned. I was given a drill with a box of metal pieces on one side and an empty box on the other. My job was to drill a hole in each piece and throw it into the 'out' box. It was all day, every day, for the best part of a year. It drove me absolutely crazy. Sometimes my bosses would vary the job so I was put on a lathe and had to cut lengths off steel bars for a change. Needless to say, that wasn't much better so I stuck at it for about seven months then just had to leave.

I knew Jim Oliver had a mechanic's job coming up so my dad had a word with him and I got the job without even an interview because Jim had seen how good I was at working on bikes. So that was it – I became an apprentice motorcycle mechanic at TB Oliver's in Denholm and that was the last real job I ever had. I did everything from fixing and servicing bikes to repairing cars, lawnmowers and tractors. I was an apprentice for four years before becoming a fully qualified mechanic and I worked there for another four years before quitting to become a professional racer.

It was when I was working at Jim's garage that I really started to hear a lot about Jimmie Guthrie. Naturally, every kid in the Hawick area had heard of the town's most famous son but at the garage he was revered. Old men were always dropping in for a chat and talking about him. I loved listening to all those stories from the old fellows. I was more of a listener than a talker (how things have changed!) back then because I was very shy but I learned an awful lot about life just from listening to those guys shooting the breeze.

I have since met Jimmie's widow, Isabel, and his son, Jimmie Guthrie Junior. Young Jimmy's one ambition was to win a race on the TT Mountain circuit on which his father had won six times and he actually achieved that in the late '60s when he won the Manx Grand Prix. After that, he quit racing and moved to

OFF THE RAILS 41

South Africa but he came back to Hawick in 1987 to commemorate the fiftieth anniversary of his dad's death. I had just won my first TT a couple of months prior to his visit and I met him at a reception. He was really friendly with me because I'd won a race and because he had known my father. Little did either of us know then that I'd go on to win even more TTs than the great man himself and at speeds that Jimmie could never even have dreamed of.

The first proper steps I took towards achieving a TT victory came in the spring of 1979 when my dad asked if I wanted to have a stab at road racing. Too bloody right I did! He bought me an old Bultaco rolling chassis and we slotted the CR125cc Honda engine from my motocross bike into it. Well, believe me when I say you have never seen such a fucking lash-up in all your life. We had bits of plywood and all sorts of other crap acting as brackets until we got the chain lined up and then we got the local black-smith to machine some better parts out of metal. They made the bike look marginally better but it was still a hell of a mess to look at. There were no shiny new race bikes for me when I started out.

But I must make a bit of a confession here before I go any further. I have always told the press that I started racing in 1983 but my first road race was actually in 1979. I didn't do a lot of racing between '79 and '83 (for reasons which will become clear), so I didn't want the media to think I'd been racing seriously for all those years and hadn't gotten anywhere. It's a bit like the way many racers these days lie about their age because they think it will improve their chances of getting a decent ride. You know who you are.

But anyway, my first race was actually at Croft near Darlington in North Yorkshire in 1979 and my outstanding memory of that meeting was a moment in practice in a combined 125/250cc session. I was riding my little 125 with my orange novice bib on and going down the main straight as fast as I could, thinking nobody could get past me. There was about two feet on the outside of the circuit between the grass and myself as I lined up for the next left-hand corner. As I shut the throttle and sat up to brake for the corner the local 250cc champion came past me on the outside between me and the grass and hooked up another gear! He wasn't even thinking about braking then and yet I was thinking, 'Fuckin' hell, these boys are a bit fast.' I still enjoyed it though and ended up finishing twenty-first in a field of around 30.

In my second race of the afternoon I was lying about twelfth following a big group of riders off the starting grid and into the first corner. They were all sitting behind each other like a row of ducklings and I wondered why they were doing that. I thought, 'Fuck this, I'm going to ride round them all and take the corner.' Bad move! So in only my second race, I had my first crash. I actually got past four or five of the riders but then some bloke lost the front end, slid off, and took me out with him. Served me right for trying to be a smart arse I suppose!

When I wasn't tinkering with my race bike back

home, I'd ride my Yamaha RD125 road bike to my papa's in Jedburgh, dump it there and meet up with my mates in town for a few under-age drinks. We weren't old enough to buy drink then so we'd give our money to some older boys and ask them to get some beer for us. Then we'd sink it in the River Jed to cool it before drinking it straight down and heading off to the Town Hall dance. There was usually a live band on at the Town Hall in those days and I invariably pulled a girl I knew from school and tickled her tonsils for a bit or even got to have a bit of a fumble if I was really lucky. If she got unlucky, I'd puke on her good dress before stumbling back to my papa's, quite often finding him lying in the gutter on the way home!

He drank a lot after my nana died and nine times out of 10, I'd find him lying by the side of the pavement drunk and have to pick him up and help him home, poor old sod. Then I'd jump on my bike and ride the back roads home. I had passed my test by that point but I'd have soon lost my licence if I'd been breathalysed on one of those trips though somehow I managed to avoid getting caught.

I could have had a 250cc bike if I'd wanted to but I prided myself on being able to thrash bigger bikes on my little 125. I used to smoke Suzuki X7250s and Yamaha RD250s with no problem. It was even more fun because I knew who everyone else was when I saw them on a bike and you can be sure they knew who I was. I loved kicking other riders' arses like that.

I'm sure some of the old boys in the area tell tales

nowadays about me tearing round the farm roads on bikes just like the tales I used to hear about Jimmy Guthrie. 'Aye, that young Hislop eedjit – ah remember him hairin' roond thay roads thinkin' he was a TT racer whun he wuz jist a slip o' a lad.'

But my carefree youth, playing at silly buggers came to an abrupt end on 27 September 1979 in the early hours of a Friday morning. Mum, dad, Garry and I had eaten our tea that night and dad then finished off some bookwork in his little office before we all went to bed. In the early hours of the morning I heard this terrible moaning and groaning coming from my parents' room so I bolted through to see what the hell was going on. My mum was running out of the room in a real panic shouting, 'It's your dad, it's your dad – there's something wrong!' I ran to the bed and turned my dad on his side thinking he might be choking on something. I put my fingers into his mouth and pulled his tongue out too so that he could breathe freely but then he just suddenly stopped groaning and went totally limp as I held him. He died right there in my arms. It was like a scene from a movie that you hope will never happen to you; holding your own father as he dies. As far as we knew, he had been in perfect health up to that point but he died of a massive heart attack right there and then at just 43 years old.

I'm still haunted by the thought that maybe I could have done more to save him and I often wish I'd known more about first aid but I suppose there was nothing else I could have done. Needless to say, we were all completely and utterly devastated by our loss. I was so close to my dad and he had done so much for me, not just with bikes but in every aspect of life. He had given up his beloved racing so he could pay for our upbringing and he had worked really hard to get us little extras. I'd probably never have gone into bike racing if it hadn't been for my dad because he was the one who really encouraged Garry and I to ride and race.

In the end, I think dad just took on too much. He had his business to run, he played in a band, he took Garry and I racing, did his own racing and rode horses in many of the Border's festivals. Even by a younger man's standards that's a busy schedule.

I was just 17, Garry was only 16 and we had lost our dad who was as much a friend to us as a father. It was a terrible thing to have to come to terms with at an age when we really needed him for guidance and it's a blow I've never really recovered from. I'm sure I'd be a very different person now if my dad were still alive.

I took a few days off work and then went to the funeral a week later and that was it – all over. We were now a single parent family and knew that life was about to get a whole lot tougher. My mum said there was no way she could continue living in the house which our father had practically built from scratch as the memories were just too painful, so we sold up and moved to Denholm in early 1980. It was only while writing this book that she told me we actually needed to sell the house for money as well because there was some kind of 'death tax' that had to be paid.

Mum continued working at the mills in Hawick but money was tight for us all and I was forced to quit racing. There was no way I could carry on with a wage of just over £26 a week, especially as I had to help out with money round the house now that I had no father to bring money in. Garry was too old for schoolboy motocross by that point so he packed that in and it looked like the end of racing for our family. My little 125 Honda sat in the garage along with my dad's 350cc Aermacchi and neither turned a wheel for a long time. It appeared the dream was over.

From that point on, the three of us just worked and survived in a kind of numbed quietness, and it was at this time that I started taking an interest in cars. I had to get my licence to test cars at work anyway but it proved to be easier said than done. I failed my first attempt for being far too confident and driving too fast; I was just being too cocky and thinking, 'Right, I'll show you how to drive.' Then I failed the second time round for trying to go too slowly; I was labouring and stalling the thing everywhere. But on my third attempt, which only lasted for 15 minutes, I drove perfectly in snowy and icy conditions and passed so I went out and bought an old Mark 1 Ford Escort.

It wasn't even a week before I put the bloody thing straight through a hedge by driving like a twat and that really was the start of my downward slide: in the months and years following my father's death I went completely off the rails. I couldn't come to terms with my loss and started drinking a lot; it just seemed the norm. On top of that, I seemed to be crashing cars every other week almost as if I had a death wish. I didn't even stay at home much on weekends, I'd just go out with friends, get pissed and end up sleeping on a sofa or the floor. It was a case of doing whatever I could to numb the pain; I would go out and crash out. But I always made sure I went to work during the week and I always stayed with mum on week-nights. Even if I was going to pieces, I wanted to try to be strong for my mum because she never wavered in her support for both Garry and me.

I bought an old Mini after the Escort and managed to crash that twice in the same night. The first time I spun it on icy roads and went through a fence back-wards, then later on I put it into a ditch. Looking back on it, I don't know how I survived that period. I could so easily have ended up dead in a car wreck or have ended up a drunken bum with no prospects in life at all.

No matter how many times I crashed, I didn't slow down. After the Mini, it was onto a Ford Escort 1600 Sport and I ended up wrecking that twice as well. I had no sooner fixed it up from the first accident when I rolled the bastard thing again while trying to race somebody on slippery wet roads. Every farmer in the Borders must have had a hole in his hedge at one time or another caused by me smashing through it in a car.

Eventually I did get myself together enough to do a couple of bike race meetings but, to be honest, my memory of racing in those years is very hazy because I was more interested in drinking, driving cars and getting off with girls. In fact, if it weren't for the result sheets that were compiled for me by a guy named Les Boultwood, I'd probably have forgotten all about those races. Those results show that I entered a few races in 1980 and 1981 with a best finish of second at East Fortune in 1980. However, I certainly couldn't afford to race often and since I can hardly remember any of the events now it's almost as if it never happened, which is generally why I've told people I started racing in 1983 because that's when I began to take it seriously.

When I did race, it was more of a lark than anything else – just a chance to play on bikes and another way to fill in a weekend. Garry, however, was taking a big interest in road racing at this point and with a wage of around £60 a week from helping run dad's joinery business, he could afford it. He started entering races on my little 125 Honda and I sometimes went along to help with the spannering. We didn't have a van, just an old car with a trailer attached and even they were both borrowed from a mate.

Wullie Simson and Jim Oliver became almost substitute fathers to Garry and I after my dad died. They even ended up buying us 125cc bikes to race to stop us going off the rails so in a way, I think those guys salvaged my life from going to the dogs. I dread to think where I'd be now if it weren't for them. My dad would have been so proud of all they did for his boys and I'll never be able to thank them enough.

Garry seemed to cope with our dad's death a bit

better than I did. Maybe he just wasn't as daft as I was, but he certainly never seemed to go over the top with the drinking and stuff as I did. Apart from losing a father, I think I lost a really good mentor when dad passed away. He knew his stuff about bikes, he knew lots of people connected with racing and was just a lot more worldly than I was in general. I'm sure my career would have worked out very differently had he still been around. Carl Fogarty's a good example: his dad George used to race and he guided Carl through his early career in a way that really benefited him.

Despite my reservations, my mum married a guy called Jim Thompson in the winter of 1980–81 and they decided to pool their resources and buy a pub called The Horse and Hounds Inn at Bonchester Bridge, so we all moved in there. Mum never really had a problem with Garry and I racing or riding bikes; if my dad had been killed on one it would probably have been different but he died of natural causes so there was no reason to hate bikes. On the contrary, she felt the racing gave us something to focus on so we weren't just getting drunk all the time and Garry actually started getting some decent results and even a couple of wins at Knockhill.

The two of us went for a holiday to the Manx Grand Prix in 1981 and Garry got so into the whole thing that he decided he was going to race there the following year. Then the month after we got back from the Manx, we had to deal with another tragedy when my friend Eric Glendinning was murdered in Hawick. He was standing outside the local chip shop eating chicken and chips when he was attacked and beaten to death by a group of yobs, one of whom was charged with murder and sent to jail. All for a fucking bag of chips! Hawick is a tiny little town and you'd never expect anything like that to happen in such a sleepy place but it just goes to show there's evil everywhere.

As it turned out, 1982 was the year when my brother really began to prove himself as a rider. He bought a brand new Yamaha TZ125 and did quite a lot of races that year and had some very good results. But the big one came in September when he won the 350cc Newcomers' race at the Manx GP on Jim Oliver's TZ350 Yamaha – exactly one year after he'd vowed to give it a go when we were on holiday. It was an amazing win because he'd only done 14 laps of the course before the race started. These days, many riders do hundreds of laps in cars or on bikes before they actually race for the first time so they know the course intimately. Everyone commented on how smooth Garry looked and he lapped at over 102mph on that little four-year-old bike. He didn't think he had any chance of even being on the leader board when he went there, never mind winning the race, so it was a fantastic achievement and I was really proud of him even though I couldn't be there with him. I simply couldn't afford to go, so I tuned into Manx Radio and listened to the commentary at home instead which was nerve-wracking stuff.

After the Manx, Garry met Ray Cowles, who was a madly keen racing sponsor, and Ray offered him a ride on his RG500 Suzuki at the Macau Grand Prix, which is an annual race held in China not far from Hong Kong. For a kid who had never been out of the country, it was an amazing opportunity and Garry was really excited about going; it would have been his first big step towards becoming a full-time professional rider but it was a trip he was destined never to make.

Because he wanted to stay sharp for Macau, Garry entered a club race at Silloth in October despite me saying he was daft because it was already winter and it was not the weather to go racing in. Besides, Silloth was a bumpy old shit-hole and I said as much but he was determined to go and that was that. He asked me if I wanted to go with him but I refused as I didn't like the place and I had to respray my car because I'd rolled the fucker again. I just said, 'I'll see you when you get back tonight,' and off he went. Those were the last words I ever spoke to him.

I went into Hawick and resprayed my car as planned, then drove back to mum's pub at about 6pm. As I was driving down the hill into Bonchester, I could see the silhouette of a transit van heading the other way. As it passed me, I realized it was Jim Oliver's van and thought, 'Garry's home early', as I didn't expect him to be back for another couple of hours. I didn't think much more of it and walked into the pub as normal. But when I went into the kitchen my mum was sitting there crying her eyes out. I asked what was wrong and she told me that Garry had had a bad accident. That didn't alarm me because racers were always having accidents; it was nothing unusual and at least it explained why the van was home so early. Garry had been taken to Carlisle Royal Infirmary and Wullie Simson had brought the van back.

Mum told me he had serious head injuries but I still thought he'd be okay so I didn't worry in the slightest. Even as we were walking into the hospital the following day I was still being cocky and cracking jokes, getting ready to say to Garry, 'You daft bugger, what happened to you?' We spoke to a doctor who told us Garry was in the intensive care ward and warned us that he was very ill. I remembered doctors telling me I might never walk again just because I'd busted my knee up, so I always took what they said with a pinch of salt. It was only when we walked into intensive care that the severity of the situation hit me like a sledgehammer, smack in the bloody face at full force. When I saw Garry lying there I just thought, 'Fucking hell, no. Oh fucking hell, no, no, no, no.'

My legs turned to jelly and my heart was in my mouth as I stared at him. He was completely wrapped from head to toe in silver foil in an attempt to raise his body temperature and there were pipes and tubes coming out of him everywhere. In fact there was so much machinery around him that it was hard to believe my lively little brother was in there, somewhere. But the one thing that really caught my attention was the huge artificial lung pumping up and down next to his bed – it was the only thing that was keeping him alive. That's when the joking stopped. Poor Garry was just lying there as if he was sleeping and oblivious to it all which I sincerely hope he was. I would much rather think that his final memory was of leading a race as he had been, than of lying helpless in a hospital bed.

I had never seen the 'death' side of racing before so I suppose I wasn't fully aware of just how dangerous the sport could be. I was now getting the toughest lesson about the harsh reality of it. Surely mum and me weren't going to lose Garry too, so soon after dad? Surely life couldn't be that cruel? As a family, we'd never done anything to harm anyone so why were we being so cruelly ripped apart like this? It just didn't seem fair.

We sat with Garry for a while and then we were asked to go and see the specialist in his office. I knew it had to be bad news. He told us they had tried everything to get a response from Garry but there was just nothing there. He then informed us that Garry was actually clinically dead and it was only the artificial lung that was keeping him going. Words cannot describe what it feels like to be told that about someone you love – about your own brother. 'Actually Steven, you're brother is already dead.'

Think of all your worst nightmares, put them all together and you're still not close to how that feels. And this was one nightmare I wasn't going to wake up from.

The specialist then asked if we would give per mission to donate any of Garry's organs and at that point I couldn't believe what I was hearing. I don't even remember what happened after that, because

I was so numbed by the experience my brain just went into shutdown mode and I became little more than a zombie. It was only when I spoke to my mum while working on this book that she told me what actually happened. Apparently, mum and Jim were staying in Carlisle that night so they drove me to Langholm where Eileen Douglas, a close family friend, picked me up and took me back to the pub where I stayed all night on my own. But I still can't remember any of that journey or that night no matter how hard I try.

What I do know is that my mum and Jim went back to the hospital the next day and at 11am on Tuesday 19 October 1982, the doctors decided there was no choice but to switch the machine off. Again, until writing this book, I had always thought my mum made that decision but she now assures me that it was actually the doctors. But mum did give permission for them to use Garry's kidneys and corneas; two -people got life out of his kidneys and someone else got sight out of his eyes.

I wasn't at the hospital when they switched the machine off so I didn't know my brother was gone until my mum got home at 1.45pm (I have the exact time noted in my diary from that year) and told me, although I had been expecting the worst. Ironically, I was watching a documentary about the TT races on television at the time, still madly keen on bikes. It was hard to believe but I was going to have to learn to accept that I didn't have a brother anymore. Or a father.

4 Tales from the Riverbank

'I poached salmon and sold them to pubs to help pay for my racing.'

Many people have asked me why I didn't turn my back on bike racing when my brother was killed and it's still a difficult question to answer.

I think I just had an inbuilt desire to achieve something in my life and racing bikes seemed the only way I could do that. I certainly never blamed racing for Garry's death as it was his choice to race and I never hated the sport because of what it had taken away from me. Bikes have always been part of my life and I continued to ride them after Garry died just as I always had done.

When I went to the inquest I learned that my brother had been leading the 350cc race and had broken the lap record before he crashed. There was a hairpin corner on the track and it was flooded from heavy rain in the morning so the organizers reshaped the corner using road cones. When it dried, the track surface became silty and dusty in the same way as a puddle dries when it's stopped raining. Garry must have just clipped that silty surface next to the road cones and was high-sided off the bike – racing speak for being thrown over the top of the machine. Instead of landing relatively harmlessly as he would have done nine times out of 10 in such an accident, he landed on the back of his head and the back of his helmet caved in causing Garry to fracture the base of his skull. Ironically, that was the last race ever to be held at Silloth.

Garry is buried in Southdean cemetery, near Chesters village, right next to my dad: they died just three years apart. My dad was 43 and my brother just 19. Each headstone has a little motorbike engraved on it and Garry's stone has an inscription reading, 'He died for the sport he loved.' Apparently it was me who asked mum if she would have those words engraved on it although I can't really remember asking her.

Just before he died, Garry was being tipped as one of Scotland's most promising riders and I'm sure he would have achieved similar results to me had he lived long enough. He was keen to turn professional in 1983 but, sadly, we'll never know just how good he could have been. As I said, I don't blame racing for what happened but I have often questioned the existence of a god since I lost my brother and father. What kind of god would take them away from me?

To cheer myself up a bit, I decided to go to the Isle of Man in June for a three-day break to watch the TT races but little did I know then that trip would change my entire life.

My first ever trip to the Isle of Man had been to the Manx Grand Prix in 1965 when I was just three years old and my dad took me over to support Jimmy Guthrie Junior. I went again to the Manx in 1975 but my first trip to the actual TT was in 1976, which was the last year the races counted as a round of the world championship. I watched my very first race from the Les Graham memorial near Bungalow Bridge. I could hear the bikes coming towards me from miles away because they were so loud back then; they were pure race bikes with pea-shooter exhaust pipes, not just glorified production machines like they race today. John Williams on the Texaco Heron Suzuki was the first rider I remember seeing and he was quite simply the fastest fucking thing I had ever seen in my entire life. He just blew my mind. Unbelievable! He did a 112mph lap that day which was the first sub-20-minute lap ever of the TT as far as I remember. But because he went so fast, he ended up running out of fuel and had to push his bike for a mile at the end to finish the race!

I was pretty much hooked on the TT from that moment on and went back there again in 1979 when I was 17 with Wullie Simson and another friend called Dave Croy. I helped Wullie and Dave in the pits, working for a rider called Kenny Harrison so it was my first real hands-on experience of the event. As it turned out, Wullie and Dave were the guys who helped me for years when I started racing, right up until I got involved with Honda. They were both a great help to my career.

Anyway, as I said, after Garry was killed I didn't race very often and I certainly had no intentions of ever becoming a professional racer. I had also never really thought about racing on the Isle of Man myself. However, that all changed when I went to the 1983 TT races, this time with Wullie and a man called George Hardie who later was to become my mum's partner and still is as I write this.

We were sitting on the banking just after the eleventh milestone munching on our pieces (Scottish for sandwiches!), enjoying the fresh air and watching the traffic go by before the big Senior Classic race got underway. Like everyone else around the course, we had our little transistor tuned into Manx Radio to listen to the race commentary, so that we knew who was who and what was going on. The men of the moment were Joey Dunlop and Norman Brown who are both tragically no longer with us. Norman was killed while racing in the British Grand Prix at Silverstone just a couple of months later and Joey, as everyone knows, lost his life in an obscure race in Tallin, Estonia in 2000 just a month after completing his famous TT hat-trick.

I could hear the bikes setting off over the radio but it was some time before I could actually hear them on the road for real. Eventually, I picked up the sound of Norman Brown's Suzuki RG500 engine screaming along the mile-long Cronk-y-Voddy straight towards us, then he blasted into view and shocked the life out of me. Having seen the normal road traffic going past for the last couple of hours, words cannot describe the difference in speed as Brown went past our spectator point. Fuck me, he came through the corner at the end of Cronky down towards the eleventh milestone, lifted the front of the bike over a rise in the road, braked hard and back-shifted two gears before changing direction and blasting off towards Handley's. He was going so fast that he almost blew me off the bloody banking.

Joey Dunlop was hot on his heels on a Honda RS850 and he had it up on the back wheel too and was pushing every bit as hard as Brown. My reaction was, 'For fuck's sake!' I just couldn't believe that anything on earth could go that fast. I was completely blown away with the whole spectacle.

In those split seconds that it took Brown and Dunlop to hammer past me, my life had changed forever. I determined there and then that if I never did anything else in my meaningless life, I would try to ride round the TT circuit like those boys. My mind was totally made up.

Having finally realized what I wanted to do with my life, I wasted no time in going about it when I got back home. As an amateur, I decided that my first attempt on the Mountain course should be at the Manx Grand Prix, which was being held in September, just three months away. I didn't have long to go from being a TT spectator to a Manx GP competitor.

The bike was not a problem, because I had already bought Cookie's Yamaha TZ250E for £800 and had enough spares to convert it into a 350 as well. But somehow I had to find money to fund the trip as well as getting hold of a van and getting all my entries organized. I was granted a Scottish national licence with no problem because I had a few races under my belt, then I blew £200 on a new set of leathers and then I had to save almost every penny of my meagre £36 a week salary to fund the trip.

I soon realized that wasn't going to be enough cash so I started selling things as well. First to go was my father's 350cc Aermacchi racing bike which netted me around £2000 then I sold my beloved Ford Escort Mexico – a mega car which I was really proud of. I had swapped it for the car I was spraying on the day Garry was killed but, true to form, I put the bugger straight through a hedge within a week. At least I was consistent. After the crash I spent a lot of time working on it and buying new parts but I needed cash to go racing so I sold it at a loss because I was so desperate. So for the first time in years I didn't own a car but being a bike racer is like being a junkie; you'd sell your own granny to get what you need.

I even had to change my lifestyle to save money. I stopped going out to the pubs with my mates and refused to go for a pint even when they called round to the house. When I wasn't working on my bikes, I just stayed in and watched television. I even knocked back the chance to go to Ibiza on holiday with the rest of the lads but it never got me down because I was so focused and all I thought about was lining up on the grid on the Isle of Man.

When I filled in the entry forms for the 350cc Newcomers race and the 250cc Lightweight event at the Manx the only person I told was Wullie Simson because I knew most people were against me racing after what had happened to my brother. I felt a bit sneaky going behind peoples' backs and not telling my mum or anyone else about my plans but that's the way it had to be; I really didn't want to upset anyone but I knew I had to race. I even prepared my bikes in secret and just told anyone that asked that I was doing overtime at the garage.

But it wasn't long before my little secret got out thanks to the race organizers. Once I'd posted off my entry forms I'd forgotten all about them until I came home from work one night and the shit really hit the fan. My mum and stepdad looking thoroughly miserable confronted me. I just said, 'All right? How's it goin' folks?' but Jim's response was to slap a postcard down on the table in front of me and shout: 'What the hell is this?' It was the confirmation of my race entries written on a bloody post card for the whole world to see! Shit.

'Dear Steve, just to confirm we have received your entry for this year's Manx Grand Prix.' I thought 'Fuckin' hell, I've been rumbled here.' Jim went absolutely apeshit screaming at me, 'How can you do such a thing to your mother?' giving it all that guilt-trip bollocks. I explained it was just something I had to do and defended myself as best as I could but it was obviously falling on deaf ears. My mum and Jim continued arguing and then she said something I'll never forget. He was rattling on about me bringing more grief into the house after Garry had already brought enough when my mum shouted, 'Why the hell should Steve live his life in the shadow of someone else?'

It was a brave thing to say. I mean, I know I'm a selfish person for doing what I do (as I think all bike racers must be) but my mum saw beyond that and recognized my real passion for racing. Jim hated the idea of me racing but I never expected him to understand and I didn't care about his opinion anyway. But I really appreciated what mum said because she obviously realized it was unfair to deprive me of something I wanted so badly just because my brother had been killed doing the same thing. We don't stop driving cars because someone else has an accident, do we? To me, bike racing was no different.

My mum was the only person who didn't try to discourage me from riding bikes after Garry's death. Everyone else, aunties, uncles, colleagues, the whole lot of them said, 'Well, that'll be the end of the racing in your family then, Steve', but my mum was different and I still respect her for that. She even walked out on my stepdad for a while when I went to the Isle of Man because they had been arguing so much about me racing and she refused to side with Jim when he wanted to stop me.

In a bid to get in shape for my Island debut, I cycled the 12 miles every day to work and back on a borrowed pushbike for six weeks. Some nights it was freezing cold and pissing with rain and just thoroughly miserable as I was cycling home and my hands would be red raw with cold but I just kept an image of Joey Dunlop and Norman Brown in my head and that drove me on.

I entered some races at Knockhill in Fife a few weeks before the Manx just to make sure the bikes were going OK. I still had the little 125cc bike that Garry had ridden and I wanted to sell it so I figured a good race result would also be a good advert for the bike. I finished second to Roddy Taylor who was Scottish champion at the time so I was quite pleased with that and managed to sell the bike as well. I was then lying about fifth or sixth in the 350cc race when I fell off and I remember being really pissed off about that because I scuffed my brand new leathers that I'd bought specially for the Manx!

Anyway, with everything packed up in the van, Wullie Simson and I caught the ferry from Heysham and four hours later we were on the Isle of Man and I was itching to get out onto the course to start learning it. One of the questions I still get asked a lot is how I learned the TT course so well. There's no real secret, it's just about putting the time in and having an aptitude for it. I'm very good at learning things like that and within a couple of laps of any foreign circuit, I was usually on the pace. But I know of some good riders who went to the TT and just couldn't get their heads round the course.

The TT is different to learn compared to short circuits because it's got well over 300 corners and you need to know where every one of them goes, where every bump is, every drain cover and every rise in the road. You need to find the quickest but safest lines to take as well as knowing where all the damp patches tend to linger after it has rained. You must know where the wind is likely to get under the bike and lift it or blow you sideways. You must know your braking points for every corner on different types of machine and you've got to know what gear to be in for them all too to get the optimum revs, grip and drive. On top of that there's cambers to learn, both converse and adverse, and loads of little tricks to gain time like using kerbs or bus stops to run wide, meaning you can take certain corners faster. And when you've learned all that, you need to find out how you can go quicker still by shaving off fractions of a second each lap. In short, it's the most difficult and demanding course in the world to learn and you never, ever stop learning it. There's never been and never will be a perfect lap of the TT.

But I had a bit of a head start as a kid because I used to sit in the back of cars and vans when my dad and Wullie Simson went round learning the course themselves. I listened carefully to everything they said about each corner and where the apexes and peel-off points were and I learned an awful lot that way. It was just through boyish enthusiasm because I never thought I'd ever race at the TT but somehow all of that knowledge stuck in the back of my mind and I put it all to good use when I eventually did come to race there.

I can't actually remember it but my mum tells me that I used to be able to recite the main points on the TT course when I was just five years old because

I'd heard my dad and all his pals talking about it so much. When I used to sit on the arm rests of the sofa with Garry as kids playing at racers apparently I'd do a running commentary, 'And Jimmie Guthrie's coming round Quarterbridge and heading on out to Braddan', or, 'He's coming down the Creg and heading for home.' Mum says my dad used to sit gob-smacked listening to me and wondering where the hell I'd got it all from!

After I'd progressed from sofa racing and actually got onto the TT course for real I wasn't one of those guys who did 300 laps in a van before practice. In fact, I only ever did about 12 complete laps on my own before lining up for the first practice session. Ten times TT winner and 15 times world champion, Giacomo Agostini, went to stay on the Isle of Man for two weeks before he first raced there and spent six hours every day going round and round the track to learn it. I never had to do that.

The first lap I ever did on a bike was in 1983 after watching Joey and Norman Brown in that Classic race. Jim Oliver had a little Yamaha RD250 with him and he let me do one lap on it after the race before we all went out for some beers that night. It was a good time to go round the track because most people had already been there for two weeks and had had their fill of laps so it was pretty quiet. I made sure I took a stopwatch in my pocket and started it off at Quarterbridge then went for it as fast as I could, especially over the mountain section where there's no speed limit, another unique feature of the Isle of Man. Boy, I was really going over there, absolutely flat-out all the way on that little LC. I rode back round to Quarterbridge and stopped my watch; it read 32 minutes, which equated to a lap average of 78mph. I know that precisely because I still have a five-year diary from that period and I entered my time in it! That was going some for open roads so I was quite chuffed with myself – after all, some people still can't do that in a bloody race!

These days, there are so many videos of on-board camera laps of the TT available to buy that a new rider could learn the course reasonably well before ever setting foot on the Isle of Man but they didn't exist when I started out. I actually made one of those videos in 1990 called 'TT Flyer' and managed to clock the first ever 120mph lap with a camera on board. It caused quite a sensation at the time. I even wrote a book on the course itself a few years back explaining the right way to take every corner –that's how well I know the place!

Speaking of on-board camera footage, I remember getting passed by Joey Dunlop a few times in my first practice week at the Manx, as he was recording foot-age for the 'V-Four Victory' video and had a huge big camera strapped to the tank. These days the cameras are so small you don't even know they're there but in 1983, it was like having Steven bloody Spielberg sitting on the tank with a full camera crew in tow! Anyway, Joey passed me so many times that I thought there was three of the little buggers – I didn't realize that he was continually stopping to adjust the camera!

I broke down at Lambfell just before the Cronk-y-

Voddy straight on my first ever practice lap – the bike just went flat and died on me. But I had come prepared and pulled out a little girlie purse that was riveted to the inside of the fairing and contained fresh spark plugs and a plug spanner! Sure enough, one of the plugs on the bike was fouled up so I changed it, bump-started the bike and was off on my way again. That's the sort of DIY job which keeps you going on the Island and it was the norm back then as it probably still is now for riders who aren't in big teams.

But I only got as far as Ballaugh Bridge on the same lap then the bloody thing died on me again. This time the big end was gone and it definitely wasn't going any farther so my session was over. But it wasn't all bad, as that's when I first met the famous Gwen from Ballaugh. She's spent years looking after riders who break down anywhere near the renowned hump-back bridge and she always had pots of tea, cakes, biscuits and toast at the ready. You've got to remember that practice starts at 5am on the Island so I was really ready for a breakfast! So I ended my first practice session in the lap of luxury eating breakfast and drinking tea in Gwen's house which was a lot better than what I'd have got back in our van. Ever since then, I always waved or wiggled my foot at Gwen just to say hello during a race, no matter how hard I was riding. I never knew when I might need her hospitality again.

The rest of practice week went okay and I eventually hit upon a pretty good way of learning the course better. Instead of trying to follow the newest young hotshot who may have been quick but reckless, I decided to tag on behind the older boys riding classic bikes. I figured that they had all probably ridden the course for years and would know their way around intimately, even if they weren't going that fast in a straight line. It proved to be a good idea as their lines were spot-on so I really learned a lot by doing that. I remember I had to roll off the throttle on the straights so as not to pass them then I'd try to follow them through the twisty bits. But they usually lost me so I'd have to hang around until another rider came along and try to follow him for as long as I could.

The buzz of riding the Mountain course was every bit as awesome as I'd hoped for. Racing flat-out on real roads without worrying about tractors, coppers or anything coming the other way is an amazing thrill and that's what attracts riders to the TT year after year despite the dangers. My favourite sections were from Ballacraine to Ballaugh and then from Sulby Bridge to Ramsay. I never enjoyed the mountain section as it's just so bleak up there. I think I was put off from the start when I broke down there (again) later on in my first practice week and had to wait for hours for the van to pick me up. Not a good place to be stranded.

I was more like Joey Dunlop in that I loved to be in among the trees, hedges and stone walls. It was fantastic racing between them at such high speeds and that's where I always made up time on the other guys who maybe backed off a little through those parts. Those sections took a lot more learning as well, which is more pleasurable in the end because it's more of a challenge and very rewarding when you get it right.

The Newcomers race was on the Tuesday and it was the first race of the week as well as being the first of my Island career. I was 21 years old. Everyone thought Ian Newton was going to win because he had been quickest all through practice week but he was pushing himself too hard and he ripped the bales off a stone wall at the Black Dub on one lap when he clouted them with his bike. He was riding out of his skin and luckily, for the sake of his life, his bike broke down and that was that.

The race became a four-way scrap between me, Robert Dunlop (Joey's younger brother), Ian Lougher and Gene McDonnell. Gene would later die in horrific circumstances when he hit a horse on the course at full speed in 1986. The horse had panicked and jumped on to the track when a paramedic helicopter had landed in a field to pick up Brian Reid who had crashed at Ballaugh and broke his collarbone. Both Gene and the horse died instantly. It was a harsh reminder of the bizarre hazards of the TT.

Race-wise, I had my fair share of problems despite all the preparation Wullie and I had done on the bike. After just five miles my back brake faded to practically nothing, then the wadding in my exhaust blew out making the bike go flat and as if that wasn't enough, the chain started seizing up because it was too hot. The vibration from that in turn split the frame in some parts and on top of that my fairing had worked its way loose and was hanging off by the end of the race!

But despite all my problems I ended up finishing second to Robert Dunlop with Ian Lougher in third place. All three of us went on to have great TT careers and currently have 22 wins between us. As I write this, Robert and Ian are still racing there so they may well rack up some more wins yet.

Second was a brilliant result for me because I hadn't expected to achieve anything when I went to the Island – I just wanted to ride the course and enjoy myself. As I said before, the bike was hanging in pieces at the end of the race so I was really lucky to get a finish at all and I even put in a lap at 103.5mph which was pretty quick back then for a 350cc machine.

The only disappointing thing was that I didn't get a trophy. Only the winner of the 500cc class, the 350cc class and the 250cc class (all classes ran in the same race) got replicas. I just got a little finisher's disc, which was a bit of a bummer. But I did get a trophy for my eleventh place in the 250cc event later that week which kind of made up for things even though the bike was a total nail – I could have kicked my bloody helmet round the course faster. But I had a great night at the presentation ceremony with Ian Lougher. We got totally legless and I remember pissing myself at him trying to dance to UB40's song *Red Red Wine*, which was in the charts at the time. It was hilarious. Ian's much better on a bike than he is on a dance floor!

When I got on the ferry and headed for home I started thinking about how much I had enjoyed myself over the last couple of weeks. The racing, the nights out, the atmosphere; it was just a great event and I decided there and then that I had to do it again the following year so I started saving for the 1984 event as soon as I got back home. I didn't even consider racing a full season on short circuits because all I wanted to do was race on the Isle of Man again. Anyway, I couldn't afford to do a full season with the money I was making.

Looking back now, I wish I could live my life over again. Those were good years when I was still young that I just pissed away, waiting for the Manx and the TT to come round again. What a bloody waste! Had I committed myself fully back then and somehow found some sponsors, who knows where I could be now? I certainly feel as if I should be sitting here with a couple of world titles under my belt, either in World Superbikes or Grand Prix but racing's full of 'ifs' and 'buts', so I try not to dwell on it too much.

I did one more race at East Fortune at the end of 1983 and finished sixth on the 125 but that was it for the year. So I just plodded on with my job in the garage over winter, rode my Yamaha DT175MX trail bike to keep my hand in and daydreamed about racing in the TT.

I did, however, have one other way of getting an adrenalin buzz when I wasn't racing – poaching! For years, my mate, Rod Heard, and I had been mastering the black art of illegally catching salmon and by this point, we were experts. My upbringing on the farm with all the fishing and sneaking up on crows to shoot them had made me a natural at poaching. I either used a shark hook for the job or sometimes I made my own hooks from an old pitchfork. I remember bending and forging specialized hooks in the garage just for poaching. We called them 'cleeks' where we came from and there's a definite knack to using them but seeing as I started poaching when I was about 10 years old, I had mastered it. I even put motorbikes to good use when it came to poaching because I made a huge halogen floodlight which I powered with a bike battery!

I remember on one occasion, when I was about 13, I was hanging over the edge of a banking by the river and looking underneath the overhanging riverbank. There was a huge salmon in there just snoozing with its tail lightly swishing so I grabbed my cleek, held onto a tree and stretched out over the river as far as I could to get some leverage. I thrust the cleek into the 'tail wrist' of the fish (between the bones before the tail fin) and then all hell broke loose. Fuck me, the thing nearly pulled me right off the bank and into the water it was so strong. With a massive effort and not a lot of dignity, I managed to get it out of the water and onto the bank. When we finally got it home and weighed it, it was 11 pounds (or five kilos in today's money) which is fairly big for a salmon.

Problem was, it was so big I couldn't get it home on my pushbike so I had to conjure up another way of getting it onto the kitchen table. I hid the fish then walked into Bonchester village and rummaged through a few bins looking for empty lemonade bottles then took them to a shop, got about 20 pence back for them and used the money to call my dad from a phone box. 'Dad, I've caught a fish but it's a bit on the big side. Can you bring the car to take it home?'

So dad turned up, threw the salmon in the boot, and off he went with me peddling home after him. I sort of got into trouble that night because my mum and dad knew I had been poaching but at the same time, dad was chuckling a bit. After all, his son had proved his resourcefulness and there was a bloody great salmon for the whole family to eat, completely free of charge.

I only poached occasionally as a kid and it was mostly for laughs but by the time I was in my late teens, my mate Rod and I were poaching far more frequently. By then we had our own cars to transport the fish so we caught lots of them and started selling them to local pubs who would then serve them up as bar meals. It was a nice little earner.

We got chased many times over the years by water bailiffs, the police and various farmers but one night in particular stands out. We had caught about 16 salmon (which a top angler couldn't even dream of doing on a two-week fishing holiday) and left each one hidden under a different tree while we caught more. That way, anyone turning up wouldn't see a whole mound of fish, which would really have given the game away. Besides catching fish from under the overhanging riverbanks or 'hags' as we called them, we would wade into the river up to our waists with a torch because the fish were drawn to the light and stayed in it when you shone it on them. Then we'd simply hook them with our cleeks and throw them on the bank.

It was important to never wear wellington boots because we soon learned we couldn't run fast enough in them when we were being chased. Waterproof trousers were a no-no too because they were too heavy for running when they got wet and tracksuit trousers were just as bad. So it was jeans and training shoes only; after all, getting soaked was better than getting caught. We might have got away with it as kids but poaching is a serious offence when adults are involved.

Anyway, that night we were doing fine until we saw lots of spotlights heading straight for us. When that happened you forgot the fish and ran like buggery. We got as far as we could on our legs then dropped to our hands and knees and scrambled through ditches and bogs keeping as low as we could out of the spotlights. It was like a scene from *The Great Escape*! It was about nine o'clock and pitch black and I remember lying in a ditch watching all those cars and vans and all the commotion as the 'lynch mob' tried to find us. We were absolutely shitting ourselves.

Eventually, we made our escape down a railway line, crept into Rod's house and got changed out of our wet clothes and sat about trying to look innocent in case there was a knock at the door. Rod's mum thought it was all quite funny and she eventually took the dog for a walk to see if there was anyone still down by the riverside. When she said there was no one there we grabbed our torches and went back to try and find the fish that we'd hidden but every one of them was gone. Bastards! We had done all the hard work and they'd pissed off with our fish. How can you own fish swimming in a river anyway? I could never understand how taking fish could be a crime so I just took them. They're as much mine as anyone else's.

On most other nights though we did pretty well and managed to make some decent cash from selling our catch to local pubs. It's fair to say that more than one customer has enjoyed a nice bar lunch of poached salmon (and I don't mean the way it's cooked) in a Borders pub without knowing it! Probably paid through the nose for it too.

Mostly, Rod and I used the extra cash to pay for petrol to arse around in our cars but I'm sure that sometimes the savings I had in my bank to go racing were boosted by my poaching activities. I guess I must be the only bike racer ever who poached salmon to help pay for racing! Just a shame I never managed to catch enough to fund a full World Superbike season.

5 The Flying Haggis

'The sport which took my brother's life actually gave me a life.'

Many people, including fellow racers and team bosses, have criticized me over the years for not trying hard enough if my bike's not set up properly, and that stems from my training as a mechanic when I was a young lad.

I've always prided myself on being meticulous when it comes to setting up or fixing bikes, whether they were mine or someone else's; I suppose in that sense I'm a bit of a perfectionist. So if a team expects me to ride a bike which isn't handling properly or is unreliable or just plain uncompetitive, they've got another think coming. Why should I risk my neck on a bike which isn't working properly and which could pitch me off at any second? It's my bloody neck, no matter how much I'm getting paid to lay it on the line, and I won't risk it unnecessarily to gain a position in a race because racing's really not that important. Don't get me wrong, if I'm feeling comfortable and confident on a bike I'll push as hard as anyone out there but only if the machine's right.

Maybe that's been a big downfall in my career and it's certainly caused some friction within teams I've ridden for, but that's just the way I am. A commercial pilot wouldn't take off in a plane if he knew it was faulty so what's the difference with a racing bike?

I've never been a big crasher and that's partly because I refuse to push bikes which aren't up to it but I'm certainly not afraid of crashing – it's all part of the territory in this sport and you have to accept that. But many accidents are avoidable so, if I can, I avoid them. Some team managers have complained that my team-mates seem to manage to get decent results on an identical bike to the one I'm riding when it's not working right, so why can't I? But that same team-mate was usually riding by the seat of his pants, crashing a lot and taking all sorts of risks just to get the occasional decent result. To me, it makes much more sense to work on getting the bike right and then the results will follow.

And it's not that I'm a quitter either, as some people probably think. I've heard people say, 'Oh, Hislop will chuck the towel in if things aren't going well,' or, 'He'll come apart like a cheap watch when the pressure's on.' But it's total bullshit. I will try everything I know to get a bike set up properly and I'm prepared to have some scary moments while I'm experimenting with different set-ups, too, if that's what it takes. The 1994 TT is a good example. The Honda RC45 I was riding that year was a real handful round the Island

and I don't know how many near misses I had in practice, but I worked away at it all through practice week until I had it a bit more under control. My team-mates, Joey Dunlop and Phillip McCallen, had too many other bikes to set up so I concentrated on the RC45 to try to find settings for all of us. Both Joey and Phillip were happy enough with my set-up advice and Joey even borrowed my spare set of forks for the races. I haven't seen them since but, knowing Joey, they're probably still lying around in his pub somewhere! The point is that initially the bike was so bad that Joey didn't want to ride it and that's really saying something because Joey could ride anything round the TT. But I persevered because I thought there was light at the end of the tunnel and in the end I won both races on it.

It was the same with the Norton in 1992. It was an absolute nightmare to ride at the beginning of practice week, bucking and weaving everywhere but I stuck with it, too, and got it going right for the Senior class race which I won. But sometimes bikes are beyond help and I flatly refuse to risk my life on an under-powered or poor-handling bike just to get a sixth place. No way!

I certainly had plenty of time to get my Yamaha ready for the 1984 Manx Grand Prix because it was the only race I did all year except for one outing at Knockhill that I treated as a shakedown session for the Manx. My bike was a 1978 model, which was obvi-ously getting a bit long in the tooth, so I spent a good bit of cash upgrading it that year. I bought an alloy frame to make the bike lighter and new bodywork to make it look more modern, together with some other smaller parts. It ended up looking really good, even though it was a bit of a hybrid. I really enjoyed my race at Knockhill. It's always been a good track to ride on smaller bikes but I think it's too tight and twisty for modern Superbikes so I've come to dislike it in the last few years, even though it's my 'home' circuit in the British Superbike championship.

Wullie Simson came over to the 1984 Manx with me as did Wendy Oliver, who I was seeing quite seriously at the time and who was the daughter of Jim Oliver, my boss. I had entered the 350 in the Junior and Senior events and practice went okay apart from some problems with my new frame, which broke a couple of times. I got it welded up again but I wasn't sure if it would last race distance. Sure enough, I was running in about third place in the Junior race when the bike started mishandling badly because the frame had broken again so I was forced to pull in and call it a day.

You never stop learning at the Isle of Man. Every time out on the bike, there's something different whether it's the weather, changes to the road surface or any number of other things; I was still learning that course the last year I rode it in 1994. I even used to lie in bed at night and visualize my way round it – every corner, every bump, every straight, lap after lap after lap. Sometimes I'd wake up and think, 'Shit, I only got to Ballacraine last night. That's no good.' Some people count sheep when they can't sleep but

I used to do as many laps of that damned course as I could before sleep took over.

Anyway, after I'd pulled out of the Junior class race I doubted whether I'd be able to ride in the Senior event with the same dodgy frame. Luckily, I met up with Ray Cowles who had offered my brother a ride on his 500cc bike before he was killed. Ray was fielding Ian Lougher at the Manx but he crashed in practice and broke his collarbone, so Ray offered me the use of his TZ350 Yamaha for the Senior. I finished fifth in the race up against much bigger and faster 500cc machines which was pretty good going and I think I was the first 350 bike home, lapping at around 107mph.

I may have become the first man in history to lap the TT at over 120mph in 1989, but back in 1984, lapping at 107mph felt awesome. If someone had told me then how fast I'd eventually end up going round that track I'd never have believed it. The 350 lap record at the TT proper was only about 112mph, so I wasn't far off the pace of the professional riders and that's when someone suggested I enter the TT and get some money back for my efforts instead of doing the Manx again. The Manx was, and is, an amateur event but the TT paid start money to riders so at least some of my expenses would be covered, and if I managed to win some prize money then so much the better.

I certainly needed the money because I was broke when I got back from the Isle of Man. So broke, in fact, that I had to sell my Yamaha RD250LC road bike. That left me with no transport at all, but Jim Oliver once again came to the rescue and gave me a Honda C70 step-through scooter just like the ones you see grannies riding to the supermarket on. All that was missing was a little basket to put the cat food and tins of corned beef in.

The bike was an MOT failure so it was worth practically nothing but I was grateful to Jim all the same. Everybody laughed at me on that thing but I rode it every day regardlessly for two years. There I was, Steve Hislop, second in the Manx Grand Prix and just six months away from becoming a TT rider and my only road bike was a daft, old granny's scooter. I even remember going to work a few times in my papa's Reliant Robin three-wheeler for want of anything better! But I eventually had the last laugh as I started a trend for riding scooters in the area. A few of my mates got strapped for cash too so they all took my lead, sold their cars and bought scooters. From feeling like an idiot riding one on my own, it actually became a brilliant laugh with all of us riding round together on them.

Looking back now I really should have spent that winter looking for sponsorship, but I was never any good at that. I was very backward at coming forward and I could probably have sold myself a lot better if I'd been a more cocky type. I did write letters to local firms, asking if they'd be interested in helping me out, but I realize now I didn't push hard enough. I hated the thought of going begging for money.

One person who did help me a lot, though, was a guy called Brian Reid who used to drink in my mum's pub. He helped out writing letters and with other things, and I used to take him to the races sometimes. He became one of my biggest supporters and even helped start a Steve Hislop supporter's club to try to raise some money for racing. One night, as he was playing pool in the pub, Brian stumbled backwards quite dramatically and we all thought he was pissed so we just laughed about it. However, it turned out to be the first signs of a rare disease of the central nervous system and he's now in a wheelchair for life. But eventually he got the coolest wheelchair around when it was sprayed up as a replica of my famous 'Hizzy' helmet in shocking pink and blue!

Brian's a great bloke and has such a passion for bike racing. He wrote to all sorts of people such as Paul McCartney and Richard Branson asking for sponsorship and eventually he landed me my first proper sponsor – Marshall Lauder Knitwear of Hawick. Not quite Richard Branson, but it was a start and I was grateful for it.

Brian was also responsible for the 'Flying Haggis' logo on my helmet. I'd been nicknamed that by commentators and Brian thought it would be a good idea to play on it to get myself noticed a bit. He took my helmet up to the day-care centre he attended and one of the art teachers painted the haggis with wings, and I've kept a variation of that design to this day.

Prior to my first TT in 1985, my employer, Jim Oliver, asked me what bikes I had to ride. I told him I only had the Yamaha TZ350 and to race that in the Senior class against 500cc machines was going to be an uphill struggle. When you make the effort to go over to the Isle of Man it makes sense to enter as many races as possible to make it worthwhile and increase your chances of winning some prize money; if you've only got one bike and it breaks down, it's all over. Jim knew this so he pointed to a Yamaha RD500 in his showroom and said, 'Take that for the Production race and enter the Formula One on it as well while you're at it.' Result. It was only a standard road bike but at least it would be good enough for the Production race. I ran that bike in on the roads of the Scottish Borders with Wendy Oliver on the back most of the time and no matter how fast I went, she prodded me to go faster. She was totally mad. As usual, I had my one meeting before the Island trip to make sure my 350 Yamaha was going okay. It was a miserable, sleety, wet day at East Fortune in East Lothian and I bagged a couple of second places, but my heart's never been in racing when conditions are like that and it still isn't. Despite what a lot of people think, I can actually ride in the wet but I just don't like it. After all, I did keep up with Mick Doohan for a whole session in the pissing rain at Suzuka in 1991 and there's no one faster than him.

Apart from my rides in the F1, Production and Senior races, Ray Cowles also gave me a bike for the Lightweight race so that gave me a ride in almost every race but the sidecars!

At least my crossing to the Isle of Man went smoothly again, which couldn't be said for Joey and Robert Dunlop that year. They took their customary means of travel, which was a fishing boat and the bloody thing sank! Joey's Hondas were being transported on a 'proper' boat, but Brian Reid and some of the other Irish boys watched helplessly as their bikes sank to the bottom of the Irish Sea. Everyone escaped unhurt and the bikes were all recovered but had to be stripped and soaked in diesel to stop the salt water corroding them.

Many people would be psychologically scarred after an event like that but Joey just jumped on a plane, headed for the Isle of Man and became only the second man in history to win three TTs in a week. The next man to achieve that honour would be me, but that was still a few years off. Just for the record, the late, great Mike Hailwood was the first to win a treble back in 1967.

Considering that 1985 was my first attempt at the TT and I didn't have the best of machinery it wasn't a bad week for me. I finished twenty-first in the Formula One race and tenth in the Production 750 (I was the first 500 home and managed a lap at about 108mph). I pulled out of the Lightweight class when Ray Cowles's bike broke down and then I finished eighteenth in the Senior class on my little 350 Yamaha.

Most people agree that you've got to go to the TT for three years to learn it properly before you can start thinking about winning races and that's exactly the way it worked out for me. So although those finishes may not look fantastic on paper, they represented a steady learning curve and, anyway, simply finishing a TT race is an achievement in itself. Jim Oliver was especially pleased because the Yamaha RD500 he loaned me got sold straight after the TT – it had been sitting in his showroom for months beforehand because he just couldn't get rid of it!

I came back from the Island quite full of myself because I felt I had done really well. I hadn't gone that much faster than I did at the Manx, but I had a lot more experience under my belt and knew I was going in the right direction. I was used to coming back from the Island in September when the Manx was finished and that was always pretty much the end of the racing season. But this time it was still only June when I got back home to Scotland and I really wanted to go racing again. That was the first time it had ever dawned on me that there was more to bike racing than just two weeks on the Isle of Man each year. It sounds stupid but I had never really considered going short-circuit racing properly – it just never entered my mind.

There was a meeting at East Fortune a few weeks later so I entered that and got a third place in one of the races. That's when a guy called Frank Kerr came up to me and asked what I was doing in September. I said I had no plans so he asked if I wanted to ride for Scotland in the annual Celtic Match Races, as he was the Scottish team's manager. It wasn't a big thing really but there were teams from Scotland, Ireland, Wales and the Isle of Man and I thought it sounded like a bit of fun so I agreed to take part. When I asked him where it was he told me it was at Pembrey. I thought, 'Where the fuck's that then?' Pembrey? I had never heard of it. It turned out to be in Wales.

There were races on the Saturday and the Sunday, and in both the 250 and 350 events I finished second to Irish rider Mark Farmer with whom I immediately became friends but who, like too many bike racers, was to lose his life at a young age. Mark's death at the 1994 TT was extra sad for me because I was the last man to see him alive. I passed him in practice between Doran's Bend and Laurel Bank when I was on the Honda RC45 and he was on the experimental New Zealand-built Britten machine. Because we were good mates, I looked back at him as I passed and gave him the fingers but then a couple of corners later at the Black Dubhe crashed and was killed. Mark had been a great friend of mine since I met him back in 1985 and his death was a great loss to bike racing.

I also got a second, third and fourth in the open class at the Match races to make me the highest points scorer in the Scottish team and we won the competition overall, too. It was a brilliant weekend both in terms of racing and in meeting new people and getting pissed up. That's when I realized what I had been missing all that time, so I decided there and then that somehow, I was going to get the money together to race a full season in 1986.

I finally realized too, that all those years of getting drunk and crashing cars had been totally wasted. I had been a good-for-nothing waste of space but now that I had decided to go racing full time I was determined to make up for it. Now I had a purpose in life – a reason for not going out boozing, a reason for working late, a reason to live, and that actually made me feel extremely good.

So from that point on, the piss-artist bum was gone and he was replaced with a focused and dedicated motorcycle racer. Bike racing may be a dangerous sport but, ironically, the sport which took my brother's life actually gave me a life and plucked me out of obscurity.

Obscurity doesn't pay much, as I was finding to my cost. My job as a mechanic never paid well and even when I left Jim Oliver's in 1988 to become a professional racer with Honda I was only on about £90 a week which is shite really. It wasn't Jim's fault; it was just the going rate.

Fortunately, as I said before, my mate Brian Reid really came good for me in the winter of 1985 by finding me some sponsorship through a guy called Leon Marshall of Marshall Lauder Knitwear. It wasn't the most obvious company to be associated with bike racing but I wasn't complaining. Leon asked me what my plans were for the coming season and I told him I wanted to do the British championships. He wondered why I didn't just do the Scottish championship but I never saw the point in that. I was living on the border anyway so I figured I might as well travel down to the big English races than waste my time riding in Scotland getting no recognition. I'm not knocking Scottish racing but I'd been there done that and was ready for a new challenge.

I had helped work on bikes for another racing mate,

called Jimmy Shanks, at some of the Marlboro Club-man events in England in 1985 and thought I could run with that level of competition, so that's another reason why I was keen to race in England.

I wanted to ride in the (now defunct) Formula Two class, both at British and world level, so Leon offered to pay for the engine and exhaust system which I needed to make my bike competitive. It cost £2600 and my first reaction was, 'What? Say that again.' I couldn't believe anyone would do that for me and thought, 'Whoopee!' Leon also gave me £100 in cash for every race meeting, which was more than I was earning in a week so it was invaluable help and I couldn't have done it without him. So my bike was painted up with 'Marshall Lauder Knitwear' on the side and I must have become the first bike racer in history to be sponsored by a knitwear company!

I didn't get my F2 engine right at the start of the year. But I still had enough parts to run my TZ350 Yamaha in the ACU Star 350 championship rounds, and it was at the Snetterton round early in the season when I first met Carl Fogarty who went on to become four times World Superbike champion. We were watching practice from the pit like two Billy-no-mates, and he just strolled up and said, 'All right, how's it going?' or something like that, and that was the start of our friendship. I don't think Carl knew that many people in racing back then and I didn't either so we just sort of latched onto each other. When they could, my mates Tosh, Cosh, Tommy and Linton would come along and lend a hand as would my girlfriend, Wendy, but they could never all make it at the same time due to work commitments so it was usually just one or two of them, if any. Otherwise I just went on my own.

At Snetterton, though, I was with Cosh and Wendy, and I remember seeing Foggy with a new 250cc Honda and a 350cc Yamaha, a shiny, new Iveco van and a mechanic working for him. That was like a full factory set-up compared to what I had. His dad, George Fogarty, used to race and the family had a bit of money through his haulage business and I thought he was a lucky bugger to have all that support. We were both pretty shy then; Foggy maybe had the edge on me in the coming forward stakes but he certainly wasn't as cocky and mouthy as he is now.

After Snetterton, I found out that Wendy had been seeing Cosh behind my back so that was the end of that relationship and I didn't particularly want to see Cosh again for a while afterwards either. I was gutted at first but it was a good thing for me in the long run because I forgot about women for a while and focused more on my racing, becoming even more selfish and self-centred, which is what a good racer needs to be.

Throughout 1986 I was just learning all the English circuits as I'd never been to them before. I was doing OK with fifth and sixth places here and there and the highlight was a third place at the Oliver's Mount circuit in Scarborough. But the 1986 TT was pretty mediocre for me. I was ninth in the Junior class on a Ray Cowles 250cc Cotton, sixth in the Formula Two event on my 350 Yamaha and eleventh in the Production B race on a Yamaha FZ750 that Jim Oliver had loaned me. I suppose I shouldn't have been too disappointed with that, as I was still improving but I had been hoping for better. Still, at least my whole year wasn't based around one event any more; I had other races to think about, too, and since they were going pretty well I wasn't overly upset about my TT, especially since I scored my first ever race win soon afterwards.

That elusive first win came at Oliver's Mount seven years after I started racing. That sounds like an awfully long time but as I've said before, I only raced on and off up until 1986 and I certainly never took it seriously, so it's not as bad as it sounds. It's probably no coincidence that Oliver's Mount is more like a pure road circuit than a purpose-built short circuit and for that reason I always liked the place. It's very narrow, twisty and bumpy but that never bothered me and I won that first race on the 350 Yamaha from my new pal Foggy, who came in second.

Foggy and I raced against each other all the time in the early years and our careers seemed to parallel one another's until Carl got into World Superbikes full time in 1992. We came through the British championship ranks together, we were team-mates at the TT and Suzuka 8 Hour races for Honda and we even battled in the Formula One world championship against each other. It's amazing how similar our careers were for about five years, then Carl just got the big break that always eluded me and his career really took off. My 1998 Cadbury's Boost team boss, Rob McElnea, has gone on the record saying that I could have achieved even greater things than Foggy but something always seemed to go wrong for me and he's right – I've had lots of luck over the years and it's all been bad. But we'll get to that later.

That Scarborough win was brilliant as a few of my mates came down with me for the weekend. For us little Borders lads, Scarborough was a huge town and we couldn't wait to get practice out of the way so we could go out and get drunk along the promenade.

Our arrangements were pretty basic when we were at race meetings. We had a little stove and oven and managed to heat up Fray Bentos steak pies, usually with a tin of potatoes and some peas, and that was about as glamorous as it got. If we couldn't be bothered with cooking we'd just grab a burger and chips from a van.

We used to shower at the circuits, too, and the toilet blocks back then weren't exactly luxurious but it was the only way we could get a wash and, anyway, it was all part of the fun. If you've ever been camping with your mates you'll know what I mean. Sometimes roughing it is a much better laugh than staying in five-star hotels, not that we had the option back then.

So as soon as practice was over at Scarborough, we got the steak and kidney pies down our necks, had a quick change of trousers, put on a clean shirt and headed off into town. It was real *Seven Brides for Seven Brothers* sort of stuff, with all of us out on the pull. It was also pure holiday-ville for us – being at a seaside town in the middle of summer – and a great way to spend a weekend when we'd have just been stuck back at home in Hawick if I hadn't been racing.

Sometimes we'd get too carried away on the booze and I'd have to race with a monumental hangover so I had to devise a little trick to get past the scrutineers when they wanted to check that my helmet fitted properly and was up to standard. Because they would have been able to smell the booze from the night before on my breath, I used to take a big gulp of air, put my helmet on, slap down the visor and stand nodding at them as they checked it over. I didn't dare breathe on them or I'd have been disqualified on the spot!

Anyway, I can't remember exactly what the prize money was for that Scarborough win but it would have been peanuts; something like a 100 quid or so. Prize money was shite back then – and still is in my opinion – but nothing could detract from my first victory. I felt on top of the world.

Another first for me in 1986 was doing the Ulster Grand Prix, a pure roads race held on the 7.4 miles Dundrod circuit in the hills above Belfast. It was a round of the Grand Prix world championships until 1971 (hence the GP tag) but was struck off the calendar the following year for safety reasons. Just getting there was an achievement in itself after the trouble I had had with my van on the way to Cadwell Park the week before. I got as far as Wetherby when the van's engine started making a horrendous noise so I stopped and noticed there were holes in the sump and oil was spilling out everywhere meaning the van had obviously broken a piston or something equally severe. Little Tommy was with me but we hadn't a clue what to do. I was Mr Depressed, as normal, and thought, 'Fuck, that's Cadwell down the toilet, then.' I wasn't an AA member and I couldn't afford to pay a private firm to tow me home so I was scratching my head by the roadside when Tosh pulled up on his Goldwing. He'd set off later than us and was his usual piss-taking self when he spotted us standing by the side of the road. 'What the fuck's wrong wae you c***s, then?' I explained the problem and he told me just to get another engine. Doh! There I was; a full-time mechanic and I hadn't even thought of that.

Tosh, who was a commercial mechanic himself, reckoned any Ford engine, like a Capri or a Cortina, would do even though they were smaller than the two-litre lump we had in the van. So I jumped on the back of his bike and we set off to find a scrapyard, which didn't take too long. We explained our plight to the owner and he said yes, he had a 1600cc Ford Capri engine and he agreed to help us out. He sold us the engine for £50 and then came back with us and towed our van to the scrapyard where we set to work on it straight away.

He couldn't believe what he was seeing as the three of us pushed and pulled and shoved and improvised like three little grease monkeys on heat to remove the old engine and shoehorn the new one in. We changed the clutch, the flywheel, changed the oil and filter and just did everything we had to do in order to get that thing to work and by 10 o'clock that night, we were ready to go: it had taken us just four hours from start to finish.

We loaded Tosh's Goldwing into the new-style 1600cc van, picked up some fish and chips and headed for Cadwell Park again, albeit at a much reduced pace as we were now 400ccs down on the old engine. As we pulled into the circuit completely exhausted at 2.30 in the morning the alternator light came on; it had completely seized because it had been sitting for months in the scrapyard. But we'd made it to the racetrack and that was all that mattered. Getting home again was tomorrow's problem.

After all that, I can't even remember where I finished in the race (I think I broke down) but I do remember we had to fit a new alternator to the van in the lunch break so that we could get home again. As it turned out, that makeshift van lasted until the end of the season with no more problems and I even got my £50 back for the engine when I sold it!

So, as planned, I finally made it over to Northern Ireland on the Tuesday to get ready for the Ulster Grand Prix. Jim Oliver was over there as a spectator and he took me for a few laps of the circuit in his Morris Marina. That was the first time I'd ever been round the track as I hadn't even been to the Ulster as a spectator before then. We only did two laps, but when I bedded down in my sleeping bag in the back of my van that night I repeatedly went over everything I could remember of the course in my head, replaying those two laps time and time again until I dozed off to sleep.

Unlike the TT, the Ulster Grand Prix has a mass start but that never bothered me in the slightest and I was straight on the pace in the first qualifying session. I didn't like the course as much as the TT but I enjoyed it all the same and reckoned I could be well up there in the race.

I became very friendly with Ian Newton at that meeting after I parked up next to his van and we've remained good friends to this day, even though he calls me Mrs Hislop because I talk so much! All that weekend it was, 'Yak, yak, yak, yak', and Ian was forced to point out to me in no uncertain terms that I, 'never stop fucking talking', once I get started which I suppose is fair comment. I'm surprised he didn't avoid me completely after that meeting!

Anyway, the Ulster race worked out great for me as I finished third behind Eddie Laycock and Brian Reid in my first ever meeting at Dundrod. It was a round of the Formula Two world championship as well so I scored 10 world championship points to add to the five I'd scored for my sixth place in the first round of the series at the TT. Incidentally, I finished fifth in that World Series despite the fact that I only competed in two out of the three scheduled rounds.

I was doing even better in the British F2 championship until the last round at Darley Moor where my old mate, Ian Lougher, knocked me off when I was in a championship-winning position and I had to settle for third place in the final standings. It wouldn't be the last time either that I was knocked off when challenging for a British title.

But all in all, 1986 was a big learning year for me and I didn't crash much, which is quite unusual for a rider learning the ropes. I found it quite easy to learn new tracks and seemed to be a bit of a natural at it. By the tail end of the season I was starting to rack up the victories with wins at Silverstone and Cadwell Park as well as grabbing another victory at Oliver's Mount. My bikes were reliable too, as my preparation had been as meticulous as always. I have always put an awful lot of time into preparing my bikes and in the end it shows in the results. Prize money was still only a couple of hundred quid here and there but it all added up and by the end of the season, my racing had pretty much paid for itself. But if things were going well on the racetrack, they weren't so rosy at home.

6 The Burger Van Queue

'If I hadn't gone for a burger I wouldn't have won that first TT.'

As if my mum hadn't had enough to cope with in losing her husband and son I found out she had more problems towards the end of 1986 in the form of an abusive second husband.

Apparently my stepdad had been hitting her for some time but mum had never said anything to me about it so I was completely in the dark until one night when I came home early from a race meeting in England. I was supposed to be racing at Donington one Sunday but my gearbox blew up so I drove home early on the Saturday night and got to the pub at about 1.30am. I noticed the lights were still on as I parked the van, went inside and then I heard a commotion. I could hear mum screaming at Jim as I walked through the door and was horrified to see her cowering in a corner while Jim stood over her brandishing a pool cue.

Now I'm only a 10-stone weakling but I have one

hell of a temper, and when I'm in a rage I don't even think about the consequences of what I'm doing and no one was going to beat up my mum as long as I was still breathing. I ran straight towards that bastard screaming, 'What the fuck's going on here?' He yelled back at me saying I was a, 'useless waste of space', as he started moving towards me. That piece of shit was ex-army and he was about six feet tall, but I lunged out and punched him on the chin so hard he went flying over the bar and landed in a heap amongst a pile of broken bottles. The combined speed of us running towards each other had been enough to launch him over the bar and he flew over it John Wayne-style. I couldn't believe my mum had been putting up with this after all she'd had to deal with.

Mum stayed with Jim for a while after that but it turned out he was still being abusive and I had another run-in with him about a year later when he came back from the golf club on one occasion, all pissed-up and aggressive. I told him to shut up or go to bed and he started telling me I was a waste of space again and went to have another go at me, so I hit back and this time broke his nose. Jim went to the police and wanted them to arrest me. The local papers even ran a story on the whole thing but the police treated it as a domestic incident and it all blew over without any action being taken against me. I ended up leaving the house after that and went to live with Jim Oliver and his wife Rae. I'd finally had enough of that bastard and my mum decided she had too so she finally left him for good, which was the best move she ever made. I've never seen that guy again since I broke his nose and that's just fine by me. I hope it stays that way.

I stayed with Jim and Rae until I found a place to rent just across the road from Jim's garage and my mum moved in with me too, but I nearly burned the place down not long after we'd moved in! The house was a bit damp and dingy so on one particularly cold night I lit a big fire with wood, old boots and anything else I could find. I then went over the road to see Jim and soon afterwards someone phoned to say my house was on fire. I ran back across the road and sure enough, my mum's bedroom was well on its way to being burned out. She had a boarded-up fireplace in there and my huge fire downstairs had set light to the board which had then fallen onto the floor and started setting everything else alight. But what really got it going was a doll mum had had since childhood, which was one of her most prized possessions. It was completely melted by the time I managed to put the fire out but after all my mum had been through lately, losing a doll didn't seem that important.

Despite all the trials and traumas of my home life, I tried to focus my attentions on the 1987 season. I couldn't wait to go racing again and as it turned out, that year proved to be a real watershed for me, when a lifetime's ambition came true and I finally put the Hislop name in the TT history books.

Everyone kept telling me that to set yourself up properly for the TT, you had to race at the North West 200 in Northern Ireland, so in 1987 I decided to give it a go. It's another pure roads course set on nine miles of public roads that link Portrush, Portstewart and Coleraine in County Antrim and it's a very, very fast circuit. Because the event is held in May, just a couple of weeks before the TT, it's an ideal way to set up your bikes and get honed back into pure road racing.

I had taken a step backwards at the start of 1987 because Marshall Lauder Knitwear folded and I was left with no backing once again. I resprayed my bike plain black and red and the only logos on it were for chains and sprockets, the usual small time product support that most racers get. I was even still buying my own leathers and helmets at that point.

The plan for the year was to race in the Super II championship in England as well as competing in the major road races which were, as always, the North West 200, the TT and the Ulster Grand Prix. I had really enjoyed the Ulster in 1986 so I was pretty sure I'd like the North West race as well.

I set off in my new van on my own, because my mates couldn't get time off work, and caught the ferry from Stranraer to Larne. I had never seen the course before so as soon as I found out where it was, I checked into a little B&B for the first night to enjoy a few home comforts before roughing it in the paddock again. I then set off to do a couple of laps in the van.

I was also taken round on the newcomers' bus which was a good idea but that was all I did before practice began. As I was setting up in the paddock for practice I met another guy who became a great friend over the years – Dave Leach. Dave was a great pure roads racer but he had a terrible accident at the

Tandragee road races in Ireland in 1992, when he was thrown from his bike and straddled a tree at extremely high speed. He literally slammed into the tree trunk with one leg either side of it and his injuries, as you can imagine, were horrendous. It took Dave years to recover from that and he still walks with a limp but he eventually made a comeback to racing, albeit as a shadow of his former self, before retiring for good in 1997.

I got a good lesson in road racing from Ian Newton and Irishman Gary Cowan (who was later paralysed in a racing accident at Daytona) during practice for the North West. I was right behind them on the run into the Ballysalla Roundabout where there's a hard shoulder at the side of the road. I had only been going out as far as the white line and not using the shoulder at all but those guys were using every inch of it, right into the gutter. They were riding the roads as if they were on a short circuit and it taught me to up my pace and use every inch of the track from then on. It's no longer any good riding at 80 per cent of the roads if you want to win – you have to ride flat out.

I was only entered on my 350 Yamaha and I had a great race with my hero, Joey Dunlop, for the first time. We were only battling for sixth and seventh but it was still awesome racing with the guy who had inspired me to race on the roads in the first place back in 1983. When the race was over and Joey had beaten me by just a wheel's length (I was still the first 350 machine home), he went to his manager, Davy Wood, and asked who I was. When Davy told him I was some Scottish bloke called Steve Hislop, Joey simply said, 'He'll win a TT one day, that boy.'

Joey was a god to me at that point so that was a real compliment but, unfortunately, it wasn't until years later that Davy Wood actually told me Joey had said that – I would have been really chuffed if I'd known at the time. I still hadn't met Joey at that point and it wasn't until I was at Honda UK's headquarters in 1988 that I met him for the first time. He was a man of very few words; he wasn't rude, he just didn't have much to say. As a Scot, I could always understand his broad Irish accent with no problem – although I know a lot of people couldn't – but there was never much to understand as he hardly ever spoke.

After the North West 200 it was time to think about the TT again. Once more I had Wullie Simson and Dave Croy helping me out and I was entered in the Formula Two and Junior races on the 350 and the Production D event on a Yamaha TZR250 which I'd been using in the TZR Challenge on the mainland. I was flying in practice and was on lap record pace for the Formula Two class on the second day, posting a 110mph lap which got everyone talking about me. They knew I was going to be on the pace that year and so did I because my newly learned short-circuit aggression was really paying dividends round the Island.

The Junior race was delayed because of bad weather but when I did set off I was riding number 28 on my 350 Yamaha with an intermediate tyre on the front and a slick on the back, hoping the course would dry out. I needed to stop for fuel every two laps whereas the 250cc machines could last three laps before refuelling so I knew that was going to be a disadvantage. But I set off at a cracking pace and as the track dried out I kept getting faster and clocked a lap at 111.5mph on the second circuit. After the pit stops had all been sorted out I was leading on lap four by about two minutes and looking good for my first TT win. But the Hislop jinx that would later become famous in the Junior TT struck on the fifth, and penultimate, lap.

I'd had some ignition problems in practice but hoped everything would be okay for the race – it wasn't. At Ballaspur on the fifth lap, the bike started coughing and spluttering and I was forced to pull in at Glen Helen. My race was over and I was gutted. I'd been holding a two-minute lead over riders as good as Brian Reid, Eddie Laycock, Joey Dunlop and Carl Fogarty and yet it all came to nothing. Bollocks!

It was nothing I'd done wrong, it was just an electrical problem with the Hitachi ignition unit I was using. But at least I got my face on TV for the first time as I was interviewed for the official TT video as I sat on the grass banking miserable as hell. I went out that night and got absolutely bladdered with Ray Swann and Roger Hurst. Those two boys were good buddies and good racers but they were as mad as fish and their friendship was to end in tragedy in 1990. Roger was driving a car while he was very drunk and Ray was in the passenger seat when another vehicle collided with them. Because Roger was drunk, he got the blame.

Ray was killed in that accident and Roger was sent to prison for quite some time but it's something he'll have to live with for the rest of his life.

Anyway, when I came out of the boozer I did what every self-respecting drunk does and went for a burger. I joined the huge queue at the burger bar and got talking to another racer called Phil 'Mez' Mellor. He asked what had happened and when I told him the Hitachi ignition had packed in he asked me if it had been a new one. I said I couldn't afford a new one because they cost hundreds of pounds so mine had been a reconditioned one. Mez, in his comedy Yorkshire accent said, 'Reconditioned units are shite mate. Throw that ignition in t' middle o' Irish Sea and get a new 'un.'

When I repeated that I couldn't afford a new one another voice piped up from further back in the queue. It was a guy called Roger Keene who just happened to sell Hitachi ignition units. He said he'd sell me a new one for £150, which was really cheap, but I told him I still didn't have that kind of money. That's when *another* voice piped up in the queue and joined the conversation. This time it was a bike sponsor called Colin Aldridge who I'd heard of but never actually met. Having overheard my sob story, Colin and his friend stuck their hands in their pockets there and then, gave some money to Roger Keene and said, 'Get this boy a new ignition tomorrow.' I couldn't believe it! That was the best burger I ever decided to buy and it proved that fast food isn't always bad for you.

I got the ignition the next day, fitted it, and was all ready to go for the Formula Two race. Surely this time my luck would hold? I certainly remember hearing the pop group Wet, Wet, Wet singing *Wishing I was Lucky* on the radio just before the race and thinking 'I wish I could be fucking lucky this time around.'

Brian Reid was leading the race on the second lap when, ironically, his ignition packed up just as mine had in the Junior race. As soon as I knew he was out I thought, 'Yes, I'm in with a chance here,' then I set a new lap record at 112.1mph on the following lap and built up a 20-second lead over Graeme McGregor and Eddie Laycock. My lead was up to 40 seconds by the end of lap three but then Laycock upped the pace and started catching as I backed off a bit trying to make sure my bike would hold out to the finish this time.

I was getting signals all round the course telling me what was going on in the race but you have to be careful with those sometimes. Most riders have their own crew doing signals but you always get some from other people who just do it to try to be helpful. That's fine most of the time but those people can often get it wrong. Sometimes I'd see a 'Hizzy third' then a 'Hizzy fifteenth' on the same lap or something daft like that so I tended to go with the most consistent times and hoped they were right.

It wasn't until I was heading over the mountain for the last time that I started thinking, 'Yes, I can really do this.' Then I became really distracted by the thought of winning and started talking to the bike saying, 'Come on, come on, please keep going, don't let me down this time, girl,' just urging my little bike on. I always muttered away to myself on the Island, cursing mistakes and encouraging the bike to make it home. If there had been a microphone inside my helmet it would have made for some pretty entertaining listening on occasions.

I had a big scare at Cronk-ny-Mona just a few miles from home when my rear tyre let go and nearly highsided me at speed. But I managed to keep upright and flashed across the finish line on the Glencrutchery Road 17 seconds ahead of Eddie Laycock: I had won an Isle of Man TT race.

To explain what that win felt like is not really possible. My father had raced on that course, my brother had won a Manx GP on it and I had been trying to win there for five years. I had even been going to the Island since I was a kid and dreamed that one day I'd stand on the winner's rostrum And this wasn't the Manx GP either, it was the TT proper and I simply couldn't have been more elated – and relieved. If I hadn't got drunk and gone for a burger, I wouldn't have won that TT; it was all down to having a new ignition that lasted race distance.

To win in front of Wullie Simson and Dave Croy was great, too, but I remember feeling really sad because my dad couldn't be there to see me win that race. Strangely enough, I thought about my dad more than about Garry but that's probably because my dad had got me into the whole racing thing and I knew how proud he would have been. If Garry had been alive, he'd probably have been on that rostrum too.

When I got back to the Doric hotel that night there were flags and banners hanging everywhere and the atmosphere was just brilliant. We all stayed in there that night and had a wild time and I got totally lashed-up for the second time that week!

My next race was the Production D event for 250cc two-strokes and 400cc four-stroke machines and it turned out to be a real giggle for me. I started off four places behind Carl Fogarty on my little TZR 250 Yamaha and caught him pretty quickly so we were racing together on the roads even though I was in front of him on corrected time. That's when the fun started. Because they were production bikes, like the ones you could buy in a showroom, they had horns fitted so we were peeping at each other all the way round the course! I would be saying, 'Get the hell out of my way Foggy you ugly bastard. Peep, peep!' Then he'd stuff it up the inside of me and switch his indicators on as he peeled into the next corner It was like that throughout the race and we had a brilliant time on those little bikes because they felt really slow which is why we had time to mess around. The straights went on forever and we'd be looking over at each other making faces or flipping the bird just to pass the time until the next corner.

It was great going back home after that first TT win as there was so much interest and support from the local people. All the newspapers ran stories and there was even a reception held for me in Denholm Town Hall, which was fantastic. After a few days I also started receiving some interest from the major manufacturers and that was what I really wanted. Andy Smith from Yamaha was the first to make contact when he called me at work. He said he'd be keen to give me some production bikes for the following year's TT and asked me to keep in touch.

The next call I got was from Mick Grant (a seven times TT winner himself) at Suzuki who also congratulated me and asked about my plans for 1988. Again, he offered me production bikes for the TT and asked me to stay in touch. But then came the big one. To me, Honda were the top dogs so when Bob McMillan called, I thought, 'Fuckin' hell, now we're talking.' Bob said he'd been watching me and liked my riding so he too offered me production bikes for the 1988 TT and I said I'd think about it.

The reason all the firms offered me production bikes as opposed to full race bikes is because they're a much cheaper way of getting results and there's less commitment required as far as preparing them goes. You can try out a rider on a relatively cheap production bike and if it doesn't work out there's not much lost. Putting a relatively new name on a precious and rare factory Superbike is a different matter. Anyway, Honda had the factory bikes covered with Joey Dunlop at that time, so there was even less chance of me being offered one.

I was flattered to have Honda's attention but still wasn't sure whose offer to accept; Yamaha had some good production bikes going at the time and I had always been a bit of a Yamaha man so I was quite happy to stay on Yams – until I saw Honda's RC30. That bike was getting lots of coverage in the press and it was hyped up to be the greatest road-going sports bike ever. To this day, I still think it is, as far as being revolutionary is concerned. To me, no bike has moved the game on as much as the RC30 did when it was launched in 1988. And so I kept in touch with Honda and towards the end of the year they said I could have a production RC30. They also said that if someone could come up with about £6000, they would give me another RC30 complete with a Formula One kit to upgrade it for the quality racing classes.

Jim Oliver agreed to pay for the F1 kit and Honda also offered me a CBR600 so that I could ride in the CBR Challenge on the mainland as well as in the 600cc Production and Formula Two races at the TT. It all sounded great but being promised bikes is one thing and actually taking delivery of them is another as I was about to find out.

Anyway, the rest of the 1987 season went okay for me and I picked up some more wins at Oliver's Mount, Knockhill, Cadwell Park and Jurby, which is a short airfield circuit on the Isle of Man.

Short-circuit racing requires a totally different style of riding compared to the TT. For starters, you're riding elbow to elbow with 20 other guys pushing and jostling for position whereas at the TT you're on your own. You can also afford to fall off more often because there's generally lots of run-off space enabling you to take greater risks, whereas if you take a risk on the Island you're into a brick wall more often than not. On top of that, there's the fact that short-circuit surfaces are a lot smoother and offer more grip so you can corner faster and lean the bike over to a greater degree.

Because of these and other differences, very few riders have been good at both disciplines, especially in more recent years since the TT has lost its prestige and there's less incentive to have a go at pure road racing. Carl Fogarty is one exception and Michael Rutter is another: they have both proved to be good road racers and good short-circuit riders and I'm the same in that I never had a problem changing my style to suit either discipline

In fact, I thought the two disciplines could complement each other. Towards the end of 1985, I realized I would have to do some further short-circuit racing if my TT results were to improve. I felt I needed to ride more aggressively and to attack the course more and I could only learn that sort of style by scratching round purpose-built racetracks neck and neck with other riders. My theory worked as my results really picked up at the TT after I started full-time short circuit racing in 1986.

Many riders say they don't ride the TT course as hard as they ride short circuits but that's absolute bollocks. If we didn't, why would there be crashes? Why would we be suffering huge tank-slappers at various points around the course? Why would there be huge dark lines of rubber exiting corners as riders wind on the gas to the max and get the rear wheel spinning up? There are lots of TT videos showing riders such as Carl Fogarty, Phillip McCallen and myself getting bikes all crossed up because we're trying so hard. Have a look at any one of those videos and you'll see what I mean. There's a lot of money at stake at the TT (well, there is nowadays anyway) and there's only one TT each year so there's also a lot at stake as far as sponsors and manufacturers are concerned. You simply can't afford to ride well within your limits or you're going to be left behind.

Admittedly, the style of riding is different in that you can't use every inch of the road as you do on a short circuit but even that's not always the case. Watch riders exiting the Gooseneck and you'll see them skimming the grass banking. And I used to use the bus stop at Schoolhouse Corner to give me a few more inches of tarmac when I needed it. The sheer bumpiness of the course means you can't take some corners as hard as you would if they were smooth like a short circuit but generally speaking, if someone says they're riding at 80 per cent of their abilities and still winning TTs, they're lying. If you want to win a race on the Isle of Man you'd better be prepared to ride flat out, make no mistake.

Over the next few years, I would ride the course faster than any man in history.

7 Money, Money, Money

'I rode all year for no money at all.'

Money, or rather the lack of it, has been a problem for me throughout my racing career.

While other riders – who I consider to be no better than myself and who I have beaten on numerous occasions – have made fortunes out of the sport, I feel I've never been paid what I'm worth. That's probably partly because I'm not pushy enough when it comes to money and have not had a manager to push for me and partly because I'm too honest with the press, which is a part of my character that a lot of teams don't like.

A few people tried to muscle their way in as my manager when my career started taking off in the late '80s but back then I thought, 'Fuck that, I'm not giving them 20 per cent of what I earn. I don't earn enough as it is.' What I didn't realize is that a good manager can actually make you more money by setting up deals and pushing you in different directions so they really end up paying for themselves. But I was so naïve in those days that I didn't realize that and it's one of the biggest regrets of my career.

I mean, until the start of the 1988 season I paid for everything myself with the help of a few local sponsors and that was fair enough because it's the way most racers start out unless they come from a wealthy family. But even when I got involved with Honda for the 1988 season, I agreed to ride their bikes without being paid so the only money that came my way was a small allowance for spares to keep the bikes going. I should have dug my heels in there and then and demanded some cash but I didn't.

I had to rely on prize money that year for income and I didn't even have any insurance to cover me if I got injured so if I'd had a bad crash I would have been in a right mess. Even when I'd proved myself with Honda and signed up for another season in 1989 I was only paid a wage of around £6000 for the whole season, which was pathetic really and not much more than I was making as a mechanic. Still, at least I was getting good bikes, a full allocation of spares and eventually a good mechanic in Slick Bass, which I felt was more important than heaps of cash. I wanted to ride bikes and I wanted to win races so I didn't think too much about money and, anyway, I'd never had any to begin with so it's not as if I was missing it.

It's only been in more recent years that I've realized the mistakes I've made regarding money because I don't have the nest egg for retirement that I should have. With retirement looming, my bank balance is becoming more and more important to me, not least because I've got two kids to look after.

The most I ever got paid to race a bike was in 2002 when I was on £70,000 for riding in British Superbikes on the MonsterMob Ducati and that was only after I refused to ride for anything less. The year before I was only on £35,000 for the same team and there was no way I was going to ride for that again when I knew rivals like John Reynolds were on two or three times that amount. I didn't get any bonuses for winning races or championships with the MonsterMob team either, so when I say I got £70,000, I mean £70,000 and that's it – no more and no less.

That may sound like a lot of money to a regular guy who works a nine to five job but racing is a short-lived career and you have to make as much as you can while the going's good so in those terms £70,000 isn't that much.

As I said before, I've always tried to get the most competitive machinery rather than the fattest pay cheque. In 1998 for example, I rode all year for no money at all just to get a chance on the Cadbury's Boost YZF750 Yamaha that Niall Mackenzie had proved was good enough to win the British title on. Niall has admitted in his own biography that as my team-mate he made about £130,000 that same year, including his personal sponsorship deals, so where was I going wrong riding for bugger all and still beating Niall half the time?

When I signed for Kawasaki in 1999 I only got £13,000 which is bloody pathetic for risking your neck week-in week-out, and Yamaha only paid me £45,000 when I rode for them in 2000 when I actually *did* break my neck! People like Neil Hodgson are probably on about £300,000 a year for racing in World Super-bikes and within another couple of years he'll be a multi-millionaire like Foggy is while I'll probably be cleaning their bloody windows. I don't begrudge those guys the money they've got, I just feel I should have been paid a lot more over the years.

I suppose I'll have to get a proper job when I retire which will feel really weird after 20-odd years of racing but what's a bike racer qualified for apart from being able to ride bikes fast? It's practically all I've known all my whole adult life so it will be hard to find a decent 'proper' job. I'd like to be a helicopter instructor but it's cost me nearly £20,000 so far to get my private pilot's licence and I would need to find another £40–£50,000 to train as a commercial pilot, so that's out of the window. It's strange but most people who see me on TV or come along to the race meetings probably think I'm loaded after so many years of racing at the top level but it's just not the case.

However, in the spring of 1988 I had other things to worry about than money as there was still no sign of any bikes from Honda and I was starting to panic. Taking delivery of bikes early is crucial if you want to have them prepared properly for the start of the season.

I also thought it was crucial to change my image around that time because I was riding for Honda and wanted to look a bit more presentable. I've always hated my hair, ever since I had a cow's lick as a kid, and used to say that the single thing that would improve my life most would be a better head of hair! So for the new season I decided to cut off my hair, which was always quite lank, and go for the hedgehog look. I came in for a lot of stick over that hairdo and lots of people called me 'lavvy brush' for years so in the end I decided to just shave the bloody lot off.

Anyway, Honda eventually called and said I could go down to London and pick up the CBR600 but there was still no sign of the RC30s that I was really after. I was desperate to keep my hand in by racing as often as possible so I asked Honda if I could take the Yamaha badges off my 350, paint it in Honda colours and race that as well as the CBR600 until my other Hondas turned up. I was totally upfront about what I wanted to do (which in any case was perfectly legitimate), so they agreed and I actually started the 1988 season yet again on my trusty 10-year-old TZ350 Yamaha as well as riding in the CBR600 Challenge series.

I had some more wins on the 350 but never really gelled with the 600 because it was on treaded road tyres and I didn't like them so my best result on that bike was a ninth place. I quit the CBR Challenge halfway through the year because I really only wanted the bike for the 600cc Production TT and I didn't enjoy racing against all those real production bike nutters – they're totally mad.

Just before the North West 200 in May, Ron Grant from Honda UK finally called and said he had some big bikes for me. I was to get my production RC30 in time for that race and since they didn't have enough Formula One kits I would be allowed to ride Roger Burnett's full-on F1 machine for the North West and the TT. I was really chuffed as it would be my first time riding a proper full-blown Superbike.

I set pole position for both the Production and Superbike races at the NW200 and was really pleased with myself but the races themselves didn't exactly go to plan. My 350 seized in one race, my brakes failed in the first Superbike race so I could only finish in fourth place and then to cap it all I crashed in the Production race and destroyed my brand new RC30.

I had been leading by one-and-a-half minutes when the bike hit a false neutral, spat me off and burst into flames as it smashed into a church wall. I was really annoyed because I had told Honda there was a gear-box problem but no one believed me. I noticed it when I was running the bike in on the Borders roads but when I mentioned it to Ron Grant and Bob McMillan they thought I was just being inaccurate with my gear changes and they dismissed my claims.

But what pissed me off even more was thinking that I'd ruined my chances with Honda in my first big outing for the team. On top of all the problems I've just mentioned my full-blown RC30 broke down in the second Superbike race as well so the whole meeting was a total disaster for me. I knew the breakdowns and crashes weren't my fault but I thought others would see it differently. Anyway, I went to a Honda function that night and Dave Hancock from Honda

UK was full of praise for the way I had ridden despite my bad luck so that surprised me and cheered me up quite a bit.

I remember feeling really thirsty at one point during that party so I necked what I thought was half a pint of lemonade – but fuck me it nearly blew my head off! It turned out to be a glass of the famous Irish poteen – 100 per cent pure alcohol and I had just swallowed half a pint of the bloody stuff before I realized. Still, it seemed to amuse everyone around me and needless to say I was drunk as a skunk from that point on so it was a pretty good night. But next morning as I went to leave there was another surprise for me – someone had siphoned all the diesel out of my van just to round off a weekend of disasters. Definitely one to forget.

I went home with my tail between my legs thinking I had blown my chances with Honda and in the middle of the week when Bob McMillan rang me up I thought this was the call telling me my services were no longer required. But to my complete surprise he was very complimentary about the way I had ridden and as a reward he offered me Roger Burnett's production RC30 for the TT since mine was completely trashed. Roger had annoyed Honda by accepting a private one-off 500 Grand Prix ride the previous Sunday instead of riding for Honda UK at Carnaby so Bob was prepared to give me his brand new RC30 as a bit of a snub to Roger. I was really chuffed and when Bob asked me to come down to London to help Ron Grant salvage parts from my trashed RC30 I didn't hesitate.

It was only when we were stripping that bike that Ron found a mechanical problem with the selector barrel for the gearbox which proved I had been right in saying it was selecting false neutrals and that's what caused me to crash. I felt vindicated on the spot and it proved that I knew what I was feeling from the bike and that I hadn't actually done anything wrong to cause that crash at all. It was a big relief, especially since Ron told everyone at Honda of his findings.

I got on really well with Ron Grant and it was a tragedy when he was killed in a boating accident in Ireland a few years later. The boat's engine had stopped and as Ron was leaning over to check it he fell into rough water and drowned – another sad loss.

Even before I got to the Isle of Man for the 1988 TT I had a very proud moment. One of the biggest events in many Scottish Border towns is a festival called a Common Riding. It's an old tradition of riding round the Border boundaries making sure no Englishmen have encroached on the land. Nowadays it's just good fun and a chance to get pissed-up for most people but hundreds of horses and riders still take part in the ceremony.

The leader of the pack is called the Cornet and he is elected each year from among local people. It's a great honour and in 1988 my mate Ian 'Ses' Whillams was given the honour. I'd known him for years but couldn't stay to watch his proud moment because I was heading off to the TT on the same day as one of the major Common Riding ride-outs. It's important to understand that the whole town of Hawick comes to a standstill when the horse riding procession comes through and nothing, but nothing, gets in the way of it. The roads are all closed and ringed with policemen to make sure it all goes smoothly.

As I set off with Wullie Simson in my van for the Island I came upon a policeman who told me I would have to stop and wait for the whole bloody procession to pass before I could carry on. I was trying to catch a boat down at Heysham so I wasn't too keen on any delay but realized there was nothing I could do about it; I would just have to sit and wait until it was past.

After a while, I saw Ses leading hundreds of horses with all the banners and pomp that is typical of a Common Riding and I thought, 'I'm in for a bit of a bloody wait here.' But to my total surprise, when Ses spotted my van he reined in his huge horse and raised his hand to halt the entire procession! What on earth was he playing at? All those horses had to be pulled up and everyone wondered what the hell could possibly be holding up a Common Riding march. I was gobsmacked to realize that Ses had actually stopped the whole procession to wish local hero, Steve Hislop, good luck at the Isle of Man TT races! I couldn't believe it. Little old me, a nobody, halting the Hawick Common Riding – that's the Borders equivalent of halting the changing of the Queen's guard. It was a fantastic gesture and I set off on top of the world, ready to take on all comers.

So with the Cornet's blessing I started practice week at the TT with my first chance to lap the course on a full-on Superbike – and I hated every minute of it.

That might sound strange since every rider dreams of getting a factory bike but the truth is that it was just too fast for me round the Island at that stage in my career. It felt so scary to ride and wanted to throw me off everywhere so in the end I just backed off and admitted defeat – for the time being. I could ride the wheels off my production RC30 and it still felt very stable but that just goes to show the difference between a production bike and a factory special. It's not all about top speed either; my production Honda would probably do about 165mph and the Superbike about 180mph but it was the extra acceleration and the light weight of the Superbike, as well as the extra top speed, that frightened me. It's strange, because the more experienced you get at the TT, the more speed and power you want but back then I wanted less as I just wasn't ready for it.

I also had my first ever crash on the TT course during practice week when I slid off the production RC30 on a damp patch on the entry to Quarterbridge. I wasn't hurt but the idea is not to fall off at the TT at all as few people do it and live to tell the tale. I only ever had two crashes at the TT and that one was the slowest. The next came the following year and it was bloody terrifying but I'll get to that in time.

The first race of the week was on Friday evening and it was the 600cc Production C event. I finished third, got on the rostrum and recorded the fastest lap of the race so I was chuffed enough with that. But the best was yet to come in the Production B event the following day when I won from fellow Scot Brian

Morrison and the late Geoff Johnson. I smashed the lap record by 15 seconds from a standing start and even had to slow down to come in for fuel at the end of that (and every other) lap because the RC30 could only manage one circuit with the small petrol tank it had. That win went some way to helping me feel that I'd finally proved myself to Honda after having so many let-downs at the North West 200 and having crashed in practice for the TT.

It was a trouble-free race for me and it felt great to win another TT, even though my first win in 1987 will always be special as it was just me against the world with my old 350 whereas now I had the might of Honda behind me. I started well down the field at number 23 so I had a lot of traffic to get through but I remember passing everyone as though they were standing still. My advantage at the finish line was almost 13 seconds but it could have been much more if I hadn't rolled off the gas on the last lap to make sure of a finish. Like Joey, I always tried to win TTs at the slowest possible pace and if records came, it was only because I was enjoying myself and riding really smoothly, not because I was riding out of my skin.

After that race, Ron Grant asked me what I was going to ride in the Formula One event on the Monday and I admitted I was frightened of the factory Super-bike. I said I would probably go better on the more stable and less powerful production RC30 so that's what I ended up doing. We put the F1-spec exhaust and carburettors on, mounted slick tyres on the standard rims and that was it – the engine was left stock.

The important point is that the bike was heavier and less flighty than the factory machine so it wouldn't be so much of a handful for me.

Our plan worked like a dream – up to a point. I started off steadily then as I got used to the modified bike I started taking seven seconds a lap out of the leader who was none other than Joey Dunlop, the undisputed king of the TT at that time. Joey raised the outright lap record for the first time since 1984 when he clocked a 118.54mph lap but my best lap was only one second slower – on a near bog-standard production bike which I'd never ridden in its current state. I was definitely on the pace.

But then going through Kirkmichael village on the second last lap the bike died on me. I pulled in and tried to fire it up but it wasn't happening so I was forced to admit defeat and watch the rest of the race from the roadside at Bishopcourt feeling totally deflated. I remember thinking everyone looked so bloody fast racing through there; much faster than it actually feels when you're on a bike. It was quite frightening really and even more frightening when you consider that Roger Burnett did a 110mph lap with a punctured rear tyre that day!

It turned out to be a dodgy ignition switch which let me down but I remember being amazed when I found out I'd been catching Joey and I reckon I'd have had enough time left to pass him had my bike kept going. Beating Joey would have blown my mind though; the thought of being faster than him was too much for me to cope with back then. I knew I was second but I hadn't known it was Joey who was in front of me. As things turned out, that was to be Joey's last Formula One win until the year 2000.

I had another good dice with Joe in the Junior race on my trusty old 350 Yamaha until it got sick. Because I'd been concentrating on my Honda rides I'd neglected the little Yamaha during practice week and that proved to be my undoing. I hadn't wired up the exhaust springs and the exhaust fell off making the bike feel as flat as hell so I knew my chances of victory were over. We fixed the bike up in the pits but lost too much time to be competitive in the race so I went out again with the intention of breaking the lap record just to prove a point. And that's exactly what I did as I got round the course at 113.41mph which is still the fastest ever lap of the TT course on a 350cc machine to this day.

The only change we made to the RC30 for the Senior TT was to replace the ignition switch that had failed in the F1 race. Again, I had a low starting number so I had a lot of traffic to get through and I wasn't a big enough name at that point to demand a number change as I could in later years. I soon caught Roger Marshall, who was in fourth place on corrected time, and he tucked in behind me for a lap or so. He later told me he couldn't believe how fast I was riding the course and maybe that's why he never won a TT – he was slow in places where he could have been making up time. When Roger was my team boss at Red Bull Ducati many years later he said he would gladly have swapped any one of his 15 British championship titles for a TT victory because he had tried so hard to win one and never managed it.

I finished the race second to Joey Dunlop and was so pleased I just didn't know what to do with myself. There I was on the rostrum with the king of the roads himself; it was just incredible. I knew that when I got used to a full-on Superbike I could beat him so I couldn't wait for the following year's TT. But fate was to rob me of the chance to have a full on head-to-head with my hero as he was badly injured just months before the 1989 TT and wasn't able to ride.

It had been a good TT for me despite the fact that I'd had some problems: I'd won another race and proved I was ready to challenge for wins in the big classes once I got used to a Superbike. I probably only made about £5000 that week despite having so many finishes so it wasn't a big moneymaker by any means but it was enough to keep me going for a while.

Anyway, Honda was delighted with my performances and that was much more important to me than cash. They said I could keep Roger Burnett's production RC30 and Ron Grant would turn it into a Superstock bike for the championship of the same name which was the biggest race series in the UK at the time. The bikes were run close to Formula One spec so I could race it in some F1 rounds too with just a few minor changes.

The Superstock championship had already run three rounds by the time I had my first race at Donington Park in June but I still finished third overall by the end of the year and won a round at Mallory Park.

The Cadwell Park round turned out to be a tragic weekend as Kenny Irons was killed on the warm-up lap for the Formula One race. I didn't know Kenny that well but I was shaken up by his crash because I was right there as it happened. I was behind him when he went down and managed to avoid hitting him but Kenny was sliding backwards down the track looking straight at me as I swerved to get round him. The rider behind me didn't have time to get out of the way and he hit Kenny as he was sliding along and the whole thing was just horrific. It was a harsh reminder of the dangers of the sport and this time it wasn't on the notorious TT circuit but on a supposedly 'safe' short circuit.

By the middle of the year, I was doing OK with prize money so I decided to quit my job and take my chances on racing full time. I left Jim Oliver's garage in August of 1988 and haven't had a proper job since. Honda had been wanting me to do more and more testing and although Jim Oliver would have given me the time off, I didn't think it was fair accepting a full wage from him when I wasn't there half the time. Jim always said there was a job waiting for me if I needed it so I had his promise as a back-up should my racing plans all go tits-up.

It was becoming too much of a rush working full time and racing at weekends, sometimes hundreds of miles away. I used to get home at about one or two in the morning, grab a few hours sleep, drive to work at 7.30am, unload the bikes, do a morning's work and then work on the bikes in my lunch hour. After working all afternoon in the garage I'd get home and have a bite to eat then start work on the bikes again until I went to bed. It was like that constantly and it eventually became too much.

Since I now didn't need to go back home every week to work I usually just slept in the back of my van at Honda UK's headquarters in Power Road, Chiswick during the week. From around the time of the Ulster Grand Prix in August (where I had a second and third place in the F1 and Senior races respectively) I had a mechanic called Barry Fielder helping me. He stayed in the van too but I had to pay him out of my own pocket.

We didn't mind staying in the van and, in fact, it was a bit of a laugh but it certainly wasn't the five-star hotel lifestyle of a Grand Prix star. We ate at Pizza Hut or McDonald's or used our little stove to cook dinner then usually went for a few beers each night to help us get to sleep. All we had between us was my whatever prize money I won but we didn't care – it was like being bounty hunters, living from week to week on whatever money we could win.

Towards the end of the 1988 season Ron Grant fell out with Honda and they parted company so I was allocated a new mechanic called Anthony 'Slick' Bass. Slick is quite famous for having worked with Carl Fogarty a lot but his nickname didn't derive from him being quick at his work as you might expect – it was because there was always an oil slick under everything he worked on! He was a great mechanic though and he became a great friend too.

Honda had come up with a good offer of bikes for the 1989 season. I was to get a new RC30 Superbike as well as having Joey's 1988 bike as a backup and I also managed to wangle a new 250cc machine because I wanted a little project bike to work on while Slick took care of the big bikes.

The Honda UK guys were very much behind me but by this time Honda Japan wanted to know a bit more about Hislop-san so I was invited over in October to take part in the Two/Four international race meeting at the Fuji circuit in Japan. I had never been out of the UK in my entire life and my first trip abroad was to be to Japan! Hell, talk about culture shock – I couldn't believe it. It was an all-expenses-paid trip with a first-class flight ticket and a top hotel to boot. What a way to pop my foreign travel cherry. Sure beats the Costa Del Sol!

Most of the world's top Grand Prix and F1/Superbike riders were there, including Wayne Rainey, Kevin Schwantz, John Kocinski and Bubba Schobert. I was blown away seeing all those guys along with Mount Fuji and the circuit, which had the longest straight I'd ever seen. I qualified in about tenth place for the F1 event which was all right given the level of competition and the fact that I was only on a standard bike against many hand-built factory RVFs and similar.

On the second day of practice, I was watching the 500 GP bikes when a heavily suntanned bloke with dark hair approached me and said, 'It's Steve, isn't it?' I said, 'Yes', and he introduced himself as Mick

Doohan. He was riding a Yamaha YZF750 Superbike at the time and didn't get into Grand Prix racing until the following season but he went on to win five 500cc world championships so he's arguably one of the best racers of all time. Back then though, it was Mick who recognized me, presumably because he'd seen some TT videos or pictures. He never forgot our meeting either because I turned up at the Suzuka 8 Hour race in 1994 as a reserve rider and when Mick saw me he invited me out to dinner. I think he must have been a bit of a closet TT fan! He's certainly always been really friendly with me.

Mick passed me in qualifying for the F1 race at Fuji and to this day I have never seen anyone riding a four-stroke bike like he did. I know no one's going to believe this but I swear he was laying black lines of rubber on the road with the *front* wheel as well as the rear wheel. He was unreal and just sliding that bike every which way you could imagine. I firmly believe if Mick had concentrated on four-stroke racing instead of going to Grand Prix poor old Carl Fogarty would not have been four times World Superbike champion. Mick was doing things on that bike that I've never seen anyone do before or since.

Unsurprisingly, he won the Two/Four race. However, I finished tenth on my standard bike which was apparently enough to impress the top brass at Honda so I received their blessing for the 1989 season, although I probably wouldn't have done if they'd witnessed some of my off-track activities at the time.

I was at Mallory Park with Slick Bass and my mate

Cosh, with whom I had made up again by that point. We went to the clubhouse on the Saturday night to have a few beers and ended up getting completely bladdered. At closing time another racer, Ray Stringer, and his entourage invited us back to their caravan to have some more vodkas. It was great fun but we stayed up until four o'clock and were totally pissed so I was in no shape for practising and racing the next day. I stumbled back to my van and fell onto my bed – the bottom half of two bunk beds. I remember it felt awfully lumpy but I lay there for a while before I realized I was lying on top of my mate Cosh! He was supposed to be in the top bunk but was too pissed to climb up so he fell into mine, then I fell on top of him and he never even noticed so I just kicked and kicked until he tumbled onto the floor in a heap.

We all had to be up at 7.30am for scrutineering and I had to use my old trick of holding my breath so the scrutineers wouldn't smell the booze on me. I got through all right but I still felt quite pissed when I went out on the track. I qualified on the front row of the grid and really enjoyed practice in a gung-ho sort of way, launching the bike into the corners like a loony and shouting, 'Yee-haa!' under my helmet but by lunchtime my hangover had really kicked in and I felt absolutely awful. I actually ended up pulling out of both races because I felt so rough. Slick and I stuck together and said we had tyre problems but the truth was that I felt sick as a dog from the night before and just couldn't face racing!

On another occasion I had decided to invite my

Left: Mummy's boy. Me as a toddler, with my mum Margaret. She's the strongest woman I've ever known.

Below: With my brother Garry and our Honda SL125.

Below left: How it all began. Riding the Wassel Sachs round the field next to my house during the long hot summer of 1976 when I was 14.

Below: A rare picture of my brother Garry and I getting ready to race each other at Beveridge Park in 1980. (Left to right) Garry, Willie Simson, Wendy Oliver, Ian Hogg and me.

As a toddler with my dad Sandy. He died in my arms when I was just 17.

Like father …

… like son. My dad takes Ballaugh Bridge on the Isle of Man during the 1959 Manx Grand Prix and I follow in 1983.

My brother Garry after winning the Newcomers' Race at the Manx Grand Prix in 1982. He was killed just six weeks later.

Looking nervous before the weigh-in for my first ever ride on the TT course in the 1983 Manx Newcomers' race. My friend and mechanic Wullie Simson is on the right.

Real road racing. Muscling my number 22 bike to the front of the field at the 1987 North West 200 in Northern Ireland.

On the way to my first ever TT win – the 1987 Formula 2 race. I had been leading the Junior earlier in the week until my bike broke down.

A pain in the neck. Despite his best efforts, my future team boss Rob McElnea amazingly failed to break my neck in this crash.

Chasing Robert Dunlop on the JPS Norton at the Ulster Grand Prix in 1990.

Leading Carl Fogarty at Cronk-ny-Mona during the 1991 Formula 1 TT. I won by over 40 seconds.

After you sir, I insist. Chatting mid-race with Woolsey Coulter (on the right, who is wearing Foggy's helmet), at Donington Park in a 250cc race.

Down boy! En route to one of three TT wins and the first ever 120 mph lap in 1989. The Honda's fairing was so lightweight that the sheer speed has crumpled its nose.

The Magic Roundabout. Leading Brian Reid and Dave Leach at the North West 200 in 1989.

Wheelie bin racing. Performing with the Purple Helmets madcap stunt team on the Isle of Man in 1996. I'm in the bin on the right.

Beating my hero. Leading Joey Dunlop over the line in the 1991 Senior TT.

Almost there. On my way to 2nd place on the Norton in the 1992 Formula 1 TT. I had only ridden 8 laps of Oulton Park on it before TT week.

They said it couldn't be done. On my way to victory on the under-funded British Norton in the 1992 Senior TT.

An unusual shot of Ballaugh Bridge during the same race.

Wondering if the team has enough cash to celebrate after winning the 1992 Senior ahead of Carl Fogarty (left) and Robert Dunlop.

Orient Express. Winning the Macau Grand Prix on a 500cc ROC Yamaha Grand Prix bike in 1993. I had my last ever road race there in 1994.

Help me Honda. A rare moment leading a race on the under-powered RC30/RVF hybrid.

mechanic Barry Fielder up to Scotland for New Year's Eve – or Hogmany as we call it north of the border – so my mates and I could teach him how to drink properly. My pal Tosh was by that point working as a dispatch rider in London but he hired a car and drove up to Scotland for the big night out. When everyone arrived we decided to go out for a sort of 'practice run' before Hogmany just to get into prime beer-drinking shape. We didn't mean to have a really heavy night but that's always the way these things happen and we ended up getting totally pissed – all 10 of us.

After the pubs shut we were eating chips in Jedburgh town centre and making so much noise that no taxis would stop for us. Two guys managed to blag lifts home but that still left eight of us freezing our tits off on a December night, miles from home. Something had to be done.

Eventually we found a driver – 'I've not had too much to drink,' he slurred. Of course he'd had just as much as the rest of us but we didn't question him because it sounded like a good idea at the time so we all agreed to drive Tosh's hire car back to Hawick. It was a little Vauxhall Astra and to this day I don't know how we managed to get eight grown men into it but I swear we did. I was in the front – next to the driver – on my mate Tommy's knee (with no seat belt on) because I was the lightest and the other five guys squeezed into the back, lying across each other any which way they could, all giggling like school girls.

We crawled up the steep hill out of town with the little car labouring under all that weight but once we crested the rise, we started picking up speed. Everyone in the car knew that road like the back of his hand except for one – the guy driving. We all forgot he didn't know where he was going so there were eight back-seat drivers shouting at him to speed up, to take the next corner flat out, to give it some wellie, to do this or do that. It was only as we approached a really tight bend, which was a notorious accident black spot, that I realized we were going too fast to make the tight corner. I opened my mouth to warn him just as someone in the back yelled, 'Flat out man, keep it lit!'

That was all it took. We ran out of road, the car dug into a ditch and flipped over doing two complete rolls before it landed upright again. My shoulder smashed the front window out and the roof was caved in but we all got out and were OK though that was just the start of our problems. We obviously couldn't call for help because we were all pissed and as soon as we saw car headlights approaching everyone jumped into a ditch to hide. That was a bad move. It was really deep and extremely muddy so now we were all covered in mud right up to our waists as well as being drunk with a crashed car on our hands. It was not looking good.

The next plan was to try to drive the car over the damaged fence that we had crashed through and back onto the road. A couple of the lads held the fence down and Tosh tried to drive the Astra over it but it was just wheel-spinning in the mud. I remembered there was a gate farther up the field, so we managed to drive it through that then checked for any identifying evidence such as bits of number plate that we might have left in the field, before driving back to my mum's house.

We parked the car close to the house and went inside to get some bacon sandwiches on the go and to relive our tale. It was only when we got inside into proper light that we realized how filthy we were so we peeled off all our muddy gear and threw it into the washing machine. When my mum heard all the laughing and roaring she came down to see eight of us sitting in our underpants munching on bacon butties at three o'clock in the morning, still pissed out of our brains.

We slept on the floor that night and were woken at 10 in the morning by my mum who said the neighbours were going to call the police about our car. We hadn't noticed it in the dark but apparently it was covered in bloody handprints from the guys who'd cut their hands holding down that fence. It was also covered in mud, inside and out so the neighbours thought we must have abducted someone and murdered him or her!

We got the car cleaned up as best we could then Tosh drove it back to London and told the hire company he'd swerved to miss a deer and ran off the road and they believed him, so he got off the hook. But for some reason Barry Fielder never came back up to Scotland for New Year again. Strange that.

8 Girls, Girls, Girls

'They said I was a secret lesbian.'

One year at the TT a magazine appeared called *Utter Tosh*, which was a Viz-style piss-take of the TT and the riders who raced there.

One of its headlines read, 'Steve Hislop is a lesbian,' and the red-hot 'exclusive' inside went into lurid details about my secret lesbian sexual activities. Well, I'm sorry to disappoint anyone who might be turned on by the idea but I'm afraid it's not true – unless liking women qualifies me as a lesbian.

I've always done all right with women as far as pulling them is concerned but hanging onto them has proved to be another matter altogether: I'm bloody useless at long term relationships. I mentioned before that I gave up chasing girls for a while in 1986 after finding out that my girlfriend at the time, Wendy Oliver, was seeing one of my best mates behind my back. But by 1988 I was well and truly over that and couldn't take my eyes off the girl who presented me with my winner's trophy on the TT rostrum. I got chatting to her in the press office and found out her name was Lesley Henthorn and that she was the current Miss Isle of Man but I didn't expect to see her again and thought that was that. After all, racing paddocks are full of gorgeous brolly dollies and promotional girls so you can't get hung up on every pretty face you meet.

But in 1989 Lesley got a job as a sales executive for the company which published the TT programme so our paths crossed again at the Alexandra Palace bike show in London. We started chatting and realized our hotels were close together so we arranged to meet up for a drink. We got on really well and I was thinking, 'Bloody hell, it would be nice to get off with her,' but once the season started I was off racing again and didn't see her for ages.

The next time our paths crossed Lesley was jumping out of the back of Dave Leach's van and I thought, 'You lucky bastard,' and resigned myself to the fact that she must be seeing Dave. But some time later we met yet again in a pub on the Isle of Man and this time there seemed to be a real spark between us so we kept in touch. She invited me over to stay on the Island and I ended up going over there every weekend when I wasn't racing. I'd raced on the Island for years but had never really explored it properly so whenever Lesley was at work, I'd set off on a little trail bike her brother got for me and explored the country roads. That's when I really fell in love with the Isle of Man – and with Lesley too.

It was brilliant just touring around with nowhere in

particular to go and the scenery was fantastic. I'd never felt so relaxed and contented in my life so I decided to move to the Isle of Man in 1991 and I'm still living there today. Lesley and I had a good couple of years chilling out on the Island and, as far as I was concerned, I was still in love with her in 1992. But apparently my racing was becoming a strain on her because I was away so much and things started falling apart. Eventually she started to see another bloke behind my back when I was away and that's when it all went really pear-shaped. Yet another long-term relationship down the drain and another woman who had cheated on me.

After Lesley and I split up I started seeing another Isle of Man lass called Kelly Bailey in 1995 and this time I really did think that she was the one I would marry and settle down with. I spotted her in a pub in Douglas and was hugely attracted to her straight away. Next time I saw her we got dancing and things just went on from there and that's when I found out that she was only 16! I was 33 at the time so I could envisage other people having some problems with us seeing each other, but to me it didn't matter what age she was because I had already fallen madly in love. Kelly seemed a lot older than she really was so the age thing was never a particular issue for us, at least in those early days but it did start to tell a bit further down the line. It's always been a bit of a stormy relationship and it's been on and off several times over the last few years but more of that later.

Maybe my moods have had something to do with

Kelly and I splitting up as often as we did. I've often been accused of being very moody and I can't argue with that, but I think it's the knocks I've taken in life that have made me as I am. Losing my father then my brother, putting up with a stepdad I didn't like, being taken advantage of by race teams, never getting paid properly – those things have all had an effect on me. Maybe I'm just too selfish to make relationships work, I don't know. I think I'm a decent enough bloke but after every relationship fails I seem to put up my guard even more for the next one and that probably makes me appear hard when I'm not – I'm just expecting the worst to happen again and am preparing myself for it.

The other thing is that I've always been a bit of a loner and maybe that's had an effect on many of my relationships too. I think that's partly due to being brought up in the country. My brother was always my best friend and when he was killed there was no one to replace him. I used to be more sociable in my twenties but mostly now I just keep myself to myself. When you think about it, everything I've done has been a one-man job. As a mechanic I worked silently on cars and bikes then at night I'd tinker with my own bikes. I often drove to races on my own for thousands of miles at a time with no one to talk to. Racing's the same: when you're out there on that bike you're on your own, concentrating so hard it almost hurts. It's an eerie, silent world out there with earplugs and a helmet on. The bike may sound awesome to the spectators but it's just a muffled drone to me and even if the crowd is cheering like mad I can't hear them. I'm on my own.

I don't need to be surrounded by people all the time to feel comfortable, I've just always been independent and like to do things for myself. I'm not being anti-social or miserable, I'm just self-reliant and I don't expect others to do everything for me even if they do offer.

Being quite a reclusive person, I don't put myself about as much as other riders do so they always seem to get the good rides and I get forgotten about, but I'm quite happy just to shut myself away from the world. I mean, even now I've got a mobile phone but it's unusual if it rings more than once a day. Most riders are always on their bloody mobiles, always in each other's pants and always kissing arse to further their careers but I just can't do that.

Getting back to girls, though, one reported liaison that I must deny is a supposed fling with a porno model, which was rumoured to have happened at the 1989 TT. I was joined in many press photographs that year by a couple of Penthouse Pets, the most notable being Linzi Drew, who was quite a famous nude model at the time. After that TT she wrote a piece in *Penthouse* magazine saying she had hit it off with a new TT star who had taken her to a golf course and shagged her senseless – presumably in the nineteenth hole!

Because I had really made my name at that TT as the new man to beat and since I had so many pictures taken with her, everyone assumed that I was the mysterious golf course shagger. I got a bit of a ribbing in the paddock about the whole thing even though it had nothing to do with me. It may be that none of the riders shagged Linzi – you have got to fill porn mags with something so it was all a bit of harmless fun.

One of the most promiscuous periods in my life was probably during 1992–94 when I had my own house on the Isle of Man but had split up with Lesley. That house became Sin City; more girls went through there than through Hugh Hefner's boxer shorts. Slick Bass practically stayed there full time as did a mate from the Isle of Man called Ian McVeighty, or 'Biscuit', as Slick called him. It was the ultimate bachelor pad and even if I went home drunk and tired from a nightclub, Slick and Ian would invariably turn up later with a 'present' for me in the form of a girl who wanted to meet Steve Hislop. Naturally, I was usually willing to oblige with the 'introductions' but none of those flings were as hot as the encounter I had upstairs in my mum's house in 1988.

I was in one bed with a girl and my mate Tosh was in another bed in the same room with his girlfriend, Mo. I was getting down to business and couldn't believe how hot things were becoming; either I was out of shape or this was the hottest girl I had even been with. I carried on regardless thinking I was setting the earth on fire until all the giggling from Tosh and Mo's bed finally put me off and I had to ask what the hell they were laughing at. Between fits of laughter they explained that, unlike me, they had realized there were electric blankets on the beds and they had been sober enough to switch theirs off before getting down to business. But there I was going hammer and tongs with 100 degrees of electric blanket wrapped round me!

Anyway, as I said before, the 1989 TT was the one that really made my name as far as racing was concerned. The plan for the year was to do the major road races again and as many world championship Formula One rounds as I could afford as well as some European 250cc championship rounds. Remember, all the travel expenses had to come out of my own pocket so there was no way I could afford to do lots of foreign meetings and that was to cost me dearly by the end of the year.

One of the first big meetings of the season was the Easter weekend Eurolantic Match races at Brands Hatch and that's when Joey Dunlop was knocked off his bike by Belgian rider Stephane Mertens and suffered serious injuries including a broken leg, a shattered wrist and several broken ribs. I actually ended up in the Brands Hatch medical centre next to him that weekend after getting something in my eye and I realized there was no way he was going to be fit in time to race at the TT. That was a real shame because I was looking forward to a head-to-head battle with us both in our prime. As things turned out, it's a battle that never really did happen. Joey's 1989 injuries affected his big bike riding for many years and by the time he was back on the case I'd stopped racing at the TT so we never actually met at our peaks.

No disrespect to Joey – and I know a lot of people

will shoot me down for saying this – but I still think I would have beaten him in a straight fight. I believe I was a better rider than he was round the TT and I have my reasons for saying that. For example, I was only fractionally slower than Joey on my production RC30 in 1988 when he was on the full factory bike and that's when he was at his peak. And I don't think he could have matched the pace that Carl Fogarty and I set in 1991 even if he had been fully fit. In fact, Joey never put in a lap of the TT that was quicker than my 123.50mph lap from 1992 despite the fact that he raced there for another eight years when the bikes had become faster.

With Joey missing the North West 200 in '89 because of his crash, I cleaned up in both Superbike races and they were my first and last ever wins there. I liked the track and the atmosphere but I'd achieved what I set out to achieve and didn't see the point of going back again and again. The same thing happened with the Ulster Grand Prix; I won a big race there in 1989 and then another in 1990 and never went back. I wanted to move on from pure road racing and concentrate on short circuits.

Talking about Joey, there's something I want to clear up once and for all. Lots of Irish fans have come up to me over the years and said I only won the big races at the TT in 1989 because I had Joey's bikes. That's not true. The truth is that at the start of the season I *did* get a one-year-old bike of Joey's as a back-up machine, but I also got a new bike built by Slick Bass with the best components Honda UK could offer.

It wasn't a full factory Japanese model, just a kitted bike. Joey's bike had had a full season of abuse and was in a hell of a state. It wasn't because he didn't look after it but because any bike that does a full season of pure road racing is peppered with stone chippings and marks, the forks get all pitted and they're just generally in a rough state. But it handled beautifully – Joey obviously knew how to set up a bike.

At the start of the season, a bike had arrived from Japan with Mr Dunlop written on the crate and that was a full factory Superbike. Joey obviously couldn't race it at the TT but I was *not* given that bike – it went to Ireland and stayed there that season. Then about two weeks before the TT another crate arrived and this time it had TTF1 – Mr Hislop on the box. I had no idea that I was due to get a special bike. But it turned out that Honda Japan had been so impressed with my riding at Fuji the year before, they decided to build me a special machine for the TT since it was such an important meeting for them and Joey couldn't contest it.

This thing was the dog's bollocks – a real hand-built, no-expense-spared, factory effort. It weighed next to nothing, had a trick exhaust system, a full-blown Formula One engine, the lot. The bodywork was carbon fibre and was so light it would have blown away. In fact, if you look at any pictures of me on that bike in either the F1 or Senior TT in 1989 you'll notice that the nose of the bike looks beaten up. The bodywork was so light that the 180mph winds were crushing it on the long straights at the TT and that's why it's so out of shape. Anyway, the main point is, it *wasn't* Joey's bike so I don't want to hear that one again, thank you very much.

I never rode the special bike until the Wednesday night practice session as it was being painted in the early part of the week. We wanted the red, white and two-tone blue colour scheme of Honda's RC30 but the paint guy said he couldn't have a complex job like that ready in time. So instead we settled on a red and white design because I'd seen Freddie Spencer using that, I liked it and it was simple and quick to do. I tried to get the go-ahead from some Japanese Honda guys but their English wasn't too good so they just grinned and gave us the thumbs up and I thought that meant OK so we went ahead and got it painted red and white.

But when Bob McMillan saw it, he said, 'What the hell's this? That's not Honda colours.' He didn't like it but it was too late to change it so the colours stayed. As it turned out, all of the official Honda UK bikes were painted red and white after the TT so someone must have liked the look of it!

Anyway, I started the week on my spare bike and when I pulled into the pits at the end of the Tuesday night session everyone seemed really excited and someone showed me a stopwatch with my last lap time on it. It was the first ever sub-19-minute lap of the TT course and the first ever lap at over 120mph. I didn't even feel as if I was pushing it; in fact I was short-shifting (changing up early) through the gears to try to keep the front wheel on the ground but the bike was just so good I couldn't help but go fast on it. Unfortunately, practice times don't count as official records as they need to be set in a race but the whole paddock was buzzing when news of that lap got out and everyone was hoping to see the first ever 120mph lap in a race.

My first race of the week was the Supersport 600 event and the plan was to blitz everyone on the first lap and gain a big enough cushion so I could control the pace. Sure enough, I was 15 seconds ahead by the end of lap one and was never troubled from there on, winning by almost 30 seconds. It was my third TT win and I was pleased enough with that but the big race for me was the Formula One and I was determined to dominate it.

The only problem I'd had on the F1 bike in practice was with the brake pads being pushed back in the callipers because of the speeds I was doing, so unless I pumped the brakes going down the straights I didn't have any stopping power going into the corners. Coming into the village of Kirkmichael on one particular lap during the F1 race, I reached for the brakes, squeezed hard on the lever and was horrified to notice that nothing was happening – I'd forgotten to pump them and I was doing about 140mph and about to enter a high street lined with houses on both sides!

There was nothing for it but to bounce up over the kerb and run onto the narrow pavement, desperately trying to haul the bike round and back onto the road before I smacked a house. I somehow managed to scrub off enough speed, which allowed me to get back on line and back onto the road with a bump as I hopped off the kerb at about 120mph. It was a scary moment but everyone has them from time to time at the TT and you've got to expect your fair share. Funnily enough, my old employer Jim Oliver and his mate Allan Duffus were spectating near that very spot and saw the whole thing which gave them a bit of a fright.

The other problem I had was during a pit stop when I got fuel splashed in my eyes. It stung like hell and lost me some time but I knew I had to get going again or I would lose the race. Fortunately, I had a big enough lead at that point so I managed to stay ahead but it was some miles before my the burning pain in my eyes eased off and allowed me to see properly again.

The quickest lap I did in the race was 121.13mph, which was slightly slower than I did in practice. However, it was still faster than the old lap record of 119.08mph set by Steve Cull the previous year. It meant that I had officially become the first rider in the history of the TT to lap the course at over 120mph and the first man to do a sub-19-minute lap. In fact, I went so fast that my entire race average, including a standing start and two pit stops, was quicker than the old outright lap record and I set a new standing-start lap record too, just for good measure! I won the race by almost two minutes from Brian Morrison, with Nick Jefferies and Carl Fogarty in third and fourth but it would have been really interesting to see where a fully fit Joey Dunlop might have finished.

Being the first man to break the 120mph-lap barrier put me in a unique club of riders who have upped the record by 10 miles per hour over the years. My fellow Scot, Bob McIntyre, was the first man to lap at 100mph in 1957. Then John Williams broke the 110mph barrier in 1976 and then I upped the pace to 120mph in 1989 and that's something no one can ever take away from me no matter how fast people go in the future.

Things were looking good in the Junior race as I was leading by eight seconds but then it all went tits-up big style as was becoming the norm in the Junior for me. I had managed to take the Quarry Bends section flat out in top gear during practice and thought I'd try it in the race too. Problem was, the strong headwind that had kept my speed slightly down in practice was absent on race day so I was going just a fraction faster on the approach to the turn. The front end tucked under and I was thrown from the bike at about 140mph and headed straight for a brick wall. I was sliding backwards on my back staring straight at the sky and I can clearly remember thinking, 'Fuck, no, this is it. I'm going to die.'

I dug my heels in and pushed the palms of my hands downwards, spread out in a star shape, just doing anything I could to try and scrub off a bit of speed but I must still have been sliding at over 100mph. I went down the track like that for about 200 yards, just waiting for the impact that I knew was going to kill me; waiting for the dull thud that would end it all. It was a horrific experience. With a lot of crashes you don't have time to know what is going on because they happen so fast but this one seemed as if it was taking ages and I was sure there was only one possible outcome. I knew the track intimately so I knew I was heading for a wall and you don't hit a wall at 100mph and walk away from it.

Luckily I slid along past the wall and mounted the next kerb. As I struck the kerb, I was flipped up, sent sliding down the pavement and I finally ground to a halt. I was alive and I couldn't believe it; the birds were still singing, the sky was still blue and what's more, I was perfectly pain-free. My leathers and boots were worn through but they had worked wonders because I was fine. It was a miraculous escape; I really should have been dead.

There were bikes still whizzing past me and marshals running towards me as I ground to a halt so I tried to stand up but nearly fell over again as the heels were completely worn off my boots from sliding down the road. The paramedic helicopter arrived in no time at all but I said I didn't need it so it flew back to base. As I walked back up the pavement, I noticed a very small damp patch on the corner where I crashed and figured that must have been enough to bring me down at the speed I was travelling at. It was nearly a very severe punishment for a relatively minor crime.

I went to Sulby Glen for a beer while I waited for Slick Bass to pick me up in the van. There was another race to come, so I stayed to watch that and was feeling very lucky to be alive, drinking beer and soaking up the sunshine. But while I had been extremely lucky, little did I know what was in store in the next few tragic hours for some of the other riders.

After the race was over I headed back with Slick and we backed the van down a slip road to pick up my trashed bike. As I jumped out of the van, something lying on the road caught my eye but it seemed to take a few seconds for me to register what it actually was. It was a horrible realization when it finally dawned on me that I was looking at a black, PVC body bag and it definitely had a body in it. There was nobody standing nearby, just the bag with a crash helmet placed on top. As soon as I saw the helmet I recognized the design and knew it belonged to Steve Henshaw which could only mean one thing – Steve had been killed.

I couldn't believe what I was seeing and Slick broke down in tears as soon as he recognized the helmet. He was in a terrible state as he had known Steve quite well. I knew him too but just to casually speak to; we weren't best buddies or anything like that but I knew he was a nice bloke.

I did know Phil Mellor well, however, and unbeknown to me at that point, he had just been killed minutes before in a separate incident. It was only when we got back to the paddock that we heard the whole tragic story.

Phil had crashed at Doran's Bend and died later in hospital. His team-mate Jamie Whitham had seen the wreckage and crashed a few miles later, exactly where I did at Quarry Bends, but was unscathed. Maybe Jamie had been distracted after seeing the wreckage of Phil's accident, but Steve Henshaw had then crashed trying to avoid the wreckage of Jamie's bike and was killed instantly. Another rider, Mike Seward, was badly hurt in that same incident as he too struck the pile of wrecked machinery.

It was a terrible fortnight for the TT with five competitors being killed in total – one of the blackest years in the event's history. Many teams withdrew from the rest of the meeting after those accidents and quite a few riders flew home, Brian Morrison and Carl Fogarty among them. Jamie Whitham also went straight home and never returned to race on the Island again.

For me, there was never any question of going home. I stayed on and fully intended riding in the Senior race in a bid to become only the third man in history to win three TTs in a week. I don't mean to sound cold or heartless, and I mean no disrespect to the memory of any of the riders who died that week, but I had already lost my father and brother at an early age so I just think I was better placed to cope with the fatalities than some other people. Naturally I was very sad but I had a job to do and I was prepared to do it even though my heart wasn't really in it.

It was a subdued and much depleted grid that lined up on Friday for the Senior TT. The pace was a good bit slower than in the F1 race just a few days before as all the riders had so recently had such a harsh reminder of the dangers of the course they were racing on. I was still a bit spooked after my Quarry

Bends crash as well as being upset with the fatalities. I took it very steadily through Quarry every time around; after all, I was still alive and Steve Henshaw wasn't, despite the fact that we both had our accidents at the same section of the course on the same day. That proves what a lottery crashing is and in the back of my mind, I felt as though I should have been dead too.

I must have been thinking too much about all the tragedies of the week during the first two laps because I couldn't seem to get dialled in properly and my riding was very ragged. But I forced myself to concentrate and eventually won the race by about 38 seconds from Nick Jefferies. It was a relief when that race was over. My hands were badly blistered from hanging onto viciously powerful bikes for two whole weeks and I was just glad everyone else finished the race safely.

Inside I was chuffed to become the only rider, apart from Mike Hailwood and Joey Dunlop, to score three wins in a week and pleased to have been the very first man to lap the course at 120mph. But there was no big celebration as there would have been any other year. It's ironic that my most successful TT to date had also been one of the most tragic for others. That was a TT I was glad to get home from – after all, five people never made the return trip.

But racing goes on despite all the tragedies it throws up and I had the Formula One world championship to think about after the TT. The F1 series was the forerunner of the World Superbike championship as it was the original World Series for four-stroke, production-based bikes. The big difference was that most of the rounds were held on closed public roads like the TT.

I had missed the first round of the series because it was held in Japan and I simply couldn't afford to go there. Carl Fogarty, who was the reigning F1 champ, did go and he scored two valuable points over me. But it wasn't so much being poor that lost me that world title, it was the fact that I burned my bollocks in the Dutch round at Assen!

I had a four-point lead over Foggy when we went to Assen because I'd won the F1 race at the TT, but Assen's where it all went wrong for me. I was running up front and doing fine until I came in to refuel. That's when a fuel filler valve jammed and I pulled back out onto the circuit with my petrol cap open and fuel flooding onto my rear tyre – and my bollocks!

I had no choice but to complete a full lap to get back to the pits but the bike was sliding everywhere on the fuel so I had to wobble round and dropped down to eleventh place. When I got to the pits, Slick hammered the jammed fuel cap shut. I went back out for the rest of the race but my crotch was killing me – it was burning like hell and my eyes were streaming with the pain so I simply couldn't concentrate on going that fast.

As soon as I came in to pit lane after the race I threw the bike at Slick and ran like Linford Christie to the shower block in the paddock, taking my helmet off and peeling my leathers down mid-stride as I went. I was so desperate that I didn't even strip naked to get in the ice cold shower, I just pulled my leathers down past my crotch and held my poor burning wedding tackle under the water. I can't explain what was a blessed relief it was, though it was too late to save the skin from my private parts, which had already burned off!

That stupid little mistake in the pits not only caused me a great deal of pain, it pretty much saw me lose any hope of winning the F1 title as Foggy had gained 15 points on me at Assen. I won in Portugal and again in Ireland but Carl's further victory in Finland was enough to give him the championship for the second year – by eight measly points. That really should have been my first world title.

To round off the year, I went to the Macau Grand Prix, the race that my brother was planning to go to just before he was killed. Now, if you can imagine the Chinese authorities shutting off the streets of Hong Kong (which is not far from Macau) and allowing 190mph motorcycles to race full speed around them, you've got a pretty good idea of what Macau's like: in other words, it's fucking mental.

There is no run-off room whatsoever as the whole track is lined with armco, walls and high-rise apartment blocks. And because it's on the coast, you could hit a wall and be thrown over into the sea at some corners! On one particular hairpin bend, the braking area is a regularly used bus stop, which is always covered in diesel and oil! All in all, there is absolutely no room for error at that place.

Despite all this, riders still race flat out at Macau

and just have to put thoughts of crashing from their minds as it simply doesn't bear thinking about. But the race still used to attract a lot of big-name Grand Prix stars because the organizer, Mike Trimby, is involved at a high level in the GP scene. He also organizes free holidays for the riders in Thailand after the race, which proves a big attraction for obvious reasons!

I was well used to racing on roads so the track never fazed me but as it turned out, the 1989 event was a total farce. They never run races in the wet at Macau as it's just too dangerous so, since it was raining, the organizers decided to wait and let us go out after the car race if it had dried up. Mike Trimby, quite rightly, said there would be too much rubber and oil on the track after the car race so that would also be too dangerous for the bikes. The solution, everyone hastily agreed, was to stage a race at a safe pace but to make it look like we were actually challenging each other. Lots of passing on the straights and anywhere else that seemed relatively safe but no balls-out, real racing. After all, it wasn't a championship round or anything and safety had to come first. The alternative was to let down the spectators by not staging a race at all.

Well, that was the plan anyway but there's something about Irish riders which means they just can't seem to back off. They always have to beat each other so they can say they're the best man back home. Robert Dunlop and Phillip McCallen had a history of not liking each other anyway so I should have known that neither of them would settle for second, even in a fake race.

For the first part of the race we all hammed it up for the spectators and TV cameras and no one was riding too fast so it was actually quite good fun. Everyone was getting prize money based on their practice performance anyway (which meant I got most because I was the quickest) so there was no point in going fast to win cash. But about halfway through the race I noticed Robert Dunlop was starting to pick up the pace – and Phillip McCallen was going with him. I watched from a distant third place for a little while, not too bothered, then the racer in me came out and I thought, 'Fuck this, if they're racing for real so am I.'

I pinned the throttle and immediately pulled away from the riders behind me. As I got up to real racing speeds I set the fastest lap of the race closing down the gap on Robert and Phillip but I'd left my charge too late and had to settle for third. Still, there was always the delights of Macau and Thailand to sample and I was looking forward to that even though some of them are strictly not for the squeamish – or for animal lovers.

One particular restaurant's speciality is monkey brains, which may not sound that bad until you realize that the monkeys are still alive as they have their brains eaten! The poor little buggers are clamped under the table with the top of their skulls cut off as gruesome diners tuck into their custard-textured live brains. It's cruel beyond belief and I never went there but I know some people who did.

Macau is also famous for its brothels and massage parlours and one of the most famous stories relating to them was when former racer and current BBC race commentator, Steve Parrish, blew up a brothel with a huge bomb made out of fireworks. Steve knew some of the riders were inside the brothel being 'treated' so he thought he'd surprise them but ended up surprising himself. The bomb was far more powerful than he'd imagined and the whole joint was practically wrecked in the explosion. Steve was chased out of the country by the police and just avoided being captured as he fled to Hong Kong. The authorities impounded his hire car and charged him for it and he's still banned from the country to this day. That's not the kind of bang the Chinese want in their brothels.

9 Bored

'I aimed the bike at the toilet block and crashed straight into it.'

I get bored with things very quickly. In fact, it's amazing I've held it all together long enough to write this book!

It's probably been a bad thing for my career but I just can't help it; it seems to be an inescapable part of my psychological make-up. A bike magazine recently took photographs of my hands and sent them to a palm reader without her knowing who I was and even she noticed straight away that I got easily bored, so there must be something in it.

By 1990, I was bored of the TT, even though I would still be riding round the bloody place four years later. I'd done what I set out to do there and it was time to move on but for various reasons, which I'll go into later, I became sort of trapped there.

But it wasn't just riding at the TT that I got bored with; I sometimes get bored riding bikes even now. At three-day race meetings such as the British Superbike championship, I'm usually revved up for Friday's practice session and maybe even still on the Saturday qualifying. But many times by Sunday's race day, I've had enough of riding round and round and it's pretty difficult racing against 30 other extremely focused guys, all desperate to win, when you can't be bothered to prove anything.

Maybe I've just been racing for too long. Sometimes I'm so uninterested that I'll sit on the start line and think about some of the niggling little problems in my life instead of concentrating on the race ahead. You see other riders gazing steely-eyed down the track so focused that it's scary while I'm often thinking about what's on TV that night or what I'm going to have for my dinner.

But those kinds of weekends are an exception: other times I'm so on the case that I'm almost untouchable. It's not that I'm not committed and determined to win because I am, but it's very difficult to maintain that level of dedication week-in, week-out over so many years. I think that if some other riders were more honest instead of just saying what their sponsors want to hear, they'd admit to feeling the same from time to time.

If I like a circuit and I'm feeling good then I'm more than capable of setting pole position, winning both races and smashing the lap record in the process as I did at Cadwell Park in 2002; it just depends. But I lose heart in things quickly, there's no doubt about that so it's surprising that I've had the success that I've had, although that probably explains why I've not had a lot more. I just go through phases when I love racing and other times when I can't be arsed.

Speed becomes normal when you spend so much time going fast. For most people, going at the speeds racers do would be an awesome thrill, as anyone who's had a pillion ride with a racer will testify. But when you've been going that fast for 20 years it actually becomes quite boring.

Another example of the way I can go off things is selling my Yamaha TZ350, which was once my most prized possession. It meant a lot to me because that's the bike that I got noticed on and my plan was always to restore it to mint condition. However when I moved to a smaller house in 2001 I just didn't have room for it and I got sick of tripping over the bloody thing in my garage so I finally sold it just to get it out of the way.

It's the same thing with all my trophies. They used to sit in a glass display cabinet in my house until I got bored of polishing them all the time so they're now in boxes up in the loft. I don't have a single trophy on display any more and I give all the ones I win now to whichever team I'm riding for. I used to treasure the smallest little plastic plaque that I won for racing but over the years I've become jaded with the whole affair and I simply don't have room to display trophies in the house I'm in now so they too had too. I also like to get away from the whole racing thing so I don't like to have too many reminders round the house.

Some riders keep all their leathers and helmets

as souvenirs too, but I've given all mine away or sold them to collectors. What would I want with old tattered leathers?

A lot of racers get overly obsessed with what they do and don't seem to have a life outside the sport. I can't understand the ones that talk about bikes constantly – every bloody conversation is the same and it just drives me nuts. That's why I started staying in hotels during race meetings, so I can get away from the paddock and arrive back at the circuit relatively fresh come race day.

The paddock is a poisoned little village filled with backstabbers and people who would do anything to ingratiate themselves with a team boss just to get a better bike. I can't be bothered with all that bitching and I've learned to let it go clean over my head. I don't give a shit what anyone has to say about me because they don't really know me or who I really am anyway. They usually have ulterior motives like trying to out-psyche me or upset my team or trying to line themselves up for my ride the following season. Fuck them all. I learned a long time ago just to do my own thing and to hell with anyone else. That's not to say there aren't any decent people in the paddock, because there are but I've been around this game too long to be bothered with childish backstabbing.

So, as I said, in 1990 I was getting bored with the TT and I asked Honda if they would support me on a 250cc machine on the short circuits. They said, 'Yes,' and teamed me up with Alan Carter for an assault on the British championship; a seven-round series run on

Britain's top short circuits. It's the first time I seriously attacked a major British championship and, much to the amazement of everyone who thought I was only a public-roads racer, I won it.

It was a damn close-run thing, though, and in the end I only beat Carter by one point. I don't usually get nervous before a race but with only four points in the lead going into the last round at Donington Park, I was crapping myself. Carter actually fell while leading that race but remounted and still won while I held on to fourth, which was exactly where I needed to be to win the title.

Incredibly, the 1990 British 250cc championship was the first championship of any kind I'd ever won and it meant so much to me. Not only because it was the first, but because it was held purely on short circuits and should have been all the proof my detractors needed that I could ride on those kinds of circuits as well as on the roads. That's when I really reinvented myself and started making the shift from road racer to circuit racer and very few people have been able to do that.

It may not be obvious to the casual observer that there's such a difference between the two disciplines but believe me, there is. Road racing is about stamina, it's about ignoring the dangers and not being afraid to clip brick walls and brush hedges and it's about nursing the bike over extremely bumpy and taxing roads. On short circuits, it's a flat-out sprint from the start over a relatively short distance and you're bunched up tight with 30 other riders, literally leaning on each other. Also on short circuits, you're leaning the bike over more, decking everything out on the absolute limits of adhesion. Because there's more run-off space, you can afford to ride that bit harder, too, because crashing is safer than on the roads. I suppose it's like the difference between a 10,000 metres cross-country run and a 100 metres sprint and there are not many athletes who excel at both of those disciplines.

Anyway, as I said before, I thought my 250 British title would have been enough to prove my worth on the shorts but it wasn't. Most people ignored that title because Superbikes were everything and no one cared about 250s but whatever other people thought, I was pleased with myself and the progress I had made so I decided to move up a stage and compete in the European 250cc championship in 1991. Back then, you had to finish in the top 10 of that series to be eligible for a place in the Grands Prix which was where I really wanted to be.

I used to have some hilarious times doing the Euro races alongside other British riders like Ian Newton, Ian Lougher, Woolsey Coulter and Alan Patterson. We'd all travel in convoy with our vans across Europe and invented no end of games to ward off boredom on the featureless motorways and autobahns. Mobile food fights were one of the favourites. All our vans were evenly matched on top speed but we'd still try to overtake one another on long straights. I remember on one occasion pulling alongside another van and I was just about to draw level with the passenger door when it opened and I was bombarded with missiles. Eggs, tomatoes, sandwiches, anything which could make a mess was all fair game until my van looked like a huge mobile pizza.

Eventually, the vans would get so messy that we'd have to stop in a service station to power-wash them. We got some strange looks in those places I can tell you. Once, I had just spent ages cleaning my van and was jumping back into the driver's seat when there was an almighty crack as an egg pelted off the inside of the door: the attack was back on. Before I'd even pulled away, my van was absolutely plastered again! It was like being in school all over again except we were travelling around Europe and racing motorbikes and there were no teachers in charge!

I think I could have been very good on 250s if the support had been there but because everyone in the UK was into Superbikes that's where all the good rides were. I certainly feel I could have been competitive in 250c Grand Prix racing because I proved myself against future GP stars such as Max Biaggi, Eskil Suter and Jurgen van den Goorberg in the '91 Euro series when I beat them all on occasions throughout the year.

Max Biaggi is a classic example of how well the Italian system for bringing on young riders works. They spot talent when it is young and back it up all the way to world level with good sponsorship deals, technical support and sound advice from experienced riders. The Italian government even puts money into bringing on young talent, which is something I could never imagine our government doing. That's why the country has produced riders like Valentino Rossi, Max Biaggi and Loris Capirossi. The talent is in Britain – without question – but there's simply no infrastructure in place to bring it on properly. It's getting much better now with initiatives such as the Red Bull Rookie team, which provides rides for youngsters, but there was nothing like that back in the early '90s – back then, you had to do everything for yourself. I mean, I was racing alongside Max Biaggi and beating him on occasions and he's now a multi-millionaire multiple world champion with a luxury home in Monaco and I'm living in a semi-detached on the Isle of Man. That's the difference proper backing can make.

However, Max was a brilliant rider even then and I told the press at the time that he would be world champion some day. He has since won the 250cc world championship four times and is now a top MotoGP rider. He used to slide a 250 bike like I'd never seen anyone do, laying big black lines of rubber out of the corners as he got on the gas. It's usually only 500s that have the power to do that but Max did it on a 250. I remember watching him power-sliding on a dry track and thinking, 'OK, very impressive but he'll be on his arse as soon as it rains.' But when it did actually rain in one of the rounds Max took off and I didn't even see which way he went!

I was still every bit as fast as the leading Euro riders though and if someone had supported me properly I don't see why I couldn't have kept running with them in Grands Prix. It's just another example of the 'ifs' and 'buts' that have littered my career.

As well as the lack of a proper infrastructure for bringing on riders, the state of circuits in the UK and Ireland are a joke compared to the rest of Europe. Mondello Park in Ireland was in such a mess when we arrived for a Euro round in 1991 that one of the Dutch riders poured gallons of diesel on the track and drove straight back home in protest. It was a total shambles. Donington Park is currently one of the UK's best circuits but many Grand Prix riders rate it as one of the worst on the international calendar! When you consider that World Superbike races attract upwards of 120,000 people through the gates, you'd think it would be time to invest some of that ticket revenue back into our circuits. There are just too many greedy promoters around for my liking.

Anyway, I'm getting ahead of myself here because I haven't mentioned the 1990 TT yet and it was a complete disaster for me. After winning three races in 1989 I didn't score a single victory in '90 while my arch-rival Carl Fogarty had his best week ever but, as usual, he went to extremes to achieve his results.

Knowing that I was the man he had to beat, Carl refused to speak to me all through TT fortnight, even though we were team-mates and based in the same garage! It was even more ridiculous because we'd been good friends since 1986 when we were both nobodies, but Carl has to do things like that to win. He has to hate his rivals in order to beat them and he's always trying to out-psyche them in any way he can. I never understood that but I suppose it seemed to work for Foggy. And at least he admitted to the press the following year that he had been a 'right twat' for ignoring me.

That's when Carl Fogarty really started to change. He was fine at the 1991 TT and we had a good time there together but from then on, he transformed into Foggy the World Superbike racer and he became a really obnoxious little bugger just full of aggression, arrogance and hatred. Some people say that's what you need to be like to be world champion but then how do they explain easy-going guys like Troy Bayliss or Colin Edwards who are both WSB champions? I don't think you need to be an arse to win races.

Anyway, Foggy won the F1 race after I'd overshot the course twice in one lap with a warped front brake disc. I had to come in and change the front wheel which took ages so I rejoined the race in thirty-ninth place with just one intention – to break my own lap record. I wanted to salvage something from the race so I went hell for leather and made up 30 places in four laps to finish ninth at the end, upping the outright record to 122.63mph in the process. Job done.

The Junior race that year has become the stuff of legends. It remains the only major race at the TT that I've never won after a catalogue of disasters that the press came to call my 'Junior jinx.' In 1985 and 1986 I retired with mechanical problems, then in 1987 I was leading the race by miles when my ignition packed up. In 1988 my exhaust fell off, then in 1989 I crashed heavily at Quarry Bends but I was sure 1990 would be my year. The bike was going great and I was on form and determined to beat my jinx.

It's no exaggeration to say that the last lap of that race was without question the hardest I ever had, and ever would ride a motorcycle round the Isle of Man. I had that thing sliding and decking out everywhere, I was brushing hedges and flying over jumps and just kept the throttle pinned to the stop. I rode the bloody wheels off that bike and thought nobody in the world could have put in a quicker lap but in the end it still wasn't enough. My old buddy from the Manx Grand Prix days, Ian Lougher, must have made a pact with the devil that morning because I just couldn't catch him no matter how hard I rode. He had never won a TT before and it was a long time before he did anything special again but on that one day he was simply unbeatable.

We both absolutely shattered the 250 lap record but Ian beat me by 1.8 seconds after 150 miles of racing. It was the fourth closest finish in the 83-year history of the TT. On the last circuit, Ian put in a lap at 117.8mph when the old record had only been around 114mph. Lap records usually go up by fractions of a second, not by more than three seconds. It was an incredible ride by Ian and even though I lost a lot of time in the pits when my petrol cap fell into the bike's body-work, I can't take anything away from Lougher – apart from the fact that he's a shite dancer as I've already said!

My steering damper broke in the Supersport 600 race so I was forced to retire and the Senior was a total farce. It was raining on some parts of the course and dry in others and just too dangerous to continue.

In my opinion, it should not have been held; I'm not about to risk my life for anyone in conditions like that. I'm no chicken but that's just plain stupid. Riding the TT is dangerous enough in the dry but in dodgy, changeable conditions, it's lethal. As soon as the rain came down I rolled off the throttle and just toured round to the pits. Joey Dunlop and most of the other riders did the same but Foggy and Phillip McCallen went at it head-to-head like nutters until McCallen crashed and Foggy was left to take the victory.

But I wasn't too concerned about my TT results because I had my short-circuit riding to concentrate on. The only thing that annoyed me was that the TT usually represented my biggest payday of the year but because I'd had such a crap two weeks I made practically nothing. In fact, my accounts from July 1989 to July 1990 showed I banked just £12,000 and I was one of the top riders in the UK. Pathetic!

The other thing I did on the Isle of Man during 1990 was to make a couple of onboard camera videos round the TT course. The first was in January for a video about the history of the TT. It was filmed over just one part of the mountain section with the police blocking some roads for me so I could go for it. It was freezing cold and there were none of the usual safety bales at the side of the track, as you'd get at TT time. I was still going stupidly fast though and being filmed from a helicopter that was hovering just above me on the run-down to Creg-ny-Baa corner. I was so focused on the helicopter that I missed my braking point and realized I wasn't going to get round the corner. Shit. A police car was blocking the slip road and I didn't really want to hit it so there was only one thing for it – I would have to try and scrub off as much speed as I could and lay the bike down.

There's a pub right on the corner at Creg-ny-Baa and in those days there was a low wall and outside toilets block right at the edge of the road so that's what I aimed for. I stood on the back brake until the bike skidded round sideways but I was still travelling at speed when I smacked into the wall, got thrown clean over it and landed head first in the little alleyway leading to the toilet. Not the most glamorous of crashes but I was very lucky to walk away from that one. Riding motorbikes at racing speeds into toilet blocks is not recommended.

I had a bit more joy filming the video *TT Flyer*. I suppose it was quite dangerous, too, because I carried all the camera equipment in a rucksack on my back and if I'd crashed, all that weight could easily have snapped my spine. Fortunately, those backpacks are banned now and they're not needed anyway because technology has moved on so much so the filming equipment is much smaller.

Anyway, it turned out to be the first ever onboard camera lap of the course at over 120mph and it got an amazing response from people. Brian Kreisky, who was behind the whole thing (and was sadly killed in an aeroplane crash some years later) was also involved in filming the Grand Prix at the time and he took a copy over to the Austrian GP. Wayne Rainey, who won the 500cc title that year, was apparently amazed by that video. While he was watching it, he kept asking Brian, 'Is this guy still on the same lap, man?' because he only knew short two- or three-mile tracks and the TT is almost 40 miles long. He couldn't believe the speeds I was doing on normal roads and apparently he even watched the video to psyche himself up for the Grand Prix that weekend.

Wayne was so fascinated with the TT that he asked me to take him for a spin round the course in a car when he later came to the Island to visit another friend involved in covering the GPs for TV. I've also taken other Grand Prix stars like Kevin Schwantz, Daryl Beattie and Scott Russell for laps in a car and they all loved it even though they'd never ride there.

My own brief career in Grand Prix was pretty disastrous, mostly because I never had a competitive bike. When you reach that level, a bike that's good enough to win a British national race is hopelessly outpaced, sometimes by about 20 miles per hour and over a race distance, that puts you down by about one full lap. That's the situation I was in with my little Honda.

I got an entry for the French GP in 1991 because of my Euro 250 standings (I was in third place by mid-season) but my bike was so slow I could do no better than twenty-fifth place. People were passing me as if I was standing still. I could have pedalled round quicker.

The British GP was even worse as I got knocked off on the second lap and that was the end of that. To make matters worse, I had opted to miss a world endurance round so I could race at the British GP and I'd had every chance of winning that championship, so it was a double disaster for me.

Endurance racing is gruesome. Some events are only six hours long but many last for a full 24 hours with three riders taking turns on the bike, so it's one hour on and two hours off, all day and all night. And believe me, you don't always feel like riding at 180mph in pouring rain at four o'clock in the morning when there's a warm, dry bed in the motorhome.

You may think you can rest between stints but it's practically impossible. By the time you get out of your leathers, have a shower, rehydrate and have something to eat, then debrief with the team, it's your turn to ride again. The pace is just relentless and the mental strain is huge.

A race usually starts at 3pm so you've had a normal night's sleep the night before if you don't get too nervous. There's a warm-up session in the morning so you're normally at the track by 8am then it's a case of loading up on some pasta or whatever and hanging about for the big start which is really hyped up. For the first hour it's like a World Superbike race with everyone riding flat out and jostling for positions then as the first rider pits for fuel, it's the next rider's turn. That goes on all afternoon, all evening, all through the night and through the cold light of dawn and then through morning and early afternoon until the 3pm finish. It's one hell of a slog and easily the most gruelling form of road racing.

The one and only thing that keeps you going is

adrenaline. Without that you'd be sound asleep by four in the morning. But when it kicks in and your eyes are wide as saucers in your head and your heart's pounding, you somehow manage to focus on the job in hand. Riding 180mph Superbikes in the dark takes immense concentration. The headlights are much better than the ones you'd get on road bikes (there are two lamps and one tilts up when the nose of the bike dives under braking so you can still see what's ahead clearly), but it's still a weird sensation. For me the worst period is dawn; that's when your eyes are burning from the strain, your body is a mass of aches and pains from lack of sleep and from being crouched on the bike for so long. Anyone who's ridden a long distance on a road bike will tell you how sore you become and how much it saps your concentration. Try to do it at mind-numbing race speeds and it gets a hell of a lot harder. You are physically and mentally shattered after a 24-hour race and you never get used to it. I usually ended up being so tired that I'd relive the whole race in my dreams that night too and sometimes I'd wake up kicking and thrashing around reliving a crash.

Some riders have been tested during the 24-hour period for reactions and problem-solving skills and their results, unsurprisingly, fall away quite noticeably during the night. Their natural biorhythms are messed up and it feels like a kind of jet lag but somehow we all seem to manage in our own different ways and there are not as many crashes as you might expect.

Whether it was because of the relatively long TT

races or not, I don't know, but I took to endurance racing quite easily and really enjoyed most things about it – except for the fatigue. Honda had linked me up with a private team under Howard Lees at the beginning of 1991 and our first race was at the famous Le Mans 24 Hours in France. The fastest rider in the team always starts the race, so he can try to gain an early advantage so I went out first and was running with all the top factory bikes on our unsponsored Honda RC30. After 20 gruelling hours of struggling against superior machinery our team was handed the lead as the bike which had been out front suffered mechanical problems. I was riding at the time and when my pit board told me I now had a six lap lead I thought 'Whoopee! We're going to win this on a private bike.'

But later on I was riding along quite happily when all of a sudden there was a huge 'BANG!' and I was down on my arse. A six-lap lead with just four hours to go and I had binned the bloody bike. I can't imagine what the team must have thought of me at that point; all that effort, all the travelling and all those hopes dashed in a split second. We got the bike fixed up and salvaged a fourth place but we really should have won that race.

To this day, I still don't know what caused the crash. I wasn't going any faster than normal but the front wheel just tucked under. Maybe it was because we couldn't afford tyre warmers like all the other teams and perhaps the tyres were still cold or maybe there was some dust on the track, but I suppose

I'll never know. Poor Howard Lees was killed in a plane accident the following year and I'll bet he's still turning in his grave over my crash. Sorry Howard.

Our second place at the next race at Spa-Francorchamps put us second overall in the world championship, which must have impressed Honda as they signed me up to ride one of their proper factory bikes in the most important round – the Suzuka 8 Hours. In endurance racing, a rider can switch teams and still win the title so I still kept all my points.

The 8 Hours is the single most important race in the world and it means more to the big four Japanese manufacturers' pride to win that event than even a world championship. Suzuka circuit is owned by Honda, which only adds to the battle of corporate pride. In the early '90s, more than 300,000 fans would turn up over race weekend making it one of the biggest sporting attendances anywhere on the planet. The pressure, heat and humidity are immense but so was the bike Honda gave me – a full works 1989 RVF750. It was the very same bike I'd raced at the TT in 1991 (more of which later) and I loved it.

Because Suzuka is 'only' an eight-hour race, there are only two riders and I was teamed up with my arch TT rival, Carl Fogarty. As usual, the rider who is fastest in qualifying gets to start the race, which means they get to line up on the grid and get all the attention from the media, the brolly dollies, the crowds and the television cameras. For the last two years that I'd ridden there with Foggy, he'd been fastest so he had started first but both times the silly bugger had fallen off in the first half-hour trying to go too fast. So in 1991 on the way to Japan, our team boss Neil Tuxworth told Carl that I'd be starting first no matter who was fastest in practice. Well, Foggy was not a happy boy. He sat in a huff all the way to Japan with his chin buried in his chest not speaking to anybody. He needn't have bothered because as it happened, I was quickest in qualifying so I'd have started the race first anyway.

As usual, the competition at Suzuka was formidable as the manufacturers pulled out all the stops to enrol the world's best riders for the weekend. So to finish third for us was a fantastic result, especially when you consider the winning team was made up of the 1987 500cc world champion, Wayne Gardner, and his fellow Australian and future five times 500cc world champion, Mick Doohan, for many people the greatest rider of all time. I raced alongside Mick for an hour or so in the wet and he was awesome to watch but having said that, I still managed to stay with him for the whole session.

Behind Foggy and I at the finish were big name riders like Daryl Beattie, Shinichi Itoh and Aaron Slight, so we were really pleased with our efforts and Foggy was smiling again. But more importantly, that third place put me in the lead of the world championship. Even though I'd only started racing in endurance for a bit of fun, all of a sudden I was looking like a world champion and this was a chance to make up for losing the Formula One world title in 1989 when I'd splashed petrol on my bollocks.

I missed the next round of the endurance series to compete in the 250cc British Grand Prix, as I've already said. Then I finished seventh at the Bol d'Or round to keep my championship hopes alive with just one round remaining in Australia and that's when it all went tits up. There was big talk of Honda supplying an RVF and that Mick Doohan or Daryl Beattie would partner me in the last round. But Honda UK didn't bother doing anything about it and there was talk that they couldn't afford the £20,000 cost of the trip so that was it all over – I didn't even get to go to Australia. Honda had a world title waiting to be won and they did naff all about it so Kawasaki was handed it on a plate. That never made any sense to me. What's the point of going racing if you're ready to pass up on world titles? That was the second almost certain world crown I missed out on after my F1 mishap and on top of that Honda had already pulled me back from European racing to help Alan Carter win the British title. Now they'd not bothered their arses to back me up in the world endurance championship either. As much as I liked Neil Tuxworth, I was learning to hate him and I really felt as if Honda was holding me back in my career.

Incidentally, I partnered Carl Fogarty and Terry Rymer in the Bol d'Or 24 Hour race in the 1992 world endurance championship and we won the event, which was enough to secure the world title for them. I wasn't credited as a world champ though as I hadn't raced the full season with Carl and Terry as my team-mates. I'd been riding in another branch of the team in selected rounds so I only finished sixth equal in the final standings.

Looking back on 1991 I realize I had ridden in too many different disciplines. I raced all sorts of classes at the TT, I raced 250s in the UK and Europe, I raced in the world endurance championship and I did a bunch of one-off non-championship meetings like the Macau GP. I was spreading myself too thinly instead of concentrating on one class and one championship and that's what you have to do if you want to win titles. But it's only with hindsight that I realize that – I certainly didn't at the time. I was trying to keep too many other people happy and not thinking about my long-term career and I paid dearly for that attitude when I raced at Mallory Park in early September.

As I said, I'd been pulled back from doing the European championship when Honda realized that Alan Carter was struggling to win the British title. They wanted me to back him up and get in the way of other riders. It's common team tactics in bike racing and you've got to expect to do it at some point but I desperately wanted to defend my top three position in the European championship rather than pissing about helping someone else in the UK.

Anyway, that's why I was racing at Mallory but I was actually riding a 400cc machine to try and get some extra prize money when I had the biggest crash of my career up to that point. I don't tend to crash very often but when I do, I always seem to have big ones and I always get bloody hurt. Some riders like James Haydon seem to be able to crash hundreds of times and just bounce their way to a standstill with no injuries. Not me – I got beaten up badly at Mallory Park.

I was on the gas coming out of the Devil's Elbow (well named) and looked over my shoulder to see who was behind me. As I turned round, the movement of my arm caused me to open the throttle a bit wider than I would normally do and that was all it took; the bike spat me off like a rag doll. I was thrown over the front of the machine and started sliding down the track but the bike followed and slammed me into the Armco at the side of the circuit. I was knocked unconscious, crushed three vertebrae, broke a rib and shattered my ankle.

I thought I was looking at a long stay in hospital but there's nothing you can do with crushed vertebrae in the lower back and consequently they never really heal properly. I still have problems with that injury to this day when I put any strain on my back. There wasn't much the doctors could do with my rib either so they simply plastered my ankle and sent me home the same day in a great deal of pain. It seemed like pretty basic treatment after they'd left me lying on a trolley in a corridor for about three hours but I suppose there's no point hanging around in hospitals if you don't need to, so I was pretty glad to be going home.

10 The Impossible Dream

'I laughed when they asked me to ride a Norton at the TT.'

To understand fully all the implications of my 1992 Senior TT victory, which remains one of my greatest ever triumphs, I'll need to mention the 1991 TT.

I was still living on the Isle of Man with my girl-friend, Lesley Henthorn, at the time and her neighbour was away on holiday so we arranged for Foggy and Michaela to stay at her house. Michaela was pregnant with Danielle at the time and I remember us all sitting around sunbathing and having a great time – while the press were saying we hated each other and refused to speak to one another!

But there was a lot of pressure on Carl and I that year because Honda had shipped in some really exotic, one-off bikes for us to make sure they won the Formula One TT as that would give them 10 F1 wins in a row. They didn't care which one of us won it but one of us *had* to.

We were busting each other's guts during practice

week as I would put in a 121mph lap then Carl would go out and do a 122mph lap. Then I'd go out and lap at 123mph and it went on like that all week. These were speeds that no one had ever seen round the TT course before and we were breaking records almost every time we went out for a lap.

Mr Oguma, the chief of HRC (Honda Racing Corporation) had come over to the Island from Japan and he was going mental at our antics, terrified that we were going to crash and kill ourselves. He called a meeting and sat Foggy and I down at a table like naughty little school children. We got a real bollocking for going so fast; apparently we'd scared Oguma-san shitless when he watched us at the bottom of Bray Hill! He was a fierce-looking man and he pointed a big, stubby finger at both of us in turn and shouted, 'You and you, not enemies. Honda and Yamaha are enemies. Honda and Suzuki are enemies. Honda and Kawasaki are enemies. You two not enemies. Must decide now which one will win big race.'

So there we were, both completely determined to win the Formula One race and we were being told to draw lots over it. No way! As we left that office I said to Carl, 'I had a shit TT last year and there's no way I'm going to lose this.' Carl was equally determined to win so we agreed between us that the first man to reach the finish line would be the victor; there was just no way either of us were going to concede that race without a fight.

The morning of that 1991 Formula One TT was the most tense experience I've ever had in racing.

Michaela Fogarty came over to me on the start line and said, 'Steve, you're a bit more sensible than that idiot (meaning Carl). You'll back off if it gets scary won't you?' I was thinking, 'No bloody way will I,' but I just nodded sweetly to reassure her.

There was so much adrenaline pumping as Foggy and I both knew we'd have to ride round the most dangerous circuit in the world faster than anyone else had ever done before if we wanted to win. And boy did we both want to win.

As it turned out I had the race won in the first 10 miles because my tactics were to go flat out from the start to try and get a gap on Carl and mentally defeat him. At the thirteenth Milestone, my board came out and said '+5 seconds' and I could just visualize Foggy seeing a minus five signal and imagined how demoralizing that would be for him. I caught him on the road on lap two at Ballaugh Bridge as I'd made up the 30-second starting-time difference and for a while we raced neck and neck on the roads. Carl had some kind of problem with his bike cutting out at high speeds but I didn't care; I won by over 40 seconds and set a new outright lap record at 123.48mph. It was a brilliant race as we were wheel to wheel on the road all through laps three and four which was great fun and good for the spectators.

Foggy didn't ride in the Senior race the following Friday because he was off on World Superbike duty so Joey Dunlop got his RVF. I beat Joey by 80 seconds after catching him on the road towards the end of the last lap. It was really nice to ride alongside him and put on a show for the crowds but to be honest, I wish Carl had been there to push me.

I won the Supersport 600 race that week too so it was a brilliant TT for me apart from my usual Junior jinx; this time the bike seized solid at the start of the second lap. But the important points to take away from that meeting were that I'd beaten Carl on an identical bike and I knew he wasn't happy about it. I knew we would never again have such exotic machinery at our disposal for the TT. We were unlikely ever to be on identical bikes again either so it looked like being the last time Carl and I would have a head-to-head on the Island, especially as Foggy and I both said we'd never be back to race there again.

Well, we did come back for different reasons and the 1992 Senior race is still talked about today as one of the best ever seen in the long history of the Tourist Trophy. It was the fastest race in the history of the event as well as being one of the closest and Foggy set a new lap record during it which wasn't bettered for seven years. But most of all it's remembered because a small British team on a shoestring budget won the race with a British bike which started life as a crazy project in the back of a shed.

It's hard to believe now that I actually laughed when Norton's team boss, Barry Symmons, asked me to ride that bike at the TT but I did. I thought, 'You must be joking – that thing will never last one lap of the Isle of Man.'

By winning that race on the Norton by just four seconds from Foggy, I beat not only Carl but also the might of Honda, Yamaha and all the other teams. I also created history by becoming the first rider to win the Senior TT on a British bike since the late, great Mike Hailwood in 1961.

For the team and myself the victory was a dream come true. We'd had just one month to raise the £25,000 needed to compete. Furthermore, I had only completed eight laps of testing before arriving at the TT (We couldn't do any more because the bike blew up!) and no one had thought we had a chance of even finishing the race, never mind winning it. And the 40,000 patriotic spectators who had made the journey over to the Isle of Man went absolutely wild at the sight of a British bike back on top of the world again – it was a real throwback to the 1960s when the British bike industry led the world. There was hardly a dry eye on the whole island.

That night I went into Douglas and got absolutely legless. I was even caught by the TV cameras singing the worst karaoke rendition of *Country Roads* ever heard, but I didn't care. As far as I was concerned, I had achieved the impossible and deserved to get drunk. So I did.

I made the most of my night out and all the media attention the win had attracted because it had been a bloody long, hard slog to achieve it. At one point I didn't think I'd be riding at the TT at all because in the space of just six months, I had been dropped by Honda, joined Yamaha, and then left them one month before the race because I didn't feel they were giving me enough support.

When Foggy decided to leave Honda to go World Superbike racing on a private Ducati in 1992, Honda thought I was the right man to replace him. Team boss Neil Tuxworth sat me down at the end of '91 and said I should give up my 250cc racing and ride Honda's 750cc RC30 in the British championships and at the TT. He offered me two bikes, a full squad with good mechanics, the whole deal. I thought it sounded fantastic but the more I pushed for a contract over winter, the less I heard from Tuxworth. Honda had me on a promise and so I didn't look anywhere else for a ride. But when I finally managed to speak to him in early January of 1992 he was very abrupt and just told me that there was a letter in the post then put the phone down on me.

In hindsight he was probably embarrassed by their U-turn and decision to sign Simon Crafar after an impressive Honda ride at Brands Hatch, but when I received the letter the following day I couldn't believe what I was reading. In a nutshell, it stated that Honda no longer required my services. What? I'd won seven TTs for Honda as well as the British 250cc championship, then they'd promised me the earth for 1992 just to turn round and slap me in the face like that. I thought, 'Bugger me, they've dropped me right in it.' Honda had opted to employ Kiwi rider Simon Crafar instead of me because he'd put in one good performance at Brands Hatch towards the end of 1991. Loyalty works only one way in bike racing.

Anyway, I thought, 'What the hell am I going to do now?' All the other good rides had been taken and it looked like I was going to be left out in the cold for most of the '92 season. The only thing I managed to arrange was a ride with Kawasaki France in the world endurance championship but that was for just five races over the whole season and, although I enjoyed endurance racing it wasn't really the way I wanted my career to go.

Eventually I got a call from Andy Smith at Yamaha saying he would love to give me a bike for the TT. That was fair enough but I told him that I needed a bike for the whole season, not just for one event. Andy eventually agreed to supply me with two good 750cc bikes and a good mechanic for the British championships, to be run under a dealer-supported team called Tillston's Yamaha, as well as a 600cc production bike and 250cc race bike for the TT. Things were looking good again.

But when I actually tried to get hold of the special parts I'd been promised, things started falling apart. Rob McElnea, a former Grand Prix racer and TT winner who was running the official Loctite Yamaha team as well as riding in it, refused to give Tillston's the parts saying he needed them for his own team. I called Yamaha straight away and asked what was going on. Andy Smith told me to leave things with him but weeks went by before we got any equipment and it was obvious straight away that it wasn't what we'd been promised. The bikes and parts were outdated and that's when alarm bells really started ringing.

I raced at Oulton Park early in the season and could only manage seventh because the Yamahas I had were so uncompetitive, but at least I beat Crafar on the Honda that should have been mine. Still, I wasn't happy and had no interest in riding under-par bikes all season. Yamaha had paid me a £10,000 retainer to race for them at the TT but I was prepared to give it back and not ride for them if they wouldn't give me better parts for my British championship bike.

That was a big sacrifice for me as I wasn't being paid to race in the British championship that year – the only money I got was a couple of grand for wearing an Arai helmet. I was hoping to earn some good prize money at the TT to supplement my meagre income so it was really important for me to race there even though I'd said I would never go back.

When I gave Andy Smith my ultimatum – give me some parts or I'm backing out of the TT – he said, 'You won't do that Steve,' but I thought, 'Just you bloody watch me.' I was really pissed off so I phoned my friend Michael Brandon from Abus Locks, a bike security firm based in Hawick. Michael was one of the sponsors of the Kawasaki team, which was fielding John Reynolds and Brian Morrison that year and when I told him I was thinking of throwing the towel in with Yamaha and didn't know what I was going to ride he said, 'Leave it with me. I'll see what I can do.'

The next morning he called and said he'd arranged a Kawasaki for me to ride at the weekend. Reynolds was cleaning up in the British championships on the Kawasaki so I knew it was a good bike and because I was contracted with Kawasaki France for the world endurance races I even had some Kawasaki leathers!

I was told to turn up at Donington Park with my leathers and that John Reynolds's spare bike would be waiting for me. It sounded perfect so I called Andy Smith at Yamaha as promised and when he said there was still no word on any better equipment, I told him I'd be posting his £10,000 cheque back to him and he could stick it where he wanted. I'd had enough of being fobbed off.

As a supposed Yamaha rider I turned a few heads in the paddock at Donington Park in my Kawasaki leathers but none more so than Barry Symmons's who was managing the JPS Norton team with Ron Haslam and Robert Dunlop as his riders. I told him the story about Yamaha and the TT and I could almost see his brain going into overdrive straight away. He had been looking for someone to ride Haslam's Norton at the TT. Haslam had a broken leg at the time but he wouldn't have been going to the Isle of Man anyway so Barry was sniffing around for another rider. He told me, 'Christ, let's get you on the Norton for the TT. That would be awesome.'

I provisionally agreed to it since I had no other offers but inside I was thinking it was a bit of a joke. I'd always seen the Norton as a kind of wacky project bike and didn't think there was any chance it would last six laps of the punishing TT course. After all, a guy called Brian Crichton had developed it from a slow, old, Norton police bike in the back of a shed. Surely it couldn't win a TT race?

I finished sixth at Donington on the Kawasaki and

then was second at Brands Hatch the following day as I got more used to the bike. After that race two mechanics that I knew, called Dave Collins and Jeff Tollan, approached me and asked if I'd be interested in riding in the Malaysian Superbike championship. They were running a Kawasaki team there with Kiwi rider Andrew Stroud and asked if I'd fly out to test their bike. With nothing else on offer I agreed and flew out to the Shah Alam Grand Prix circuit for some tests. What I'd forgotten was that the circuit was notorious for snakes and I hate snakes – I mean I'm fucking terrified of them – but I just tried to put them out of my mind and get on with the job in hand.

We unloaded the bike from the van amid all these little Indian and Malaysian boys running around the paddock and that's when I realized it was a track day open to the public rather than a private test day which is more usual when testing a race bike. Now, here in the UK, track days are populated by riders with full-on sports bikes capable of 160mph but in Malaysia, the only bikes were little souped-up, step-through scooters such as Honda C90s and the like. They called them 'Underbones' for some reason and there were hundreds of them, all with a top speed of about 80mph so it was going to be difficult to navigate between them all but at least I could be sure of being fastest.

Anyway, the track finally went quiet for a while so I headed out and took it easy as I felt my way round for the first time and I was just hooking into fourth gear round the back of the circuit when this bloody great cobra slithered across the tarmac! I was terrified and gassed the bike as if my life depended on it to get the hell out of there – I probably went through that corner quicker than any rider before or since to get away from that snake.

I pulled straight into the pits and shouted at the guys, 'There's a snake on the track, there's a fucking snake on the track! I'm not going back out there,' but they all just laughed and sent me out again saying it would be gone by the time I got back round. I didn't see the slithery bastard again so I started laying down some good lap times and was really sliding the bike around because the high temperatures were just destroying the tyres, but I loved every minute of it.

In my first Malaysian races I got a first and second place which I was pretty pleased with because there were some very good Australian riders there like Chris Haldane on a Marlboro Yamaha and Trevor Jordan who rode for Lucky Strike Kawasaki. After that I was offered a ride for the rest of the championship at a rate of £3000 a round on top of all expenses. The prize money was crap, just a few bloody roubles or something daft like that, but it was worth it for the laughs we had and I eventually ended the season in third spot, which I was quite happy with.

Barry Symmons worked feverishly trying to sort out the Norton TT deal while I was testing in Malaysia. The biggest problem was that we needed to raise £25,000 to cover costs and there was less than one month from the time that we first discussed the idea to the start of practice. The people from cigarette firm JPS, who normally sponsored the bike in the British championships, weren't interested for some reason so I called my old friend Michael Brandon again and explained the situation.

I was desperate to ride the bike by now, not because I thought it could win, but because I really thought it could be the making of me as far as publicity went. Public interest in the British Norton was huge and I knew there would be even more nostalgia about it at the TT where they used to go so well decades ago; in fact, Rem Fowler won a TT on a Norton in the event's very first year in 1907. I just felt it would really put me back in the spotlight and that was something I needed badly if only to secure a solid ride for 1993.

Anyway, Michael Brandon got his head together with Andy Freeman at EBC brakes and together they reckoned they could raise about £10,000. That was brilliant but we still needed another £15,000. A deal was being arranged with Manx Telecom for the extra money but they pulled the plug at the eleventh hour and we were left in the lurch again.

Then, at the very last minute, I approached Brian Kreisky who produced TV coverage for the TT races and told him I would put cameras on the bike or do whatever he wanted filming-wise if he would help with our effort. Brian had good relations with the Isle of Man Tourist Board so he took me to see them and we sat down to try and get some money. Brian was amazing in the way he twisted their arms up their backs and persuaded the board to sponsor us.

They eventually came up with around £10,000 which was still a bit short but Barry Symmons did some calculations and said, 'That's enough, that'll do, we'll be there boys. We're going racing.' It was a real *Rocky* moment.

So I finally got to test the Norton for the first (and only) time at Oulton Park on the Thursday before TT practice started when most racers were already on their way to the Isle of Man. The team told me there were a few things they wanted to try on the bike so I said fair enough and out I went, eager to see what the Norton was like. As I got to the first proper corner I went to gently tip the bike in and the bloody thing nearly fell on its side. I thought, 'Fuckin' hell, what's this all about?' I'd never ridden a bike that steered so quickly. Much too quickly in fact. It nearly pissed off and took the corner by itself.

Apparently, that's the way Ron Haslam liked his bikes set up for short circuits but there's no way you can ride the TT with a bike set up as nervously as that. Stability is everything on the Island and I knew we had to make some vital changes but the team's suspension guru, Ron Williams, argued that the bike didn't need changing and he actually got quite stroppy about the whole thing.

Eventually, Ron allowed the mechanics to lessen the severity of the steering and it felt a little bit better but then after six more laps, just as I was getting used to the thing, the engine locked up solid. The team had been trying some kind of turbo system on it and it was just too much so the engine cried enough and that was it. That was all the practice I had on the Norton before the TT.

In total I'd done about eight laps and when I came back into the pits everyone asked me what I thought of the bike. I said, 'Boys, to be quite honest I don't think that thing will ever last one lap of the TT, never mind six. It can't even manage 10 laps round Oulton Park without shitting its pants.'

Anyway, I flew over to the Isle of Man and when the team arrived Barry said I could make some more changes to the steering. Apparently he'd had a word with Ron Williams and explained that it was my neck on the line and therefore I should be allowed to set the bike up the way I wanted to.

The first practice session got underway at 6pm on Monday evening in miserable wet conditions and to everyone's surprise, I ended up at the top of the practice leaderboard ahead of Foggy, who was riding the Yamaha OWO1 which I had originally been meant to ride.

He was desperate for cash to fund his privateer World Superbike campaign so he'd accepted the ride on that basis, even though he didn't really want to ride at the TT again.

The rest of practice week was a wash out weather-wise but when I woke up on the Saturday morning for the Formula One race, the sun was beating down and conditions were perfect. Well, they were perfect for sunbathers and ice cream salesmen but not for my Norton. On the very first lap it started overheating in the hot conditions and I had to keep a close eye on the temperature gauge from then on. Robert Dunlop's JPS Norton expired completely on the first lap, which wasn't exactly encouraging.

I came in after the second lap for my pit stop and my crew ripped the front mudguard off to allow more air into the radiator but that cost me about 20 seconds and Foggy was long gone by then. His glory was short lived though because he was so hard on his Yamaha that he broke the gearbox on the fifth lap and handed the win to Phillip McCallen on the factory Honda.

By the time I got out of the pits and got going again, the bike was weaving all over the road and I had to fight it all the way round, constantly trying to analyse the instability problem. But the top speed was awesome and I really started enjoying myself and clawed back as much time on McCallen as I could in the remaining laps to finish second.

After that I was pretty convinced that if we could sort out the problems with the bike during the week, I stood a real chance of winning the big one – the Senior TT held on the Friday. We took the bike up to Jurby, a disused runway on the Isle of Man, and got to work. One problem I had in the race was that the wind was pushing my body back on the bike and this meant I was pulling the front forks up and making the rear suspension squat at the same time. That meant there was no weight over the front of the bike, which in turn made it unstable. We got round the problem by simply fitting a taller screen so I could get really tucked in out of the air.

We certainly never lacked top speed; the Norton

was tremendously fast in a straight line and a radar gun clocked me at 193mph down Sulby straight at one point. But it was the weirdest bike to ride because of its rotary engine. It had very little engine braking and I just got sucked really deep into corners so I had to change all the braking points that I used on 'normal' bikes. I remember many times I was hammering down the gearbox and pulling the front brake lever like hell only to find I was still heading into the corners way too fast.

Anyway, between the Formula One and Senior races we added the taller screen, ditched the front mudguard, added wider and higher bars to help stability over the bumps and made some little fork protectors to stop them getting chipped with stones now that the mudguard was gone. With those changes made, the bike was stripped and every single component checked and rechecked to enhance our chances of making it to the finish line. Then all we could do was wait until Friday.

11 A Day at the Races

'For the first time in my life I thought victory maybe wasn't as important as living.'

Under a baking hot sun and a cloudless blue sky I lined up on the famous Glencrutchery Road start line for the 1992 Senior TT.

Carl Fogarty was starting at number four and I would set off at number 19, three minutes behind him.

I'd finished second three times that week and was desperate for a win at this point, especially on the Norton as I was fully aware of how important that would be for my career.

Earlier I'd been chatting to a spectator who said I looked like I was trying too hard in the F1 race and he thought that was what was actually slowing me down. Smoothness and consistency are the key factors round the Isle of Man so I decided to ease myself into the race rather than go gung-ho from the start.

The first signal I got was 13 miles out and it told me I was in second place. I had expected to be fourth or fifth at the pace I was riding but there I was only two seconds off the leader and I knew it had to be Carl. Even though there were other top names like Joey Dunlop, Phillip McCallen, Robert Dunlop and Trevor Nation in the race, I'd no doubt it was Foggy who was leading. No one else could touch us at that pace so I didn't give the others a second thought.

Foggy was still leading after the first 37.74 miles lap and he'd posted an average speed of 121.90mph from a standing start. We were setting an amazing pace on bikes that were really quite inferior to the factory Hondas of the previous year.

I started to up my pace on the second lap having found a rhythm and I set about trying to catch Carl. By the end of the lap I was 2.8 seconds ahead as we pulled in for our first pit stops. I took the precaution of fitting a new rear tyre because I didn't know how badly those speeds would tear up the rubber. Foggy only took on fuel and blasted out of pit lane having retaken the lead with his quicker stop. Once again, I had to do all the work of catching him up and I knew I'd have to ride really hard from then on.

I got back on the gas but was still treating the bike with respect. In the F1 race I'd tried to ride it flat out everywhere but it was simply too fast on top speed for that and I had been totally out of control. This time I was in control of the bike instead of having it take me for a ride. But I was still hitting bumps and getting lifted up out of my seat and the wind at those speeds was really wrenching at my neck and shoulders, threatening to blow me off the back of the bike. Bigger bumps caused the bike to shake its head viciously from side to side while gentle rises in the road sent the front wheel skyward, which is always dangerous because the wind can get under the front wheel and loop the bike over.

By the end of the third lap I'd pulled back five seconds on Foggy and was just one second behind him. I knew that would demoralize him and play on his mind but I kept charging all the same.

Because of my low starting number I had to pass lots of slower riders and they can be a real threat round the TT course as they've no idea when someone's behind them. They can move right over in front of you in a corner at the last moment and force you to squeeze between them and a stone wall to get by. Sometimes I revved my throttle like mad to let them know I was there but it's not always possible if you're already flat out and have no more revs left.

At the end of the fourth lap as we came in for our pit stops I was 7.4 seconds in the lead. I wiped my visor clean of flies while the team refueled the bike. Races can be won or lost in the pits and it's a precise art, which my team and I had practised in the garage time after time to get right. We worked on ways to save fractions of seconds here and there. Our solution was simple – keep it to the basics. The more things we changed, the more could go wrong. Some riders change visors and earplugs and some even change helmets but I didn't do any of that. I cleaned my own visor, which meant there was one less person to get in the way, took a quick drink through a bottle with a long straw attached to rehydrate and let my mechanics get on with dumping the fuel in.

But no amount of practice can account for nerves. My team was so tense and so desperate to win the race that one of the mechanics fumbled with the petrol cap and we lost vital seconds. It took team boss Barry Symmons to interject and tell everyone to slow down before the cap was popped into place and I was push-started down pit lane again.

The stop took me 35 seconds which was way too long and it left me just one second ahead of Fogarty after all the hard work I'd put in to catch and pass him on corrected time.

Seven miles out at Ballacraine, Foggy had pulled out a lead of three seconds over me but by Ramsey on the fifth lap I had overtaken him again and pulled out a lead of 6.4 seconds. I knew Carl would struggle to pull that back in one lap but I also knew how good he was and that it was still a possibility. I only had to make one slight error and he'd be right back on me. There was no doubt in my mind that he'd try everything that he knew on that final circuit.

Carl and I had already shattered the lap record I set the year before on the Honda RVF, which was a measure of how hard we were trying. But Foggy pulled out all the stops on the last circuit to set a new outright lap record at an amazing 123.61mph. It was such a fast time that it stood for seven years.

The crowd was awesome throughout the race but I'd never seen anything like it on my final circuit. It must have been incredible for all those fans to see a

British bike threatening to win the Senior TT after more than 30 years and it was very hard not to be distracted by them. Every vantage point was packed with fans hanging out onto the road, waving their programmes, cheering and taking photographs – it was a spectacular sight.

On the last few miles I started talking to the bike, urging it home, nursing it every inch and mile of the way. I was well aware that I'd been unlucky in many races at the TT before and it was quite possible that the Norton could just blow up any minute at the pace I was riding. More than 226 miles flat out over bumpy roads with six climbs over the 2197 feet Snaefell mountain is a lot to ask of any bike, let alone a low budget, privately funded one.

As Foggy crossed the finish line he had a three-minute wait for me to come home to find out who had won. He'd given it everything but now all he could do was wait. As I reached Signpost corner just a few miles from home the traditional light came on at the start/finish grandstand to indicate that I was nearly there. The crowd was going absolutely mental sensing that the Norton was surely going to hold out. As I crossed the finish line and slammed on the anchors I still didn't know who had won but as soon as I saw the crowds lining the path that leads back to the pits I knew I'd done it. I remember my back being sore from all the slaps I got even though I had a back protector on. I was totally swamped the second I got off the bike and I had to push through the crowds to give Lesley a hug and a kiss. Then the throng of enthusiasts inadvertently pushed her against the bike's still red-hot exhaust and she needed first aid treatment for the burn.

Bike racing doesn't usually attract an awful lot of mainstream press but that was a fairy-tale win and there were reporters present from all the national newspapers who would never normally cover a bike race. The British bike angle itself created a lot of interest but the shoestring budget nature of the team made it even better. The fact that I'd achieved something that had not been done for over 30 years and at speeds that had never been seen before just made it all the better.

It was the fastest race in TT history with my average speed for the entire six laps being 121.28mph. Foggy may have set a new outright lap record on the last lap but it still wasn't enough to beat me – I don't think anyone in the world could have beaten me that day.

My team was ecstatic. They knew the budget was running out and that this might be the last big win for them; it was certainly the biggest they'd ever achieved. When the press asked Barry Symmons if we'd be having a party to celebrate he replied, 'If we can afford it.' That's how tight things were money-wise. But none of that mattered; we'd silenced a thousand critics and made racing history in what was probably the greatest single race of my life.

I must admit there was a tear in my eye as I fully realized what I'd achieved and people are still talking about that race to this day. Most rank it alongside

Giacomo Agostini and Mike Hailwood's epic duel in 1967 as the best race ever held on the Island and that's about as high a praise as you can get.

After the dust had settled Foggy once again announced he would never return to the TT as it was now just too fast and dangerous and this time he kept his word. I agreed and said I wouldn't be back either. There seemed little point if Foggy wasn't going to be there – he was the only guy who really provided me with a challenge.

By the end of the year the JPS Norton team had ran out of steam and cash and the bikes were put into storage. It was all over. So many things came together at the right time to make the 1992 TT something really special and many of them were never seen there again.

I was dying to hear Carl's side of the story so we got together after the race to swap tales and it was uncanny how similar his experiences had been to mine. The one section of the track that had been scaring me badly was a straight between Kerrowmoar and Glentramman, which is probably the bumpiest part of the TT course. It should be taken flat out, pinned in sixth gear at about 180mph but I was having to back off a bit because my bike was tying itself in knots and threatening to chuck me over a hedge. I was really pissed off because on every lap through that section I was thinking, 'Fuckin' hell, Foggy will be getting away from me, come on, come on Steve.' But there was nothing I could do about it because the bike just couldn't cope with the vicious bumps at those speeds. I was riding it beyond its limits and it was going into such a weave that I was totally out of control at 180mph, just hanging on and praying for the best. At that speed, instinct takes over and for the first time in my life, I actually started thinking that maybe victory wasn't as important as living but that soon passed and I got my head down again.

However, before I even mentioned this to Carl he told me that he had been really mad because on every lap he was forced to shut the throttle off a bit on one particular section of the course, and he thought I would be gaining a few tenths of a second on him each time. I couldn't believe it when he told me that, as it was exactly the same section of the course where I was having the identical problem!

That's how closely matched we were and how close we were to the limit – we simply couldn't have gone any faster with the technology of the bikes at the time. Carl had been so determined to beat me in that race because we'd been on equal bikes the year before and I'd won, so he was out for revenge. I wanted to beat him fair and square too, especially as everyone had been bitching about me and Carl having the best bikes in 1991. They said we were only winning because of our bikes so I suppose it was a good thing that we both had average bikes for 1992 just to prove a point.

Foggy's Yamaha was nothing special and I've already explained about my Norton but we still kicked everyone else's arses and proved our speed was nothing to do with the machines we were on. Even so,

I couldn't believe that I'd won on the very project bike that I used to laugh at!

Although everyone in the sport congratulated me on my Norton win and the press loved the 'David and Goliath' sentiment of it all, I wasn't exactly inundated with calls offering me rides on the short circuits as I'd hoped to be. Still, 1992 had turned out okay for me even though I had been living from hand to mouth and taking any rides I could just to keep my hand in.

Initially, it looked like it was going to be a great season with Honda until they fucked me up big style by dropping me from their plans and after that it was just a case of picking up the scraps. That's why I couldn't believe it when, at the end of the year, Neil called me up out of the blue again and asked me what I was doing in 1993. I said, 'Nowt. Why do you want to know anyway?' Then he told me that Honda Japan was sending one of their exotic factory RVFs across to Honda Britain and he asked me if I wanted to ride it. I thought, 'You've got to be taking the piss.' I was back to where I'd started.

12 The Champ

**'People said I only won because
Jamie Whitham had cancer.'**

British racing was a bit confusing in 1993 because
there were effectively two British championships for
Superbikes. One was the ACU British championship
and the other was the HEAT Supercup, which was
more prestigious because it was televised.

I finished second to Jamie Whitham in the ACU
series but had a dismal time in Supercup and finished
only sixth overall. I had fuel starvation problems at
Mallory Park, my engine blew up at Brands Hatch
and I crashed twice during the Cadwell Park round.
Not good.

But the most significant aspect of 1993 for me was
that it marked a turning-point in my career. It was
the first year I hadn't competed in the TT since 1985
and it was the first year I concentrated exclusively on
racing in the British championships instead of racing
in endurance events, pure road races, Euro rounds
and all the rest of it.

It should have been a much better season for me but my Honda wasn't as good as I had expected it to be. It handled beautifully, thanks to a 1991 RVF chassis, but we weren't given an RVF engine. We had to make do with an RC30 engine, together with some special cranks and ignition parts, that wouldn't have pulled the skin off the proverbial rice pudding and so I struggled all year against much faster opposition. Therefore I was really excited when I got the chance to fulfil a lifetime's ambition by riding a 500cc Grand Prix bike – the *crème de la crème* of racing motorcycles – but that ended in disappointment too.

A 500 is the ultimate thoroughbred race bike and I expected it to be really vicious but it actually felt pretty lame to ride. I was offered the bike (a Roc Yamaha YZR500) for the Macau Grand Prix at the end of 1993 but tested it at the Paul Ricard circuit in France before going there and I was so excited because of everything I'd heard about 500s. I only did about seven or eight laps first time out and when I came into the pits my team mate for Macau, Robert Dunlop, was all pumped up saying, 'Well, well? What's it like Steve, what's it like?' I told him it was flat as a fart and I'm sure the disappointment was clear on my face. I was not impressed.

It just felt really flat at the bottom end and it's not that I wasn't used to two-strokes because I had ridden them a lot in my 250cc racing days. It just wasn't the beast I had hoped for because it had a 'big bang' engine that smoothed out the power delivery and made it less peaky than the earlier 'screamer' engines.

One good thing to come out of that trip though was that I met a keen Irish sponsor called John Kennedy who was backing Robert Dunlop at the time. After Robert's big TT crash in 1994 John started sponsoring me and he still does today.

Anyway, the Roc bike was good enough to win at Macau and I beat Jeremy McWilliams who had been riding a 500 all year in the Grand Prix world championship. Jeremy said I had a better bike than his privateer machine and that with me being an experienced pure roads racer I had an advantage at Macau anyway. But then we all raced on a purpose-built short circuit at Sentul in Indonesia just after Macau and I set pole position, shattered the lap record and won the first race, beating Jeremy, so I felt I'd proved a point against an established 500 rider on his kind of circuit.

But all in all, 1993 wasn't the best of years for me. I soon perked up though when I heard about Honda's new bike for the following season – the RC45, which was supposed to be the absolute nuts. The plan was for me to race it in the British championships and in selected World Superbike rounds so it finally looked as if I was going to fulfil my dreams of racing at world level. However once again, the Hislop jinx struck and it all went pear-shaped thanks to a certain motorcycle publication stitching me up.

I had agreed to do a road test for a British biking magazine comparing the new Honda RC45 road bike with the RC30s I had raced round the TT so many times. As a contracted Honda rider, I was naturally expected to give the bike a glowing report and, during the official interview, I did. But during a lunch break when I thought my comments were not being recorded, I said some things, mostly in jest, that were less positive about the bike. To add to the problem, I had a quick run on a Ducati 916 as we headed off for lunch and, without my knowing, the photographer got a picture of me riding it so the scene was set for a total stitch-up.

When it was published, the feature made it look as if I'd been testing the Honda RC45 back to back with the Ducati (which I definitely had not been doing) and had slated the Honda. I couldn't believe it. All the quotes that were used were the things I had said in the pub which I had assumed were off the record and it sounded like I was really laying into the Honda. Needless to say, the staff at Honda were none too pleased when they saw the magazine and I was told in no uncertain terms that the budget for my World Superbike rides was being withdrawn. Yet again I had missed out on the chance to race in a proper world championship all because of one sneaky journalist. And as if that wasn't bad enough I nearly lost my British Superbike ride over that article too. I hope that journalist was satisfied with the hatchet job he did on me but I never understood why someone would want to stitch a rider up like that for the sake of one poxy feature.

I've often been called controversial because of things I've said to reporters but it's never been a conscious effort on my part; I've just always given my honest opinion about the way I felt at the time. Maybe the next day I'd feel differently about things but in the heat of the moment I can't help but say what I feel. That hasn't always done me a lot of favours on the PR front but I prefer to be honest rather than to wear a corporate hat all the time, spinning the same old bull-shit about sponsors and tyre manufacturers. I mean, who wants to listen to that apart from the sponsors and tyre manufacturers? I have dropped myself in hot water on several occasions with the media and I can look back through some press cuttings now and think, 'Shit, did I really say that?' because I honestly don't remember having made some of those comments.

In 1994 I rode again on the Isle of Man, but that really was to be the last time. It's not that I wanted to race there but Honda was very keen to promote the RC45 so it was written into my contract that I had to race at the TT, albeit just in the two main races – the F1 and Senior.

If I had ever needed convincing that the TT was too dangerous, riding the RC45 round there was proof enough – it was absolutely lethal at the beginning of practice week. On my first lap I clipped a kerb at 150mph on Bray Hill then smacked my leg on a wall at Ginger Hall and ripped my leathers and my knee open. The bike had a mind of its own and just went wherever the hell it wanted. It was so out of control that, for the first time in my life, I considered with-drawing my entry and going home and so did Joey Dunlop. He came into the garage on the first night of practice, threw the bike into his van and said, 'That fucking thing's not going to kill me.'

Phillip McCallen was also terrified of his bike and that's saying something because he was always out of shape at the TT. I can honestly say I had more frights in those two weeks than I'd had in the last eight years of competing at the TT. Having said that, I was still going fast because I couldn't afford not to; everyone expected me to win and I needed the money so I wasn't about to wobble round looking like a twat. I even tried to ride half a lap back to the pits with a puncture at one point in practice but I got black-flagged by the marshals and had to pull over.

I also did the fastest-ever lap with a camera on board at 123.5mph, but got a harsh reminder of just how lethal the track is when my friend Mark Farmer was killed on the Thursday of practice week. I really liked Mark but didn't go to his funeral just as I never attend any other riders' funerals. I suppose it's a bit of a defence mechanism for me because I simply don't want to see that side of my job and I know many other racers feel the same way. The only exception I made was when I went to Lee Pullan's funeral in 1996 after he was killed striking a marshal on the track at Spa-Francorchamps in Belgium, but that's only because he lived on the Isle of Man and I knew him really well. Otherwise, I just don't want to be anywhere near that scenario. It's just a racer thing and I suppose it's difficult for non-racers to understand.

As if the RC45 wasn't scary enough to ride, that year I also had to face a wet track with slick tyres fitted. For those who are not aware, slick tyres have absolutely no tread at all which is great in the dry because they stick like chewing gum, but in the rain, it's like riding on marbles.

The Formula One race started in the dry but then the heavens opened and the race wasn't stopped for another couple of laps because of poor organization. Some riders kept going at race speeds like idiots but I backed it off as soon as the rain came down and cruised round to the pits. I'm not interested in that sort of do-or-die nonsense.

The race was rerun on the Sunday in dry conditions and I blitzed it having got the handling of the bike sorted out a bit. It was still a scary machine to ride but at least I didn't have the problems Joey Dunlop had when he encountered a dog and a van on the track! The dog didn't know any better but the guy driving the van should have as he worked for the Isle of Man highways department. He'd forgotten the race was being run on the Sunday and reversed straight onto the circuit as Joey whizzed past at frightening speed. It was only because of Joey's lightning reactions that a major accident was avoided.

I won the Senior event later in the week quite easily from Phillip McCallen and Joey and that was finally it: my TT career was officially over, even if people never believed me because I'd said that so many times before. But to this day I've never raced on the Island again and there are several good reasons for that. One of them is that as I got older I became more aware of the risks. When you're young, you'll drive your car at 100mph down a back road and not care if there's a family approaching round a blind bend. But as you get older, you'll drive down that same lane at 40mph and wonder if there's something coming the other way. I was getting that way about the TT as I got older – the dangers of it just became more apparent and I started thinking about them more.

I always thought I was quite safe at the TT but some spectators say they were scared as I went past. People's perspectives are very different though and what might look scary to one person would look fairly controlled to another. Having said that, I think it's worse watching from the roadside than it is on the bike. What did increasingly scare me was the thought of component failure at the TT. It doesn't matter how skilled or safe you are on a bike if your brakes fail or your wheels break up or anything mechanical goes wrong you could be dead in an instant.

Of all the riders I've raced against at the TT, Phillip McCallen looked the scariest. I don't know if he was actually that out of control but his nervous, aggressive style certainly made him look like he was. I like Phillip a lot and I'm not trying to knock him but I've heard other people say the same thing so I'm glad he's retired in one piece as I used to worry about him a bit.

Everyone says the TT course is much more dangerous than purpose-built short circuits and I can't really disagree – it is a bloody dangerous place. But since my brother was killed on a short circuit and not while racing on pure roads, I saw things a bit differently to most. I always used to think I was very lucky to be alive after every TT race I competed in so I was perfectly aware of the dangers; it's not like I was burying my head in the sand. But all my bad injuries have happened at short circuits so I don't really think they are much safer. When you race a motorbike at high speeds, accidents can happen no matter what kind of track you're riding on.

I never wanted to see the TT banned, I just think that 600cc machines are fast enough round there now. They're still capable of lapping at 120mph and they don't take you for a ride like the bigger bikes do so I don't see why there can't be a 600cc limit – it would certainly make things a lot safer.

Another thing that influenced my decision to quit was the pressure to win once I had really established myself. I'd stopped racing at the Ulster Grand Prix years before because my nerves couldn't take it any more: everyone expected me to win since I was a 'pure roads specialist' and you shouldn't be under pressure on circuits as dangerous as that. Other riders would really push me trying to prove themselves by beating Hizzy and some of them obviously didn't give a shit whether they died or not. But I wasn't about to die just to prove a point – my ego's not that big.

So for better or worse I finally decided my future lay entirely on short circuits, riding Superbikes and I never raced on public roads again which is probably why I'm still here in one piece to tell this tale. Too many of my old road-racing colleagues are not with us any more and that's a very sobering thought.

The rest of the 1994 season was a bit of a disaster for me on the RC45, as it was a new bike and still needed a lot of development work. The fuel injection was a nightmare and the bike was also fairly slow which was why I finished a lowly tenth in the Supercup British championship, but I had been making progress towards the end of the year when the Hislop jinx struck again. I blew up my number one engine in practice at Pembrey but was still fastest for most of Friday's qualifying on my number two bike until I crashed on one of Pembrey's notorious bumps in Saturday's qualifying.

I was high-sided off the bike and my hand got caught under my body as I slid along the track and two fingers were so badly mangled that the doctors in Swansea hospital wanted to amputate one of them. No bloody way, I wasn't having that – I'm terrified at the thought of amputation. I refused to give them permission so they strapped it up as best they could and left it to heal. Today the finger's fine apart from the fact that my fingernail grows in two pieces but I can live with that. At least I've still got all 10 digits!

Anyway, that pretty much finished 1994 for me apart from a late season outing at Brands Hatch where I finished fifth and fifteenth and the next thing I knew was that I didn't have a job for the following season as Honda told me they no longer required my services. Colin Seeley, who had run the 1994 British championship-winning Norton team (a totally separate affair from my Norton TT team), was given the job of looking after Honda's 1995 British racing squad. He wanted to bring his Norton riders, Ian Simpson and Phil Borley, with him so I was out the door – simple as that. It was a bit of a shock after having been with

Honda for so long but, to be honest, I was quite glad to be out of the team because it was a total shambles back then. I was given bikes, spares and a budget and pretty much left to get on with it, which is no way to run a team. That's why Colin was brought in to co-ordinate things in a better way but I obviously didn't feature in his plans. What I didn't realize then was that it was just the first in a series of disputes and sackings from teams that would plague me over the coming years.

I was really pissed off with racing by that point because 1994 had gone so badly and I seriously wondered if I should call it a day. But I went for a meal that night with fellow racer, Ray Stringer, and he told me he was trying to put a team together for 1995 riding Ducatis under the Devimead (a bike dealership based in Tamworth) banner and asked if I'd be interested in riding for them. It looked like I was back in business just hours after being sacked.

Devimead was going to put up the money for an assault on the British title with customer replicas of the 916 Ducati that Carl Fogarty had won the 1994 World Superbike title on. Ray and I would have one of those bikes each and there would be one modified road version to share between us as a back-up machine.

It was a small team running on a relatively small budget but I like working that way. There's not so much corporate bullshit to deal with such as attending dealer days and meetings all the time. It was far more like a family atmosphere with us out to take on all the big teams and to this day, that's still the way I like to go racing. After all, I'm a motorbike racer not a sales rep and I belong out on a racetrack in a set of leathers and a helmet, not sitting at a meeting table with a bloody suit on. Sometimes I think the big bike manufacturers forget that.

The only practice I had with the Devimead team before the start of the season was on a dark, wet day at Mallory Park on the modified road bike that acted as a spare machine but it was incredible to ride from the start. It was the first time I had ridden a Ducati and my first time on a V-Twin too and I couldn't believe how good it was compared to the four-cylinder Hondas I'd been riding. One touch of the throttle and the thing just picked up and went like a rocket right from the bottom of the rev range. When we entered a pre-championship race at Mallory Park I won first time out on the Ducati. That's how good it was so I knew I was in with a shout at the British championship.

It felt good to prove it was the RC45 Honda that had prevented me from winning races and not my riding ability because sometimes I had even doubted myself and was starting to get depressed about the whole racing trip. At the end of 1994, I had reached my heaviest weight ever of 12 stones from drinking too much beer and eating too much food and I'd lost all motivation to race after having such a bad season.

But having a new team for 1995 really motivated me again and I trained hard until I was back down to my fighting weight of 10 stone. I knew this was a whole new chance for me; there would be no more TTs to upset the rhythm of the season, no more messing around with corporate seminars and hand-shaking exercises, just a competitive bike and one very determined Hizzy.

As many people will remember, the 1995 British Super-cup (the forerunner of today's British Superbike championship) was an epic duel between Yorkshireman Jamie Whitham and myself. Jamie was also on a Ducati but was riding for the Moto Cinelli team and had an ex-factory bike with full factory camshafts and exhaust system while I was on a lower-spec customer machine.

When we were racing at Misano in Italy that year we sourced some factory camshafts but Ducati wanted £1300 for them! I was desperate to get my bike closer to Jamie's so I used my prize money from the race to buy them which was a ridiculous scenario but they were worth every penny because when I fitted them in May, I was right on the pace with Jamie.

Anyway, I'm getting ahead of myself. At the start of the season, Jamie was the man to beat and I wasn't totally convinced I could get the better of him over a full season but I was definitely ready to give it a go. My new-found consistency during the 1995 season was down to both the Ducati and me. The bike was a great package at every circuit, unlike the Honda, so it was a lot easier to set up, which was a big advantage. As far as I was concerned, I was still on a learning curve at that point in my career and still improving as a rider and racing so closely with Jamie all season really helped hone my close-contact skills.

The bike was very reliable all year, too, which was another bonus and it really only let me down in a couple of World Superbike meetings where I had some engine problems. The team took in the Donington, Misano, Assen and Brands Hatch WSB rounds and, when the bikes were running OK, I always managed to finish in the points which was pretty good going for a small team running private bikes. In fact, at Brands Hatch I finished eighth and ninth, which was about as good as a privateer could have hoped for.

It's a measure of how closely matched Jamie and I were, and how far ahead of the rest of the field we were in the British championship, that we won all but one of the year's 14 races between us, scoring six wins apiece and sharing a dead heat in the Snetterton round. At that race we crossed the line so close together that the officials simply could not separate us either with the electronic timers or by replaying the television coverage. The result was declared a dead heat and that's extremely rare in bike racing because of all the high-tech timing equipment. Sure, there are many times when only a wheel's width separates two bikes at the flag but in this instance there was absolutely nothing between us.

We were having a fantastic season riding neck and neck on the booming V-Twins and it was really great fun knowing that at every round we'd be clashing fairings and ducking and diving all race long. It was anyone's guess who would win at any given round and the pendulum swung both ways so many times over the first 12 races but it all went sour just after I came back from racing in the Suzuka 8 Hour race in Japan.

I got a call from Jamie's team boss, Rob McElnea, and as soon as I heard his voice I thought it was strange that he would be calling me. He asked me if I'd heard the news. 'What news?' I said. Rob replied, 'Jamie's got the Big C.' I was stunned into silence. I simply couldn't believe it. A lively, fit, young guy like Jamie couldn't have cancer, there must be some mistake. How could he cheat death week-in, week-out racing a motorbike at crazy speeds and then succumb to a poxy disease? It just didn't seem right but it was true: Jamie had developed Hodgkin's disease, a cancer of the lymph nodes in the throat, and I was devastated for him.

I realized there and then that with just two rounds of the championship left to go no one else could catch me so I had just become the new British champion but I thought, 'How fucking hollow is that?' I didn't want it and wasn't interested if that's the way I had to win it. I felt so empty and hollow for a long time and I realized how stupid and unimportant my thoughts of beating Jamie had been all year long. He had been my nemesis the entire season and the only thought I had was to beat him. Now that was irrelevant and all I wanted was for Jamie to get better. I'd gladly have given him that championship if it could have speeded up his recovery. But I hadn't realized what a fighter Jamie was and I was about to have the shock of my life at the next and penultimate round of the championship at Cadwell Park.

When I arrived at the circuit I noticed that the Moto Cinelli race truck was there but thought maybe the team was going to give another rider a shot on Jamie's bike. After all, Jamie had already started his gruelling chemotherapy treatment and that meant poisoning his body with platinum to kill off the cancer cells. As far as I knew, he was lying in a hospital bed somewhere puking his guts up. Many people vomit all day and all night when undergoing chemotherapy but Jamie responded to it pretty well for some reason; I think he just refused to be beaten by it.

Anyway, I was standing next to my Devimead truck and when I looked up towards the paddock entrance I saw Jamie's motorhome driving into the circuit. I got a huge lump in my throat and my eyes welled up as I thought, 'Yes, the brave bugger's going to give it a go. What a bloody hero.' I so desperately wanted him to be fit enough so we could finish or dual man-to-man and not have to have the title handed to me on a plate because of his misfortune.

I followed Jamie in practice and could see he was weak and making mistakes everywhere. It was then that I realized he probably couldn't race but he still managed to qualify seventh, which was a monumental achievement. Only a handful of riders in the country could ride that fast, never mind one who was racked with cancer. I was filled with admiration for Jamie for having a go like that and was nearly in tears when he had to leave the circuit and concede the title to me without being able to fight all the way to the wire. That was the bravest ride I ever witnessed.

I was leading the championship by two points when Jamie had to pull out but despite the fact that we had been so evenly matched over the season many people thought I only won because Jamie got cancer. In fact, some people got quite nasty about it. I received an anonymous letter from a complete arsehole slagging me and my team off for having championship T-shirts made up. What were we supposed to do? Sponsors pay a lot of money to enable people like me to go racing and they all dream of winning a championship so they've got to have their reward. Many titles have been won through another person's misfortune but they're still titles and you can't just throw them in the bin, as I'm sure Jamie himself understood.

He was great about the whole thing, telling everyone from his hospital bed that I deserved to win and that I'd ridden great all year long. I really appreciated that but the championship still felt completely worthless to me. That was a shame because 1995 was the year I finally turned my whole attention to the British Superbike title on a decent bike without the interference of the TT and in that first year I won the championship. It should have been enough to prove to people that I was as good on short circuits as I had been on the roads but once again they had an excuse: 'Hizzy only won it because Jamie was forced out,' and that pissed me off more than anything else. Even when I went out and blitzed the last four races of the season to prove a point people still doubted me.

Sadly, the Devimead team folded after we'd wrapped up the championship because promised sponsorship money didn't materialize and Devimead simply couldn't afford to cover all the costs themselves, so there was no option but to call it a day. It was a pity really because it was a great team and if we could have raised the funds I'm sure we could have gone World Superbike racing full time in 1996 and done really well. It's ridiculous that the team which wins the premier bike racing title in Britain should still struggle to find sponsors but that's just the state of racing in the UK. And so I was left looking for another bike to hang my number one plate on for 1996, even if I wasn't destined to retain it.

I raced in another series in 1995 called the International Shell Oils Trophy and was all set to win that too until I cricked my neck in my sleep. It sounds stupid but the next morning I couldn't move my head at all. I went for a check-up and was told I had prolapsed the disc between the cervical vertebrae at levels 5 and 6. This, of course, was the injury that clouded my broken neck in the x-rays in 2000.

I was losing the feeling in my right hand and was all over the place on the bike so it was just too dangerous to ride and I sat out the last round and conceded the championship, otherwise I would have been a double champion in 1995. Anyway, since my bike was doing nothing at that final round I persuaded my team to give young Chris Walker a ride on it and that was his first ever ride on a Superbike.

An osteopath worked on my neck and eventually with a bit of rest (a holiday in Thailand with Kelly to be precise) it got better without me needing to have surgery. It's ironic that I injured myself in my sleep because I never crashed at all in 1995, which is pretty amazing considering the pace Jamie and I were running at.

But my biggest regret of the '95 season was just missing out on the chance to be Carl Fogarty's teammate in the Ducati World Superbike squad. I rode at the Assen round on my own bike and my old mechanic and mate, Slick Bass, was working for Foggy at the time. He told his team boss, Virginio Ferrari, to watch out for me in practice and sure enough, I finished fourth quickest on a pair of old wet tyres that Ray Stringer had used at the Mallory Park Race of the Year.

It must have impressed Ferrari because when his other rider, Mauro Luchiarri, got hurt he considered giving me his bike for the last two races of the season. It really looked like it was going to happen but at the last minute, he announced Freddie Spencer was getting the ride instead. I was really pissed off. Spencer, a former triple world champion, had been my hero when I was younger but by that point he was overweight and well past his best so I felt that it was a wasted opportunity. He rode like a total pillock in those races too, which just added fuel to my argument. It would have been great to team up with Foggy again and I'm sure I could have really made my name with that ride but it wasn't to be. Yet another missed opportunity.

So with the season over I retired to the little rock in the middle of the Irish Sea which is the Isle of Man, where I spent the most idyllic winter of my life with the girl I had met earlier in the year – Kelly Bailey. I was absolutely head over heels in love with Kelly at this point and the next few months were just a merry-go-round of restaurants, cinemas, nightclubs and general fooling around. Maybe I didn't have a job lined up for 1996 but I couldn't have cared less. I'd finally met the girl of my dreams.

13 Sacked

**'He loaded the gun and got Roger to
pull the trigger.'**

I don't remember breaking a mirror in 1996 but I
certainly started a run of bad luck as far as the British
championship was concerned.

After winning the title in 1995 I didn't complete
another full season uninterrupted until 2002 due
either to teams folding or sacking me plus a whole
catalogue of physical injuries. If you plotted a chart
of the highs and lows of those seven years for me it
would look like a map of the Himalayas.

It all started when Steve Horton, the promoter of the
Devimead Ducati team, told me he had arranged factory Kawasakis for the 1996 season and was going to
set up a new outfit called Nemesis Kawasaki. He had
new workshops, a top mechanic in Stewart Johnstone,
a good truck – the whole deal.

I still wanted to go racing but I was so loved up
with Kelly that I was living in my own little world on
the Isle of Man and I probably didn't take enough

interest in what was going on with the team. Whenever Steve called with more details I just agreed and got back to my love life as soon as I could. That turned out to be a big mistake.

The season actually started OK for me with a second place at Donington Park but from then on it was downhill. As the other teams developed their bikes and the race pace picked up, we got left behind because we didn't have the money to improve our bikes. Kawasaki had given us the machines and the race kits but it was the team's responsibility to fund any developmental work and the funds just weren't there to accommodate that. Unfortunately that outfit was built on dreams and an empty purse.

As a measure of how poorly organized the team was (it was eventually dubbed 'In-a-mess' Kawasaki by the biking press), Stewart Johnstone left before the season started and I even arrived at Mallory for a test day on one occasion to find that no one else had bothered turning up because the bikes weren't ready!

My bike blew up spectacularly in the second race at Donington right in front of the TV cameras, then I had problems with grip at Thruxton and salvaged only a couple of sixth places. A crash and a fifth at Oulton Park didn't help matters, then I finished tenth and ninth at Snetterton before the inevitable happened and the team finally folded at the Brands Hatch round. It was the second team that had collapsed around me in a matter of months.

Luckily for me however, Reve Kawasaki team

owner, Ben Atkins, still had his bikes and the entire infrastructure to restart his team even though he hadn't fielded anyone in the 1996 British championship up to that point. He had made arrangements for Jim Moodie to have a ride at the TT then decided to offer me a ride when he heard my team had collapsed. I took Red Bull (who had been backing me in the Nemesis team) to Ben's team as sponsors and they ended up staying with him right up until 2001.

At the end of July I accepted his offer and we were up and running in time for the Knockhill round, which was awesome. As soon as I got there I put in 40 laps to get used to the bike and ended up being the fastest in that first session. I was quickest the next day, too, ahead of Niall Mackenzie and Jamie Whitham (who had made a full recovery from cancer) on the Cadbury's Boost Yamahas and they had been dominating the whole season, so it was great to get one over on them.

I finished third in both races which, considering I'd not raced the bike before, was great and a big difference from the tenth places I had been posting on the Nemesis bike. When we got to Cadwell Park I was fastest again and set pole position for the race proving that my riding wasn't at fault. I had just been hindered by poor machinery.

I finished the first race in third place behind Whitham and Mackenzie and was fifth in the second leg but still really chuffed with my efforts, and I actually beat Mackenzie to second place at Mallory then took another third in the second race there. I'm sure if I'd had the Reve Kawasaki for the whole season I could have challenged for the championship but that's by-the-by.

As it was, I ended the season in fifth place overall after getting on the podium at Donington Park again in the final round. That's the difference a decent team can make; Ben's squad was organized, the bikes were well prepared and all I had to do was ride, which is how it should be. I got on well with Ben, too, and that's how I ended up riding for him again the following season. At that point he was happy with me but that was all to change before too long.

I was annoyed with the way 1996 went because I felt I'd wasted a lot of time with the Nemesis squad when I should have been challenging for race wins. So when Ben said he would be running Ducatis under Red Bull sponsorship in 1997 I was definitely up for it and felt sure I could make amends for what had been a miserable title defence.

During the winter, I moved out of my modest semi-detached bachelor pad and a bought a much bigger place for Kelly and I. It was a beautiful house and I still regret the fact that I had to move out when I split up with her in 2001 but I'll get to that later.

I was massively pumped up for the 1997 season as I felt I had the best team ever with four ex-factory Ducatis, huge team trucks, big sponsorship and great team personnel. My team-mate was to be John Reynolds who was coming back to the UK after struggling on a Suzuki in World Superbikes. John and Ben Atkins were the best of mates and that began to tell later in the season but at the start of the year it looked like being a dream team.

But my hopes were soon to be shattered as I struggled to adapt to the Ducati. It felt like a completely different machine to the one that I'd won the 1995 title on, as it was a lot more aggressive in the way it made its power. The bike had been designed around WSB rider John Kocinski's recommendations and the chassis was just crap. Foggy had the same sort of complaints when he went back to Ducati after riding for Honda in 1996 – the 1995 model had been far superior.

Our first test session was at Mallory Park and after building up the laps running the bike in I was just starting to gas it a bit. To my horror, as I rode through the Esses the throttle stuck open and I had no choice but to brake as hard as I could to lock the front wheel, lay the bike down and pray as I headed straight for the Armco wall. I was knocked unconscious and spent the night in Leicester Royal Infirmary.

I didn't do much physical damage apart from cracking my shoulder but that crash had a bit of a lasting psychological effect through the season as I lost a lot of faith in the bike. We went testing again but the Ducati still felt too aggressive and I couldn't get the power down smoothly which is the key to my riding style. It was really 'loose' too and by that I mean it was sliding and bucking and weaving everywhere which is not only unsettling for the rider but it wastes time too.

John was turning in better times than I was but he was riding by the seat of his pants and looked like an accident waiting to happen. I don't think a rider should have to do that to get results; if a bike can't be set up to run properly it shouldn't be on a bloody racetrack in the first place.

I told the team we needed to smooth out the power delivery and get some suspension experts to work on the damping. Ben refused to make those changes. It seems that he did not think the bikes were dangerous, thought I was making a fuss and pointed to John as an example that the bike was fine. He would say, 'John's getting results, why can't you?' But John was either getting a result or crashing and I didn't want to do that. It's dangerous for the rider and expensive for the team too so I couldn't understand why Ben just wouldn't make those changes. That way I could have gone faster and I wouldn't have racked up a big repair bill either.

Again, just like the year before, my season started OK with a third place at Donington Park and a fourth at Oulton Park, both circuits on which I always tend to go well at. But from there on it was downhill again and I started finishing well down the points with a thirteenth at Snetterton and an eleventh place at Brands Hatch. I was sick of banging my head on a brick wall because no one would allow me to make the changes to the bike which I knew would make it much more rideable. Eventually I just lost heart in the whole deal and gave up trying.

Matters came to a head at Thruxton where I finished twelfth in the first leg and pulled out of the second race with one lap to go. Everyone thinks I finished last in that race but in truth I didn't even finish it – the organizers and all the results sheets showed me as finishing eighteenth, and last, because they credited me with finishing the race even though I pulled in with one lap still to go.

After that race my team manager Roger Marshall, against whom I used to race at the TT, came into my motorhome and I knew by the look on his face that something was very wrong. I expected some dissatisfaction over my poor results but Roger looked very solemn. He sat down and said something like, 'Steve, we can't afford to have another embarrassing result like that' so I thought, 'Great, they're going to let me change the bikes.' Wrong! He proceeded to tell me that the team was going to have to replace me because of my bad results. I suppose I should have been expecting it but it still came as a bit of a shock. I felt a bit sorry for Roger because he'd been given the dirty work to do. As Ben had hired me I would have expected him to deliver the news but he didn't even have the bollocks to come and tell me himself, he simply loaded the gun and got Roger to pull the trigger.

A racing paddock is a very small place so it's impossible to avoid seeing people that you're pissed off with. I've learned that it's easier just to smile and pretend nothing's happened and that's pretty much what I did the next time I saw Ben Atkins. There's no point taking the huff or shouting and screaming at anyone because you can't avoid them after that.

The only way you can really hit back at someone who's sacked you is to get another ride and go like hell, hoping you can beat the riders from your old team. I always ride out of my skin on occasions like that and it's always worked for me. It's a great feeling being able to prove that it was the bike and not me that was the problem.

So although being sacked came as a bit of a shock, I realized there was no point in continuing with a team that wouldn't allow me to make vital changes to the bike and seemed to think I should risk my life to get a result.

The other problem in that team was favouritism. I like John Reynolds and have nothing against him but he was like a son to Ben Atkins and he was his blue-eyed boy who got all the preferential treatment. I think Ben just lost faith in me and didn't believe it was a bike problem. That's why it was so gratifying when I finished second and third just two rounds later at Mallory Park on a Kawasaki.

Incidentally, Ian Simpson was riding a Ducati 748 production bike for the Red Bull Ducati team that year and when I got sacked he was promoted onto my bike. Ian found the same problems I had and was almost in tears of frustration when I spoke to him about it because he couldn't do a thing with the bike the way it was. When John Reynolds crashed and dislocated his shoulder at Mallory Park, the team put pressure on Ian to get results. He said he couldn't do anything unless they made the changes that I had recommended and this time Ben Atkins listened. Surprise, surprise, when the modifications were made Ian started getting some good results including a win at Cadwell Park.

It wasn't the first time I'd been vindicated when it came to my set-up skills. From the first time I rode the Honda RC45 in 1994 I said there was something fundamentally wrong with it because it just wouldn't steer. Of course, no one believed Honda could make a bike that didn't steer so everyone thought it was just me being fussy again. But over the years, Carl Fogarty, Aaron Slight, Niall Mackenzie (who tested one for *Motor Cycle News*), Jim Moodie, Phil Borley and many others came to agree with me – the bike just didn't steer. Jim Moodie rode an RC45 quite a while after I had and I remember him saying, 'Steve Hislop was right about this bike, it doesn't go where you want it to.'

It always feels good to be proved right but it would be even better if people would listen to me at the time. Even way back in 1988 I told Honda my RC30 was selecting false neutrals but they didn't believe me until the bike was stripped and the problem found. It's me that's out on the track with whichever bike I'm riding so no one knows better than I do if it's got a problem. I just wish teams would listen.

It makes me look bad with racing fans too because they probably think I'm just moaning unnecessarily and not trying hard enough and the press don't help when they sensationalize stories of me slating bikes. Hell, it's part of my *job* to diagnose problems with bikes and get them ironed out so why should I be slated for it?

Anyway, when news got out that I had picked up my P45 from the Red Bull team I started getting phone calls from other teams offering me rides. Kawasaki offered me a test on Terry Rymer's bike at Mallory Park, which I accepted and I was on the pace straight away. Terry's team boss, Colin Wright, was impressed enough to offer me a ride at Mallory when Terry was away riding at Suzuka in Japan. He actually wanted me to have some more rides on Terry's spare bike for the rest of the season but Terry refused as he felt he needed both bikes and that was fair enough. Ultimately, it's up to the rider to decide if anyone else can ride their spare bike because it's written into their contract that they will have two bikes at their disposal.

However I still got to race his bike at Mallory and, like I said, I finished on the podium both times which felt great after all the problems I'd had on the Ducati. After that, it was time to join yet another team, this time for the remainder of the season.

My old Devimead Ducati team-mate, Ray Stringer, was running a private Kawasaki team with sponsorship from Sabre Airways and asked if I'd like to join him. He said he couldn't pay me but I was desperate to race and had no other options so I agreed to ride for him.

Our first outing was at Knockhill and I finished second, which was a brilliant result for a private team considering there were so many factory bikes on the grid. I finished fourth in the second leg to prove it wasn't a fluke and the prize money definitely came in handy since I wasn't getting any wages.

I didn't manage to repeat those kind of results

in the last three rounds for various reasons but I still finished in fairly respectable positions for a privateer, ending the season in ninth place overall. That was obviously disappointing considering I'd been the champion just two years before, but I did change teams three times during the season so I couldn't really have expected much more.

I had a good third place in a one-off ride in the Bol d'Or 24 Hour endurance race with Christian Sarron's Yamaha France team and we had a great laugh just hanging out in the South of France. Christian was supposed to be the figurehead of the team but to me he was more like the entertainments manager as he didn't seem to do anything else except keep us all amused. He hired a speedboat one day and we all went cruising on the Med. At one point Christian and I jumped into the sea and swam to a rocky coastline. When I asked him why the others wouldn't come in the water he said, 'Probably because zer are quite a lot of ze sharks round eer.' Shit, I swam back to that boat quicker than Duncan Goodhew and never set foot in the water again.

I rounded off the season at Bishopscourt in Northern Ireland with a win on the Sabre Kawasaki then after that all I could think about was the up-coming birth of my first son. Kelly had been acting weirdly one night back in March and she went out for a while leaving me wondering what the hell was going on. I didn't realize it at the time but apparently Kelly was too scared to tell me she was pregnant because she was so young and didn't know how I'd react to the news. I had never been a big fan of kids but when she came back late that night and plucked up the courage to tell me I was delighted. Me, a daddy? Fantastic! It's funny how you can go through life not being all that bothered about children but when you're told you're going to have one it's such a thrill; I just suppose I'd reached the right time in my life. So from that point on I spent most of my time getting ready to be a dad. I bought a bigger car so I could throw a pram in the boot, I started decorating a nursery in the house and I even went to antenatal classes with Kelly.

We spent a long time thinking about a name but eventually decided on calling our first child Aaron. Everyone thinks I named my son after the World Superbike racer Aaron Slight but that's not the case. I just liked the name and we chose Alexander as his middle name after my dad – who I'm sure would have been very proud to be a grandpa – and my brother Garry whose middle name was Alexander.

Aaron was due on 20 December 1997 but he was five days late and didn't actually arrive until Christmas Day. Kelly was in and out of the hospital for the best part of a week with varying levels of contractions and she ended up being in labour for over 50 hours in total, which must have been a nightmare for the poor girl. I slept on a chair next to her bed in hospital and at 3am on Christmas morning she went into the delivery room and the miracle happened at 8.55am. I was a father.

I was in tears when little Aaron Alexander Hislop

came into this world weighing eight pounds and 10 ounces – I was just completely overwhelmed with emotion. I checked him all over to make sure everything was in working order then I spotted one of his fingers was missing. I told Kelly who had a look, laughed and uncurled the little digit, which had just been folded up out of sight!

That was the best Christmas present I ever had; a healthy baby boy. It's a feeling you can't describe to anyone who hasn't experienced it but having a child is just the greatest thing on earth. When you've got a kid it doesn't matter what other problems you have in your life because they give you so much joy that everything else becomes irrelevant.

Not long before Aaron was born I'd had another surprise when Cadbury's Boost Yamaha team boss, Rob McElnea, called me up out of the blue. He said, 'I know we've had our differences in the past (Rob had refused to give me parts for my short-lived Yamaha team back in 1992) but I hope that's all behind us and I'd like you to ride for the Boost team alongside Niall Mackenzie.'

I thought, 'Fuckin' hell! Me, getting the same bikes as Mackenzie? Wow!' I couldn't believe that I was finally going to get the most competitive bike in the British championship and I'd be riding for the best team too. Mackenzie had already won the title for two years running so I knew the bikes were up to it and I couldn't have been more delighted. Well, actually I could have – if the team had paid me a wage. The catch in the otherwise perfect set-up was that I wouldn't get paid anything because the team couldn't afford it. Chris Walker had ridden for nothing in 1997 so it's not like it was just me being victimized but even so it was a bit of a bummer. Still, as Rob Mac said, he was offering me a shop window in which to get noticed again after two dodgy years of poor results and team fall-outs.

I accepted because I was desperate to get a good bike but it was annoying that my team-mate, Niall Mackenzie, was the best paid guy in the British Super-bike paddock and I was getting nothing. I just think I'm not cut out to make any money. I survived that year on prize money and personal sponsorship deals but it should have been a much bigger earner than it was.

Anyway, I agreed terms in December and the next few months were pure bliss with the knowledge that I had the best bike in the country for the following season and a beautiful little baby boy to dote on. Life was good.

14 Sacked Again

'I set pole position then got a fax telling me I'd been sacked again.'

I didn't really know Niall Mackenzie when I became his team-mate in the Cadbury's Boost Yamaha team in 1998.

We're both Scottish and of a similar age so in theory we should have got on really well but it just didn't happen. Niall had been a Grand Prix star for 10 years before coming back to the UK and winning two back-to-back British Superbike titles in 1996 and 1997. I raced against him many times over those two years and one thing I really noticed out on the track was that the other riders seemed to be in awe of him. All he had to do was show them a front wheel and they would let him through. It's as if they were thinking, 'God, here comes this GP legend, I'd best not rough him up.' I don't know if it was all in my head but that's certainly the way it seemed to me – I just thought no one had given him a good run for his money since he'd come back home to Britain so I decided I'd be the man to do it.

I had, and still have, the ultimate respect for Niall as a rider and I definitely used him as a yardstick to measure myself against. If I could beat a world class rider like Niall, maybe I could finally prove myself as a world class rider to those who still doubted me.

We attended a few pre-season functions and got on well enough but never became close buddies, which is strange because I've always been good mates with all the other Scottish riders such as Jim Moodie, Ian Simpson and Ian Duffus. It wasn't through want of trying either because I did try to be Niall's mate but it just never happened. Maybe I'd done something to upset him in a previous life, I don't know.

I did get on with Rob McElnea pretty well though and I think there was a lot of mutual respect between us. Rob was a great TT and Grand Prix rider before he took up team management and he's said some very complimentary things about me over the years, even once going as far as to say that I'm the fastest rider in the world on my day! I'm not so sure about his appraisal of me as 'flawed genius' though, but I think there's a compliment in there somewhere.

When we got round to the first tests of the season I was marginally slower than Niall but that was to be expected as I was still getting used to the bike. But the first leg of the first round of the championship at Brands Hatch was a real disappointment for both of us as Niall and I could only finish sixth and seventh respectively. As far as I remember it was down to poor tyre choice but Rob Mac rallied us a bit before the second leg and we went out and had a one-two with Niall getting the win.

But the real fireworks started at the next round at Oulton Park. The first leg was damp and I struggled to ninth while Niall finished fourth, but the track had dried out for the second leg and I was ready for a win because I knew I could run with Mackenzie at that point. We both loved Oulton Park and both of us wanted to be the 'daddy' around there so I hung onto Niall for almost the entire race distance before getting a perfect drive onto the final straight before the last corner of the last lap. I ran up alongside Niall, turned the bike in and fired it to the line beating him by a gnat's whisker and taking my first BSB win since 1995.

That represented a real turning-point for me but when I got back to the pits I noticed that Niall was absolutely fuming with rage. I thought, 'What have I done wrong?' In my opinion, that pass was forceful but clean so I couldn't understand why Niall was so miffed at me. When he was interviewed for the TV he said something like, 'Well, we know the rules now – there aren't any.'

Even watching a replay on video of that final move I still can't see what all the fuss was about and I think Niall was just pissed off because someone had actually beaten him. He was 'the man' in the UK at the time and really didn't like being beaten. He complained that I could have taken him out and ruined things for the team but, hey, this is motorbike racing –

if we're all going to be wrapped up in cotton wool then we might as well take up bowling.

Niall had an easy win in the first race at Thruxton but I was leading the second leg going into the chicane on the last lap and looking odds-on for another victory. I took a defensive line into it leaving no room for anyone to come up the inside – or so I thought. Well, fuck me, but the next thing I saw was Niall coming scuttling up the inside, his body actually hanging over the grass and his bike squeezed into the foot-and-a-half of tarmac between me and the edge of the track. His left footrest snagged my elbow and nearly pulled my hand off the bars as he scythed through and took the win.

On the slowing down lap I patted him on the back and thought, 'Well, fair play, I suppose you're just getting me back for my move at Oulton Park,' even though his was a far dirtier move than the one I had pulled on him. But whatever, I was happy to let it go and just looked forward to the next race.

But forceful as it was, Niall's Thruxton man-oeuvre was nothing compared to what he attempted at Snetterton in the next round. I blitzed the first race on a softer tyre than Niall had chosen and stuck with it for the second leg but the track temperature had dropped and the tyre started tearing up towards the end of the race, dropping me back into Niall's clutches. At one point I had a five-second lead over him with about five laps to go but as my tyre went off my pit board told me that it was four laps to go and that my lead was down to four seconds. Next lap it was down to three, then two then practically nothing on the last lap. I could sense Niall crawling all over me on the entire way round and was I thinking, 'Fuck, I can't let him beat me.'

My bike was struggling for traction and sliding all over the place as I got on the power but I couldn't risk backing off so I kept it pinned and let the thing slide all it wanted. As I fired it into the last chicane on a defensive line I thought, 'Yes, he can't get past me now.' Wrong! Out of my peripheral vision I saw a purple projectile going far too fast to make the corner. If I had seen that bike just one-thousandth of a second later it would have been too late and Niall would have knocked us both off. As it was, I managed to lift my bike up and had to ride straight over the chicane and onto the grass on the outside of the circuit. Niall went off the track too but we both got back on and finished the race albeit down in third and fourth places instead of in first and second as we had been.

Rob Mac was furious and so was I. As I pulled into pit lane I was shouting, 'What the fuck was that all about?' but Rob told me to disappear and get changed. He wanted to speak to Niall alone and didn't want me ranting and raving in front of the TV cameras, as it would have looked bad for the team. Rob had some pretty strong words with Niall and the two of them didn't speak for about a week which was unlike them. It was an out-and-out suicidal move and things were getting totally out of hand on the track even though the press were having a field day and the fans were loving it.

A lot of riders use the press to try and wind up and out-psyche their rivals. Lots of racers have told the press that I'll come apart like a cheap watch mid-season or that I'll crack under pressure but I just let it go over my head. It certainly doesn't bother me. If anything, it makes me even more determined to beat them so it actually works in my favour, not theirs. Niall said he didn't like what I was saying in the press that year but I wasn't trying to wind him up, I was just being my usual too-honest self. Anyway, the press always takes things out of context and blows up the slightest little quip into a big deal so it's not even worth getting upset about. Most riders know that it's just bullshit to sell papers so they usually choose to ignore it.

I won again at Donington while Niall crashed out but he came back to win the second race. But what was funny about that round was that I had to borrow a set of Niall's leathers so there were two Mackenzies out on the track that day. I've always had a problem with people supplying me with enough gear and that year I only had one set of leathers up to that point. So when I ruined them in a practice crash I was forced to borrow a set from Niall, which probably confused a few people.

I didn't do myself any favours at Knockhill when I crashed again on the first lap of the first race. I ran into the back of Sean Emmett and was thinking about what that would do to my championship points even before I hit the ground. I led the second race from Niall all the way until the last lap when he dived underneath me at Clarke just a few corners from the

The last TT. With Joey Dunlop and Phillip McCallen after winning the 1994 Senior.

Flying high again. Nose-diving the Honda RC45 at Ballaugh Bridge.

Look at me noo ma! Soaking up the atmosphere after my last ever TT in 1994.

Having a great scrap at Knockhill with Jamie Whitham before he developed cancer in 1995. I went on to win the British Superbike title.

Celebrating my 1995 British Superbike title. I got hate mail from some Jamie Whitham supporters.

Baling out. Parting company with my Kawasaki in 1996. Soon afterward I bailed out of the Nemesis team.

Aboard the ill-fated Nemesis Kawasaki in 1996 …

… before joining the Red Bull team later that season.

Out cold as journalist Mac McDiarmid tries to switch off my Ducati's ignition – while still smoking his fag!

Taking the private Sabre Kawasaki to a rostrum finish at Knockhill in 1997, just weeks after being sacked from Red Bull Ducati.

Now it's war. The outbraking manoeuvre I performed on Niall Mackenzie (right) which started a season-long battle for the 1998 BSB title.

And this is how it ended – with a broken wrist at Cadwell Park and no money in the bank. I didn't get paid to ride that season.

Returning the Mac. Despite our rivalry, I couldn't leave Mackenzie to walk back to the paddock at Donington in 1998.

Like a Virgin. Trying out the much maligned Yamaha R7 for size in 2000.

Winning the Le Mans world endurance race on a Kawasaki in 1999. My partner was Chris Walker.

On pole position for the Donington Park British Superbike round in 2000. Neil Hodgson is closest to camera with John Reynolds in between.

Yes, it did hurt but amazingly, the doctors failed to spot that I'd broken my neck in this spill during the World Superbike round at Brands Hatch in 2000.

Faster than ever at 40. On pole position for the Donington World Superbike round in 2001.

Proving I could still cut it with the best Superbike riders in the world. On the podium with Neil Hodgson and GSE team manager Colin Wright, after finishing third in the 2001 World Superbike round at Donington.

Closing in on the 2001 British Superbike title on the MonsterMob Ducati …

… until this happened with just one round to go. Lying in Kettering General with a broken and dislocated ankle and a broken collarbone. Another season down the toilet.

At last. Flying the Scottish flag at Donington after finally lifting the 2002 British Superbike championship. It's the only time I've ever carried a flag. I'd beaten Valentino Rossi's lap record in practice too.

Possibly the last picture taken of Steve with his sons Aaron and Connor.

The final journey. It was estimated that up to one thousand bikes followed Hizzy to his final resting place. Thousands more lined the streets to pay tribute.

finish. I took a defensive line but Niall still scuttled through and used all of the track, forcing me to shut off and lose all my drive.

I thought I could peg back a lot of points at Cadwell Park because I love the place and Niall's not too keen on it. There was a free practice day on the Friday afternoon and I had been fastest all day so I was ready to pack up and leave. Rob McElnea urged me to go back out and try a new tyre that Dunlop had come up with but I said I'd just wait and try it on Saturday. However, Rob was concerned that it might be wet on the Saturday so he persuaded me to go out and do about 15 laps just to be safe. Well, it turned out to be anything but safe for me.

The tyre was brilliant and I lapped quicker than I had all day. As I came round on my fifteenth, and last, lap my pit board told me how fast I was going but I still felt very comfortable and wasn't taking any chances. I came out of the hairpin, kicked up a gear and banked into Barn Corner and then all hell broke loose. The tyre let go viciously then gripped again and the bike spat me off right into the air. It was a huge and classic 'high-side'.

Some people let go of the bars as soon as they feel a little slide but I never do because there's always a chance of saving it. On this occasion it was a mistake; I did a huge handstand still holding onto the bars and when I finally did let go, I landed on my feet then toppled onto my backside awkwardly. Even if you have broken some bones, you don't always feel the pain straight after a crash because the adrenalin's still pumping rapidly through your body. When I stood up on that occasion I could tell I'd probably broken a couple of bones in my foot but it wasn't really that painful and I wasn't too worried. It was only when I tried to undo the chin-strap on my helmet that I realized something was very wrong.

Taking a helmet off for me is second nature because I've done it so many times but this time I couldn't do it. No matter how much I fumbled it just wasn't happening. It was only when I looked down at my hand that I realized why; my hand was so completely dislocated that it was set at right angles to my forearm and pointing outwards, away from my body. Strangely, there was no pain at first but that was all to change when I got to hospital. The x-rays showed my wrist was in a hell of a mess. The joint is made up of a lot of little building blocks and mine were all displaced as were the ligaments that held them together. In total, eight major bones had been wrenched out of place and the tip of the radius (a bone in the forearm) had been snapped clean off. The damage had actually occurred while I was hanging onto the bike and being thrown over the bars, not as I landed on the ground.

It was pretty painful once the adrenalin had calmed down but nothing like as bad as when the doctors put it back in place. They had to act quickly because my circulation was being cut off so a couple of people held me down, I was given some gas to inhale, and a doctor wrenched the wrist back into place. Christ but the pain was unbelievable – I think without the gas I would have passed out. Just take a minute to imagine your entire hand being torn from your wrist and then some bugger stretching it to snap it back into place. Then hope you never have to go through that. It's not funny, believe me.

I had an operation the same night to have a couple of 'K-wire' pins inserted to hold the building blocks in place and after that the only thing that was going to help was time both for my wrist and the broken bones in my foot.

Doctors who aren't used to dealing with motor-cycle racers take a pretty dim view of us as you can imagine. They think they're wasting their time and resources fixing us up so we can just go back out and smash ourselves up again so they always have a good nag while they're working on us and give us as much grief as possible. It's like being back at bloody school sometimes, but fortunately there's a very good surgeon called Anthony Green who works at Nobles Hospital on the Isle of Man and is totally sympathetic to my cause and never gives me a bollocking. Many times I've gone to see him with a big pile of x-rays and said, 'Tony, can you fix me quicker?' or, 'Tony, can you take this cast off?' I wanted the cast off but left it to his discretion. If he thought it would be damaging to me he would have left it on, but he said it would be OK to take the cast off and the wires out from my Cadwell crash so I could try to ride sooner, but only on the condition that I didn't try to lift any weights as that could cause permanent damage.

Even with the pins removed there was no way

I could ride at the next round at Silverstone, much as I wanted to. The broken bones in my foot were no problem but I couldn't even ride a paddock scooter without terrible pain in my wrist so there was no way I could handle a 180mph motorcycle. I had realized as soon as I crashed that my championship was over and I was completely gutted about that; it was the third straight year that my season had been messed up prematurely for one reason or another.

When I came back for the Brands Hatch round a few weeks later I went out in practice and managed about six laps before pulling in with real pain. I couldn't blip the throttle like I normally do when I change down gears and I really didn't think I'd be able to last race distance. When Rob Mac said to me, 'How do you feel?' I told him I was in pain and doubtful about the race. He said, 'Well you've just set the fastest time mate. Keep it up.'

I did keep it up somehow and got pole position before going on to win the first race. After that Rob asked me to help Niall win the championship. There was still another round to go at Donington Park but Niall could wrap the title up at Brands if I rode 'shotgun' and tried to stop too many riders getting past him. I agreed to help out and I made that YZF as wide as a bus all race long. I think Niall was having some tyre problems that day so I defended his inside to stop anyone coming through. It must have been really frustrating for the riders behind me but sometimes you've got to do a job for your team. The three riders behind me finally got past on the last corner but I had done enough to safeguard Niall's position and he lifted the title for a third straight year.

At Donington Park, the last round of the championship, Niall came to my motorhome and thanked me for helping him out at Brands so everything ended on a decent note between us. It had been a great battle up to the point where I was injured and that season really marked a turning-point in my life. I may have been 36 years old but that was the first time I'd had real top level machinery and I felt that Rob Mac and Yamaha were right behind me all the way. I wasn't treated as a second rider to Niall – we were both treated as equals (apart from salary) and that raised my expectations as far as teams went. I'd been involved in so many half-cocked teams over the years but 1998 really boosted my confidence again and I felt I'd proved myself against Mackenzie.

But, like so many times in the past, I was to find myself without a ride again for the following season as Cadbury's withdrew their sponsorship and the Boost team folded. I hung on for a while hoping Rob would get something sorted out and I even turned down an offer from Kawasaki in October, but by January Rob still hadn't found a sponsor and I thought I was going to be left out of the 1999 season.

Things weren't going well at home either, as Kelly was becoming more and more unhappy in our relationship. We were arguing all the time and it just wasn't working out. Around Christmas time we had a blazing row and she decided to leave, so I bought her a little two-bedroomed house and she moved out.

I still looked after Aaron whenever I could and Kelly and I remained friends but I was very sad about the way things had turned out.

I went up to see Kelly at her house in March 1999 and must have been in a bit of a bad mood because I made a sarcastic quip about her putting on weight. Her response stunned me – she told me she was pregnant again! It was weird knowing that we were going to have another kid when we weren't even living together anymore and I went through a real roller-coaster ride of emotions over the next few weeks. Of course, I wanted the baby because I loved being a dad but I really wanted my kids to be brought up in a traditional, old-fashioned family unit. I'm very much a believer in that since that's the way I was brought up but it seems to be more and more difficult these days to find someone else who feels the same way. People have got much more cash to throw around these days and I think that makes them more selfish. Everyone's striving to achieve things and make a name for themselves and they're forgetting the simple things in life like family. It's really sad but that's just the way things are and there's not a lot I can do about it. If I had my way it would just be Kelly, myself and the kids, as one big happy family but it looks like it's not to be. I hope the boys will understand when they're a bit older.

Anyway, by January of 1999 I still didn't have a ride and was wishing I'd accepted Kawasaki's offer back in October. Kawasaki had ended up signing an Australian rider called Warwick Nowland, but he had problems getting a work permit for the UK so they had to let him go in January. That's when team manager Simon Buckmaster rang me up out of the blue and offered me the slot which I was delighted with, even though the salary was a measly £13,000. My team-mate was to be Chris Walker and he had hogged most of the available cash but I still think Kawasaki knew I'd ridden the Boost Yamaha for nothing so maybe they tried to take advantage of that.

The bikes sounded good, though, as they were 1998-spec World Superbike machines and I also struck a deal with Kawasaki France to race in three World Endurance rounds – Le Mans, Spa and the Bol d'Or, so my season was filled up nicely.

My first test day with the team was at Donington Park in January where I rode a kitted bike rather than the WSB machines we had on order. I was within a second of the lap record in the freezing conditions, which I was really chuffed with and I really thought I was going to be challenging for the title at that point.

Our next test was at Albacete in Spain and this time I rode the WSB machine. It felt awesome and I broke the lap record and went faster than Kawasaki's WSB riders, Akira Yanagawa and Gregorio Lavilla. Chris Walker didn't like the factory bike and reverted to his lower-spec kitted machine, which proved to be a wise decision in the long run, even though he wasn't on the pace at that point.

It was only when we went on to Cartagena for more testing that I realized there was a problem with the WSB machine. I was way off the pace no matter how many adjustments I made and it slowly dawned on me that the bike was suited to some circuits and not to others. The difference between factory bikes and customer bikes is that the factory models offer much more adjustment; there are just so many more things you can change on them. That's fine if you have lots of testing time as you get in World Superbikes or Grand Prix racing but at British races you don't get nearly as much practice time before each race.

I tried endless set-up combinations at Cartagena but nothing seemed to work. It was the same when we went to the British Superbike open test day at Silverstone, I just couldn't get the thing set up to my liking.

When the season started Chris Walker was right up front dicing for the lead on his kit bike as he'd opted to race that instead of his WSB machine. I could have done the same as we both had a kit bike and a factory bike apiece but I decided to persevere with the factory model hoping things would eventually fall into place. They didn't, so at the Brands Hatch round I sat down with Simon Buckmaster and told him we needed to make a decision about the bikes. I had been jumping between the kit bike and the factory bike and it just became confusing so I said either I should have both factory bikes and Chris get both kit bikes or the other way around. I didn't mind either way. Chris said he wanted the kit bikes so I thought fair enough, I'll stick with the factory machines and at least both my bikes will be the same so I'll be chasing the same set-up. It was a fatal error.

I got on with Chris OK socially and he's a funny bloke to be around but he certainly didn't help when it came to sharing information about the bikes. I was busy trying to sort out my chassis at Silverstone and asked Chris if he'd tried a particular gearing set-up just to save me time trying them all myself. Now he may have not properly understood what I was asking, as he told me to forget about the one I asked about saying it was crap but I later found out that's the one he was actually using and he was right on the pace. I never said anything about it to him but I thought that was a shitty thing to do, not to mention un-sporting. Even when Niall Mackenzie and I had been battling for the title in 1998 we still swapped information readily for the good of the team.

Chris and I did work well together at the Le Mans 24 Hour race where we were team-mates and actually won the event which was my first world endurance win since I partnered Carl Fogarty and Terry Rymer at the Bol d'Or in 1992.

But as I said before, I shot myself in the foot when I accepted both factory bikes because I just couldn't get on with them. There were occasions when I found a set-up that worked and I'd be up there with the leaders but it was an exception rather than a rule. And it's not as if I wasn't trying; at the Donington round I was battling so hard for second place that I crashed and scuppered both John Reynolds and Troy Bayliss.

The TT was a special time for me in 1999 but it had nothing to do with racing, although I did do a parade lap on a ZX-7RR Kawasaki. After that lap on 9 June

I was watching the Supersport 600 race from Hillberry when Kelly's sister called me on my mobile saying Kelly was going into labour and I'd better hurry up if I wanted to be at the birth. As I've already mentioned, Kelly and I had split up but we were still close enough for me to be there for the birth of our second child.

So I raced up to Nobles Hospital in Douglas and arrived just in time to witness the birth of Connor William Hislop whose second name is after Kelly's grandfather. Again it was just the most amazing feeling on earth and having one kid already didn't make the feeling any less emotional, but it still felt a little weird knowing that Kelly and I weren't going to be together to bring Connor up.

After a brief period of elation I had to get back to the increasing gloom of the Kawasaki camp. I asked Simon Buckmaster if he could get hold of a kit bike for me so that I didn't have to ride the factory machines but he said there were no more available.

I was just getting ready to fly out to Belgium to fulfil my commitments to the Kawasaki France team by riding in the Spa-Francorchamps 24 Hour race, when Simon called and said he'd found a spare kit bike and had booked some track time for the following day. This was on a Sunday and I was due to fly to Belgium on the Tuesday so time was a bit tight. I knew that one day wasn't going to give enough time to get the bike working. Simon explained that he'd booked us on to a track evening at Donington – where there would be lots of normal road-riding guys on their own bikes running around – and we would only get a one-hour session to ourselves. I felt that it was a hastily arranged, half-cocked 'test' session and I thought it sounded like a total waste of time so I told Simon, 'Look, let's wait until I get back from Belgium and do this properly' and caught my flight as planned.

Things went well in practice at Spa and I actually ended up fastest in qualifying and set pole position for the race. Just after setting pole I was back in my truck cleaning my leathers when the circuit tannoy asked me to go up to race control. That usually only happens when the officials want to give you a bollocking for passing under yellow flags or pulling wheelies or some sort of rule infringement like that, so I was wondering what I'd done wrong as I trudged through the paddock and up the steps to race control.

When I got there I was handed a fax which had just come through from Simon Buckmaster in the UK. It said I had been, '. . . relieved of my duties with Kawasaki Motors UK.' In other words, I had been sacked. Again!

I thought it was very unprofessional of Simon to fire me that way. I mean, who knows how many people read that fax before I did? I was also trying to race for another Kawasaki team so it should have been in Kawasaki UK's interests to let me concentrate on doing the best job I could for the firm. But then I suppose he thought I was unprofessional in not going to the 'test' he had arranged. Either way, it didn't affect my ride with Kawasaki France but our bike packed up when my team-mate was leading the race and we were forced out. I did one more race for Kawasaki

France at the Bol d'Or later in the year finishing seventh and that was my contract fulfilled.

Kawasaki UK claimed I had breached my contract, not only for missing that joke of a test, but by not riding in the Suzuka 8 Hour race in Japan. Earlier in the year I said I'd like to ride at Suzuka but when they said they could only cover my expenses and wouldn't actually pay me to race there, I said I wouldn't bother going as I did not consider that I was contracted to do that race anyway: they didn't tell me I had to race.

After my sacking became public knowledge Colin Wright from the GSE Ducati team sent a letter into *Motor Cycle News* which said I had bitten the hand that fed me by slagging off the bikes in public. I don't know why he felt he had to voice an opinion on the whole thing as it was just another case of me being too honest for my own good. If a journalist asks me what I think of a particular bike I tell him the truth and I just said what I thought of those Kawasakis. But once again, being honest did me no favours.

Anyway, for the second time in as many years I was fired from my team and things were looking increasingly bleak, as there were fewer and fewer teams in the paddock that I hadn't fallen out with for one reason or another. That's when Rob McElnea called and said he'd like me to join Niall Mackenzie on a Yamaha again, this time under Virgin sponsorship as Rob had brokered a deal with the company just days before the 1999 season started.

I went testing at Cadwell Park and broke the lap record on my first time out on the new R7. I don't think Niall was too chuffed that I was back in the team again after our run-ins of the previous season especially when I started going better than him. On my debut on the R7 I beat Niall in both races at Cadwell. Then I set pole at Brands Hatch but the bike suffered electrical problems on the warm-up lap and I had to start from the back of the grid so I was never in the running for the lead in the race.

I finished the season on the Virgin bike with three wins at Kirkistown in Northern Ireland and Rob Mac was impressed enough to offer me a job in the year 2000 – and this time I was to be paid too! Again, I'd ridden the Yamaha for nothing in those last few races of '99 but I was glad to be riding anything and I had to thank Rob for giving me another chance. For the year 2000 though, I was to get a salary of £45,000, which was a lot better than nothing, even though it was still only half of what other riders were getting. However, what was about to happen to me in the year 2000, was a good reminder of how unimportant money really is.

15 Swearing at Fairies

'Racing is my life – it's what I do.'

Apart from thinking that I've got lots of money, the other popular misconception people have of me is of what my day-to-day life is like away from the race-track.

When they see me on TV I'm Steve Hislop the motorbike racer, dicing at high speed with some of the best riders in the world, all clad from head to toe in cool, futuristic-looking protective gear. I'm the guy spraying the crowd with champagne, the guy who pulls huge wheelies and punches the air in victory when I win a race. I must admit that it's a glamorous image but at the end of the day that's all it is – an image.

That Steve Hislop disappears as soon as I jump into my little hire car and head for the airport to fly back home. At home my life is so simple and quiet you wouldn't believe it. Some big-name riders lead play-boy lifestyles in Monaco with powerboats and flashy cars but I drive round the Isle of Man in a white Fiat Ducato van, the only mode of transport I own.

Away from the track my life follows a pretty straight routine. I get up early, make a packed lunch for my kids, take them to playschool and primary school then come back and maybe have a quick read of a newspaper. Then I do all my own washing, vacuuming and ironing and maybe I'll type out a couple of invoices or do a spot of DIY or whatever and that's about as exciting as it gets I'm afraid. There's no cruising around on luxury yachts or hanging out with celebrities and no dating super-models or staying up at all-night parties. I've got kids to look after and I want them to have as normal an upbringing as possible; they're everything to me and I don't really need anything else.

It may sound dull to people who expect to hear about a high-octane, rock-star lifestyle but I've had a remarkably 'clean' life all in all. I've never taken drugs, never been nicked by the police and never lost my driving licence. I don't want to tempt fate but as I write this, I don't even have any points on my licence. I've driven like an idiot my whole life and had lots of crashes but I've only ever been done for speeding once and that was just three points and a flat fine years ago.

I don't ride bikes on the roads much these days either. Sometimes I borrow a bike during the TT to run around on and I quite enjoy that but it's only once a year and that's enough for me. When you're used to racing exotic Superbikes flat out on purpose-built circuits, riding on our over-congested and camera-infested public roads doesn't hold much of an appeal. In fact the last road bike I owned was a Yamaha RD250LC way back in 1984.

Another thing I don't do much is watch bike racing on TV. In 2002 for example, I only saw two of my own races all year! After all, I was there when they happened and got a grandstand view of the whole thing so why watch them on telly again? That never made much sense to me. I sometimes watch a Grand Prix or World Superbike race if it's on and I'm doing nothing else but I don't go out of my way to see them. There's a whole cupboard-full of bike-racing videos in my house, which never see the light of day.

The only thing I do which is a bit out of the ordinary is to fly helicopters. I've always known that I'd need something to replace the adrenalin rush of racing when I retire so that's why I decided to start flying in 2001. I had my first lesson in December and loved it straight away. Adrenalin is the best drug on earth and if you could bottle it and sell it you'd make a fortune. The great thing about flying is that there are no idiots in the air; everyone up there has had to sit so many tests that they're all experts by the time they've got a licence. Maybe there's a lesson to be learned about car drivers there.

I studied for my written tests all through January and February of 2002 and got great results in all my exams, then I started my proper training on 11 February and passed my test on 11 September, the first anniversary of the terrorist attacks on the World Trade

Center. It's strange but for me that date will now always be synonymous with me getting my pilot's licence rather than being associated with terrorists. I get as big a kick from flying a helicopter as I do from racing so I'm chuffed that I've found something to replace the buzz of racing when I stop.

Anyway, until my big accident in 2000 I'd been having a pretty good season on the Virgin Yamaha, even though I didn't think I could win the British championship on it. Without question it was one of the nicest bikes I'd ever ridden as far as the chassis went but it was badly let down by its lack of power against much faster opposition. Still, I'd had some good results on it including a couple of seconds and a couple of thirds until that fateful day at Brands.

My recovery from that incident was slow and gradual but I persevered and bit by bit I got the strength and feeling back in my right arm. Ironically, that knock on the head actually did me some good because when the surgeons were cleaning out my neck they removed fragments of bone that had been giving me twinges and pain for the previous five years, which suddenly disappeared!

I was driven by a newly found determination during my recovery period because I really felt I'd been given a second chance at life and was deter-mined to make the most of it. I'm as committed as any other racer when it comes to training to strengthen an injury but I never bothered with all that fitness-freak stuff for the most part. Carl Fogarty was the same and he actually used it to his advantage. He knew all the other riders were training like mad to try to gain an edge on him so he would just harp on about all the pies he'd eaten over winter, then just go out and blitz them all and that really screwed their heads up.

Foggy was a lazy little shite when it came to training and I'm every bit as bad but I still never struggled with fitness during a race. I never even felt the strain during a six-lap, 226-mile TT race, which just goes to prove that it's all in the head; racing is much more psychological than physical. I laugh about it now when I see people like Neil Hodgson because he's absolutely obsessed with training; his routine is like a religion and he gets upset if he misses any part of it. Neil trains like an athlete but I can't see how it's going to make him go round a corner on a bike any faster. I've done the Suzuka 8 Hour race five times in 40 degree heat and about 90 per cent humidity and never had a problem so I really don't see the need for all this obsessive training. I'm not knocking anyone that does it, I just don't think it's necessary for the most part – not to that level anyway.

Once I knew I was going to be strong enough to ride again in 2001 Rob McElnea was the first guy I approached about getting a ride. He fobbed me off with the usual stories about lack of sponsorship so I could tell he wasn't keen on signing me again. I'm sure he thought I was washed up and didn't have the determination to win anymore. I knew differently.

Many people thought I was crazy to even want to try and race again after breaking my neck. But when you get to my age people you know start dying of cancer and other degenerative illnesses so I don't see racing as being the massive life-risk that some other people seem to see it as. My view is, you're only on this planet for a short space of time and you've got to make the most of it. People climb mountains, freefall off buildings and do all kinds of crazy shit to get a buzz – that's living. You can't wrap yourself up in cotton wool and miss out on all the good things in life. This is not a dress rehearsal after all – it's the real thing, and what would be the point of being here if the greatest thrill you ever had was sitting on your arse watching TV? Fuck, even that could blow up and kill you!

My mum never tried to stop me racing after I broke my neck nor did Kelly. I'm sure they both knew they couldn't stop me doing what I wanted to do anyway but the point is that they both appreciated that racing is my life – it's what I do.

At least, it's what I do when I can get a bike. I had burned my bridges with so many teams in the UK that there were very few I could approach for a ride in 2001. Rob had already indicated that Yamaha wasn't an option, I'd been sacked by Kawasaki in 1999, Honda wasn't running a team in 2001 and I'd been sacked by Ben Atkins's Red Bull Ducati team in 1997 so all the main teams were no-go areas for me.

But then I heard that a millionaire poultry farmer called Paul Bird was running a private Ducati team and that he had the ex-Red Bull bikes, which I knew were good bits of kit. (In fact, he gave those bikes back to Ben Atkins after the two of them fell out over a deal to part-exchange the bikes for a team truck and Paul ended up getting ex-Neil Hodgson GSE Ducatis instead.)

Anyway, the problem was that I'd always thought Paul was a bit of a show-off and I'd had a run-in with him on one occasion during the Isle of Man TT races. He was seeing Ben Atkins's daughter, Karen, and I'd upset her when I said that I didn't like her dad because he'd sacked me during the 1996 season. Paul started playing the macho man saying I shouldn't be upsetting his girlfriend so I told him to fuck off and that was that. Not a good start.

Now, I had to swallow my pride and phone Paul to see if I could ride his bikes. I didn't like to do it but I needed a team, so I had to. He offered me a contract pretty much there and then but the money was shite – just £35,000. I couldn't afford to be choosy, though, and at least Paul was showing some faith in me when no one else would, so I signed up to ride for MonsterMob Ducati in a one-man Superbike team with Stuart Easton as a stablemate in the 250cc class.

Unbelievably, Stuart is from Hawick so we knew all the same people back home and got on really well from the start. It's amazing to think that the remote area surrounding Hawick has produced so many successful riders and I really enjoyed being able to pass on some of my knowledge to Stuart during 2001 and 2002. I'm sure he has a great future in the sport.

Having signed for the team I couldn't wait to go racing again because I had once more split up with Kelly after having been back together with her for a while so I needed something to focus on. We'd been seeing each other again since January 2000 and she had moved back in with me in the middle of the year and I was over the moon because I finally had the idealistic little family unit I'd always wanted for Aaron and Connor. Things went fine for about six months but in January 2001 we had a huge argument about money and things fell apart again. One thing led to another and I ended up telling her to leave so she did and that was the end of that again – at least for a while.

My MonsterMob career started with a few laps at Donington Park on a cold day in February. Then we moved to Albacete, in Spain, for our first proper test in glorious sunshine – well that was the plan anyway. But when we got there it was really windy and even started snowing at one point. I went out on track briefly but was making mistakes everywhere and that's when I decided I would definitely not be riding at the TT again in 2001 which is something I had been seriously considering up until that point.

I knew Paul Bird had run some pretty good efforts at the TT before with riders such as Joey Dunlop and John McGuinness and I thought Ducati would be keen to back us up if we went to the TT. I also thought I could make a lot of money by going back there but I was quickly proven wrong.

To do the TT properly you really need to have a shakedown at the North West 200 so I spoke to the organizer, Mervyn White, about the possibility of my riding there again after a 12 year absence. Mervyn lives in the real world and knows what riders are worth so he offered me £10,000 start money and said he'd give Paul Bird a few grand to get the team over too. I would also get to keep any prize money I won so it was starting to sound like a profitable deal.

The TT organizers, on the other hand, couldn't have been more disinterested when Paul spoke to them. They more or less said, 'If Steve wants to ride the TT then fine but we're not going to pay him anything special to do it.' That's why there's no top riders there anymore – because no one's prepared to pay decent start money as they did in the old days of factory star racers.

Basically, most of the organizers of the TT are just nine-to-five government employees and they don't know how to promote a race properly. In my opinion, the TT should be trying to attract more big-name riders to raise its profile again but it doesn't seem to be happening so it looks doomed to be a glorified club race run on a historic course.

Anyway, when I got to Albacete I hadn't been on a bike since I'd broken my neck (apart from that brief run round Donington) and I was a bit rusty and making mistakes everywhere. For example, when you've not been on a race bike for a while you pull the brake lever hard and think you're going to stop but you don't. That's when you realize just how hard you have to pull it to slow down from 180mph. So I was overshooting corners and running onto the grass and thinking, 'Fucking hell, imagine if I'd done that at the TT – I'd be dead.' Then I remembered my fear of component failure at the TT and started thinking about all the dangers and the hassle of money and I decided there and then that I wasn't going to go back.

On the second day of the test there was a sandstorm so we packed up and headed a bit farther south to Cartagena. The bike worked great there and it seemed to work really well on Neil Hodgson's settings from the previous year, but I couldn't get on with it at Donington Park for the first race of the season so we had to change things around a bit.

Donington was the first time I had sat on a grid since breaking my neck eight months earlier but it didn't feel strange at all. I wasn't worried about crashing again and I just treated it like any other race except for one vital difference – I was motivated like never before. I realized I couldn't keep racing forever and I desperately wanted to win the British title and make some decent money before calling it a day. I was going to show the world that Steve Hislop wasn't finished yet.

No one had given Paul and I a chance that year so we started out as real underdogs which suited me just fine. Everyone thought we were two fickle characters who would fall out in a matter of weeks. Well, this time they were all wrong. I felt I had always been a consistent rider as long as my bikes were working OK so I knew that if the Ducati held together then I would be challenging for the title in 2001 no matter what anyone else thought.

A second and a fourth at Donington proved I was fit enough and back on the pace but it wasn't enough to satisfy me and I was really pissed off on the Sunday evening when the races were over. I sat down with my chief mechanic, Phil Borley, and went over everything about the bike's performance in detail with him. I told Phil that there were loads of things I wanted to try to gain an edge and I knew that as soon as I could work out a perfect set-up then I could beat everyone else out there. And that's exactly what I did at Silverstone, setting pole position after a great practice session.

I had a brilliant race in the first leg with John Reynolds and was lining him up to overtake on the last lap when backmarkers got in my way and balked me. I was furious at losing out on a win and more determined than ever to take victory in the second leg which I did, giving me my first win of the year and my first in the championship since 1998. Hizzy was back.

I remember letting John through in that race so I could follow him to see where he was vulnerable. It's hard work leading a race and it's often easier to let someone else do the grafting then just zap past them on the last lap and I did that quite a lot in 2001. Paul Bird could never understand why I didn't just try to clear off but why bust your balls for 10 laps only to look at your pit board and see 'plus nothing?' It's a waste of mental energy and the rider behind's still got the advantage on the last lap.

Another thing I like to do is make a race look more interesting for the spectators by showing the leader my front wheel everywhere and feigning moves. I don't just follow a rider flat out without thinking; I'm always weighing up where they're faster than I am or where their weak points are. That puts a lot of pressure on the rider in front and can force him into making mistakes and it's a lot more fun for the crowd too.

When you've ridden for as long as I have, the actual riding part is second nature so my brain is totally freed up to think about tactics. That's not always the case with some of the younger riders who are just going as fast as they can from start to finish. It's the rider with a cool, calculating head that usually comes out on top and that's where experience counts.

The MonsterMob team was fantastic in letting me do whatever I wanted to the bikes and I needed that sort of freedom. Phil Borley was a great guy to bounce ideas off because he's an ex-racer himself and really knows his stuff. Before long we had a great overall package, which worked well everywhere and that's what allowed me to be so consistent over the season.

John Reynolds beat me by 0.1 seconds in both races at Snetterton but then I started a winning streak that was to last for the next five BSB races – easily the most dominant run of my entire career. I set pole and won both races at Oulton Park then did the same thing at Brands Hatch. Everyone made a big issue of my return to Brands for the first time since breaking my neck but it honestly didn't bother me. I just treated it like any other race at any other circuit.

Anyway, between the Oulton and Brands rounds at the Donington round of the World Superbike championship, I put in one of the best displays of my career.

I've never been fortunate enough to have the chance of doing a full season of WSB. However, on this occasion I was up against the top Superbike riders in the world on an inferior machine and I was fastest in every practice session then quickest again in Super-pole to take first place on the grid.

I even surprised Carl Fogarty with that one. He had doubted my chances before the race but ended up saying I was an inspiration to all 40-year-old bald blokes, even though I was only 39 at the time!

I eventually finished the race in third place, which sounds great but I was actually really gutted about that. I had made a poor tyre choice that slowed me up a bit and then I made a stupid mistake with about five laps to go when I ran wide at the Old Hairpin. I got straight back into the groove though and repassed Colin Edwards, Tadayuki Okada and Pier Francesco Chili to take second spot but Chili duffed me up at the very last corner and forced me back to third. Still, considering my team had only been put together at the start of the year it was a pretty good result for us and by far my best ever WSB outing.

On the slowing-down lap after the race Colin Edwards came alongside me and held a finger up at me. I didn't know what he meant; I had duffed him up twice in the race and thought he was maybe trying to tell me that he was number one and I should have stayed out of the way. But I found out later that he was signalling 'number one' and meant that I should have won that race after the way I'd been riding all weekend, which was a nice gesture. Unfortunately,

I didn't get the chance to go one better in the second leg as my bike broke down and I was forced to retire.

Back in BSB, I won the first race at Thruxton and it was an absolute blinder with six of us racing side by side, jostling for position at every corner. We were all so tight that day that I ended the second leg in sixth place but was still just fractions behind the leader. My championship lead at that point was still only 10 points from John Reynolds so I certainly couldn't afford to relax.

It was back to business as usual on our second visit to Oulton Park, where I did the double again taking my lead up to 20 points. Knockhill was next up and it's always good to get home support in Scotland – they really appreciate their local heroes up there. The owners of Knockhill have done a great job with the track and facilities but it's just a shame that the location is up in the bloody clouds somewhere because the weather can be so changeable. You can't unleash the bikes round there either, because it's so tight and you always seem to be on the brakes. It's weird that at tracks such as Oulton Park you always want more and more power because you can use it all but at Knockhill you actually want less.

Anyway, I finished third and second at Knockhill but was dominant again at Cadwell Park taking another double win on another track that I love. Reynolds was never far away, though, and he was a great rival to be up against in 2001 as we were the two oldest guys in the series and we were still showing all the young ones how to race properly. I always got on well with John and we never had any fall-outs, no matter how close things got that season. We scored a win apiece at Brands Hatch and again at Mallory Park, which meant I was going into the penultimate round at Rockingham with a 25-point lead. It was a healthy advantage and meant that I could afford to finish behind John in the last two rounds and still win the championship but, like so many times before, disaster awaited me.

Rockingham Motor Speedway was a new, £50 million circuit in Northamptonshire. It should have been a brilliant facility but it was built more for cars than bikes and it was apparent the first time we rode there on a test day that parts of the track were going to be dangerous for bikes. In particular, the first chicane after the start/finish straight was spooking everyone because we knew that if anything went wrong on the exit there was nowhere to go except into a concrete wall and even though it was padded by air-fencing, it still looked dangerous.

The weather forecast was bad for race day so I knew I had to win the first leg in the dry to get some more points over John before the rain set in. Rockingham looked dangerous enough in the dry so I certainly didn't want to risk things in the wet.

I got a bad start and was about ninth or tenth into the first corner but then I picked my way through the field and had just caught John when the pace car came out following John Crawford's crash. That bunched us all back up and I was right behind John as the car pulled off the track and we all gassed it again.

As we exited the chicane that everyone was worried about my nightmare happened. My front wheel was just inches behind John's rear wheel when his bike suddenly slowed and I had nowhere to go but right into the back of him. I thought, 'Ooyah fucker,' and there was a puff of smoke as our wheels touched at about 130mph and I was thrown off the bike and slammed down onto the track. My foot came off the footrest and hit the road at 130mph, which dislocated it. The bike and myself then headed straight for that brick wall with me going in head first.

Somehow John managed to stay upright and carried on as I followed my bike into the wall, turning round as I went so as not to hit it head first; I'd rather have hit it with both legs and broken them than have suffered brain damage or worse. I clearly remember thinking, 'Shit no, the wall, the wall,' as I slid towards it. My bike hit the bottom of the air fence so hard that it lifted it up just in time for me to slide underneath it and smack into the wall. Then the world went black but despite what all the reports at the time said, I wasn't actually knocked out – it was just pitch black because I was stuck under the fence! When I was pulled out and could see again I noticed that my foot was twisted at a gruesome angle away from my leg, dislocated as well as broken, and that I'd broken my right collarbone too. My season was over.

As well as dislocating my foot, the impact had caused a compound fracture (meaning the bone came right out through the skin) of my right fibula and that in turn severed the tendon which supports my instep. It was a gory mess.

There's a place on the Isle of Man between the airport and Douglas called Fairie Bridge where fairies are meant to live. It's traditional for TT riders to say hello to them as they pass the bridge because it's supposed to bring luck in the races. I always used to say hello on my way to the airport as I headed over to the UK. I'd be saying, 'Come on fairies, I need a bit of luck this weekend,' but I've stopped talking to them now after all the bad luck I've had in recent years. They've been unlucky little gits for me, those bastard fairies. I've got more used to swearing at them now as I pass the bridge after a race meeting, 'Thanks for nothing you little fuckers.'

Talking of superstition and that sort of thing, I met a faith healer in 2001 and for a while I was convinced that he was helping me with my results. The guy's name was Jonny Hargill and the press had a field day when they found out that I was consulting a faith healer because that's just the sort of stuff the media loves. 'Oh, yeah, Hizzy the nutter's coming apart like a cheap watch again so he needs to see a shrink.' I could just imagine all the shit they'd be thinking.

I met Jonny through my old mechanic, Slick Bass, and at first I really thought he helped me focus and relax but I'm not so sure now. I find it hard to get my head round all that stuff and it was probably just another one of those phases that I'm prone to going through.

Jonny used to reassure me and calm me down at

race meetings and when I had a couple of great week-ends on the track I started thinking his presence was lucky or that maybe he did have some sort of power. Sometimes he'd even predict results accurately so I really started to become a bit spooked by the guy. And when he put his hands on my injuries there definitely seemed to be a heat coming from them. The whole thing was just weird and I'm still not sure what to think of it all, but half of it was probably just in my head.

But superstitions are like that: I once had a pair of Tweety Pie socks and I swore blind that they were lucky because I always seemed to win when I was wearing them. But then I crashed while wearing them and realized it was a lot of nonsense. How can you wear them again once you've crashed in them? They're obviously not that fucking lucky are they?

Paul Bird is terribly superstitious; he once made me keep a goatee beard because I'd done well the last time I raced with it! Anyway, I eventually realized it was my own ability coupled with years of experience that allowed me to win races and that it had nothing to do with a self-proclaimed faith healer so I 'lost the faith', so to speak. I'm prone to mood swings any-way and that's probably got a lot more to do with my performances than a faith healer.

But I'm not knocking Jonny and if other people benefit from working with him then fair enough. My biggest problem was that I was in an awkward position because the team didn't want a faith healer hanging around since they didn't believe in the whole thing. But I hope I can still stay friends with Jonny because he's a decent bloke. Anyway, to be fair, Jonny did say he felt something bad was going to happen at Rockingham and he was definitely proved right on that occasion.

The real reason for my accident dated back to Mallory Park when John Reynolds crashed in practice and injured his ankle. It was still giving him problems at Rockingham and that's what caused his bike to slow so suddenly; he missed a gear trying to hook it up with his damaged foot. I can't blame John for riding with an injury because we've all done it but that's really what cost me the British championship in 2001. I had 12 races including four double wins and held a 25-point lead going into the penultimate round which should have made it easy for me to ride round steadily and just pick up enough points to win the title.

I simply couldn't believe my luck as I lay in Kettering General Hospital with a plate in my ankle and another season in tatters for the seventh time in a row. I was close to tears at times and the only thing that kept me going were all the cards, messages and emails from fans and riders alike – I've kept each and every one of them. John Reynolds and his family sent me a card saying they were sorry things had worked out as they did and that meant a lot to me. My personal sponsor, John Kennedy, even told me Reynolds didn't want the championship because of the way he had won it. Kennedy had gone to congratulate Reynolds's team after the final round at Donington and said he saw John sitting with his head in his hands, distraught because the title felt like nothing to him. I suppose that's exactly how I felt in 1995 when I was handed the championship because Jamie Whitham got cancer.

One surprising message I got in my hospital bed was a text from Carl Fogarty. I hadn't heard from him in ages and thought he just wanted to wish me well. Foggy was lying around with a busted leg after crashing a Super Moto bike so he said, 'Sorry to hear what happened mate – I know how you feel.'

When I got back home to the Isle of Man Foggy phoned and asked if I was finished with racing. I told him no way, I was going to ride again and once he was convinced he told me about his Foggy Petronas team (which was still top secret at that point) and asked if I'd like to be one of the riders. He knew I was a good development rider, which was what he needed and although we didn't talk money, I knew the team would have good finances. I'm sure I could have got a couple of hundred grand out of it but I wasn't convinced that was the way to go. I still really wanted to win the British championship and for that I needed a competitive bike. Riding for Foggy would have meant going into World Superbikes on an unproven machine and no new bike is going to be competitive from the start. I thought it would probably take Carl a couple of years to really get the thing going in World Superbikes and I didn't have that kind of time on my side.

I told Carl I'd think about it but when I later told him I was going to stick with Paul Bird he understood. I didn't think Foggy would get his road bikes homologated in time to race in 2002 and he agreed with me despite everything he said in the press to the contrary and in the end his team didn't actually race that year. It was a great offer from Carl but my heart was set on winning the British championship so I turned it down though I hope when I retire he'll still want me to help with development.

What a lot of people don't realize is that racers often lie in hospital beds alone. I certainly had no one hanging around in Kettering and I was just left on my own with depressing thoughts about another season being down the drain. I briefly thought about quitting because I really felt that I didn't need the hassle and pain that goes with bike racing anymore, but as time wore on the old fire that always seems to be lurking somewhere came back again. I had made a vow to win the British Superbike championship after recovering from my broken neck and I was damned well sure I was going to do it. I faced another winter of struggling back to full fitness and I had to persuade my doubters all over again that I still had the ability and desire to win races but by now that was becoming the norm.

Paul Bird promised that he would give me bikes if I wanted to race again in 2002 and I took him up on his offer knowing I'd have precious few other offers, if any at all. I knew the 2001 championship should have been mine and I knew for sure that I was capable of winning it in 2002. All I needed was some bloody luck for once in my life.

16 2002: A Race Odyssey

'I'm going to show these fuckers how to race properly.'

Round 1: Silverstone, Northamptonshire, 1 April

We had new Ducati Testastrettas for 2002 and when we tested them at Almeria in Spain in March they felt exactly the same as the 2001 bikes. It was only when we got to Silverstone for the first round that I noticed they felt a bit different because they only had one injector per cylinder rather than three which made them harder to set up at tighter tracks.

New rules for the 2002 British Superbike championship allowed 1000cc four-cylinder bikes to compete, whereas the old limit had been 750cc, so Silverstone was the first time we were able to see how competitive they were. They weren't as strong as I thought they'd be in the early part of the year but it was obvious they were going to be on the pace by mid-season once they'd been developed a bit more.

I set pole position at Silverstone but got a real surprise to see Sean Emmett was right on the case. He was using old settings on his Ducati from the year before because I don't think his new IFC team had even tested before the first race. I expected Michael Rutter and Shane Byrne on the Renegade Ducati Testastrettas to be big threats and I also thought John Reynolds would be up there once he got the Suzuki sorted out but Sean was a bit of a dark horse.

I must admit I turned up at Silverstone thinking I was going to set pole position and win both races to show every bugger how it's done so I was really angry that I got beaten in the first race by Sean after I'd been held up by a backmarker. I was so mad with myself because I could have won if I'd been a bit more aggressive so as I climbed on the bike for the second race I turned to my team boss, Paul Bird, and said, 'Right, I'm going to show these fuckers how to race properly.' I channelled that aggression well and won leg two by seven seconds from Reynolds and Emmett proving once again that I was capable of coming back from injury and kicking arse.

I may not have achieved my goal of two wins but I still left Silverstone leading the championship so I wasn't too disappointed and there was still a hell of a long way to go in the title chase.

Results: 2nd, 1st
Points: Hislop 45, Emmett 41, Reynolds 33

Round 2: Brands Hatch, Kent, 14 April

I was well on the pace throughout qualifying at Brands even though I was on race tyres rather than super-sticky qualifiers. But I made a stupid mistake during the final qualifying session on the Saturday. My pit board showed that some other riders were closing in on my times because they were on qualifying tyres so I pushed a little harder on my race rubber and slid off at Druid's bend. It was my own fault and I should have known better but it turned out to be the only crash I had all year which was of my own doing, so that's not a bad record.

I still set pole position and won both races, too, which was awesome. It was looking like I was on a roll at this point and people were already saying that it was going to be a boring season if I kept on dominating as I did at Brands. I even had people coming up to me in the paddock saying, 'I hope you're not going to do this every weekend, you'll spoil the racing.'

They needn't have worried though – in true Hislop style, things would all start to go pear-shaped before too long.

Results: 1st, 1st
Points: Hislop 95, Emmett 74, Reynolds 69

Round 3: Donington Park, Leicestershire, 28 April

I always look forward to Donington Park because it's a track I love but the weather ruined this round. Qualifying was dry so I expected to set pole but Michael Rutter had really got his bike working well and he pipped me into second place which I wasn't happy about. It also meant I ruined my chance of winning the £20,000 bonus for anyone who could win five Superpoles in a row.

I still thought I could win the dry first race but I warped a brake disc and couldn't stay with the other guys because I couldn't brake hard enough into the corners. It was a daft mistake on the team's part because we didn't bed the brakes in properly. Normally I do a few laps then leave the bike to settle then do the same again until the brakes are bedded in. Stupidly, I just went straight into a race with new brakes and paid the price – they overheated, warped, and ruined my race.

I was really hacked off with that result, especially as Steve Plater and Shane Byrne seemed so full of themselves after beating me, but I knew I'd had a problem and could have beaten them if my brakes were working properly so they shouldn't have been too excited.

Race two was horribly wet and most people just wanted it to be stopped; I don't think there was a single rider who could feel his fingers at the end of that one. It might have been May but it was still bloody freezing and I don't think people watching at home on TV have any idea how cold a rider can get out there when the weather's bad. After all, you're sitting exposed in a 160mph wind and if you add rain to that it's even worse. Leathers are not waterproof and they don't offer much warmth either as they're designed primarily for protection and even with my daft little wet weather oversuit on I was like a drowned rat when I got off the bike.

My hands were so cold that I could hardly work my

clutch and brake levers and when I saw Emmett, my main championship rival, go down I happily left the heroics to Rutter and Byrne while I plodded around in fifth place just trying to get some safe points. To my surprise Emmett got back on his bike and flew past me to take fourth at the end of the race. I was a bit miffed at that but I just hate wet races; I can ride them if I really have to but I'd just rather not.

Results: 3rd, 6th
Points: Hislop 121, Emmett 98, Rutter 82

Round 4: Oulton Park, Cheshire, 6 May

Oulton is my stomping ground and I fully expected to set pole there but Michael Rutter beat me again by a fraction – hats off to the boy. Even so I won the first race from Rutter and Emmett which was mega but I was determined to do the double at one of my favourite tracks, so I was really pumped up for the second outing of the afternoon.

Unfortunately, the second leg turned into a bit of a farce when John Reynolds's Suzuki engine blew up and spewed oil all over the track. Normally a bit of cement dust would fix that but this time the spillage was right on the racing line at a tricky part of the course so the top riders got together for a meeting to decide if it was safe to race. After riding some sighting laps we all agreed it was too risky so I suggested that half points should be awarded based on the positions we were lying in when the second race was stopped and that's what the organizers decided to do. It was a shame to end things that way, especially for the spectators, but it was for the best. Safety must come first.

Results: 1st, 2nd
Points: Hislop 156, Emmett 122, Rutter 114.5

Round 5: Snetterton, Norfolk, 3 June

Snetterton is where things started going wrong for me.

Every rider who has a deal with a tyre company as I have with Dunlop gets a tyre allocation sheet at the start of a race meeting detailing exactly what tyres they have at their disposal. This will be made up of all the different compounds and different profiles of tyres that that particular rider favours, but on this occasion I was shocked to see lots of different numbers and sizes which I was not at all familiar with. I asked Simon Betney from Dunlop what was going on and he explained that they were new larger profile tyres which Dunlop were supplying to all the top riders and which they reckoned would be better than what I had been using. Since they didn't have any of the tyres I was used to, I had no choice but to try the new ones and I found to my horror that they threw out many of my settings on the bike such as the gearing and the ride height. The theory was that the new tyres would offer more side grip when the bikes were leant over and lots of other riders loved them but I just hated the bloody things from the start and I really struggled to get on the pace.

I couldn't get the bike to steer, I couldn't get on the gas properly and I struggled to get third place on the grid when I should have been challenging for pole. The Dunlop guys went back to their Birmingham headquarters on Saturday night and brought me some of their older tyres but I still struggled in the races because I hadn't had enough time on those tyres round Snetterton to decide which compound was best. I gambled on using the same tyres as the year before but they didn't work as well on the new bike for some reason. A second and a fourth was the best I could do in the two races while my arch rival Emmett had a double win and closed in on my championship lead. I wasn't happy.

Results: 4th, 2nd
Points: Hislop 189, Emmett 172, Rutter 130.5

Round 6: Brands Hatch, Kent, 16 June

I asked Dunlop for my normal tyres for the Brands Hatch round and was on the pace straight away even though Emmett pipped me in Superpole. But then I had more tyre traumas in the first leg despite being on my usual compounds. The rear was chattering and vibrating all over the place and all I could think of was that I had got a bad tyre. It does happen from time to time and there's nothing a rider can do about it – some tyres are just 'out of round' as we say. With so much vibration I could only limp home in twelfth place which proved to be my worst result of the year by far.

The only consolation for me was that Emmett broke down in that race so he never had a chance to capitalize on my misfortunes as far as points went. Emmett, and probably lots of other people, started saying I was cracking up once again. However I knew it was a tyre problem and had nothing to do with my riding so I just let Emmett mouth off to the press all he wanted – he was only trying to fool himself.

Between races I found out that Dunlop had been supplying the other riders with yet *another* new tyre but they hadn't given me one because they knew I didn't like their new profiles. I demanded those tyres for the second race because you have to try everything available and this new tyre might just have been perfect for me. I had no time to test it so I bit the bullet and tried it in the second race. I kept my small front but fitted the new big rear and thought, 'Fuck it, I'm just going to have to go like hell and see what happens.'

As it turned out, I very nearly won that race and still think I would have if Emmett hadn't pulled off what I considered to be a bit of a dirty move at Dingle Dell on the last lap. He practically parked his bike in front of me in the middle of that chicane to ruin my drive. When a rider slows dramatically right in front of you like that you're forced to brake hard too but he has the advantage of getting back on the power a fraction earlier so he usually gains some time. It's quite a common tactic and he wasn't breaking any rules but I think it's a bit dirty.

I was still pleased, though, because I finally got on well with one of the new tyres so I thought that might be the end of my rubber problems. It was a turning-point in my season because I'd sat totally depressed between races and had to have a word with myself, telling myself just to go out there and ride like hell no matter what. When I actually did that I was right on the pace so I think I overcame a bit of a mental barrier that weekend.

Results: 12th, 2nd
Points: Hislop 213, Emmett 197, Rutter 162.5

Round 7: Rockingham, Northamptonshire, 23 June

Naturally, I got the same old questions on my return to Rockingham that I'd got about going back to Brands Hatch after breaking my neck there. 'Was I worried about crashing again?' 'Did that corner play on my mind?' No. I don't like the circuit and that's not going to change but I certainly didn't worry about crashing there any more than I'd worry about it anywhere else.

One thing I had learned from the year before was not to set pole position. Usually that entitles you to the best place on the grid, which is to the left of the track if the first corner is a right-hander, or to the right of the track if the first corner turns left. At Rockingham, pole position is to the right of the track but having started from there in 2001 I learned that the other riders push you out against the wall and you get swallowed up in the pack as you head for the first corner. So I deliberately went a bit slower in Superpole and it worked out perfectly as I finished third and away from the wall.

As it turned out, I didn't get the best of starts and never really got dialled into the race so I ended up finishing second to Rutter, who seems to go well at Rockingham. No excuses really, I just never got into my full stride for some reason and wasn't able to pull that extra something out of the bag.

I was more dialled in for the second race, though, and starting breaking away from the chasing pack when I out-braked myself into one particular corner. It was a stupid little mistake but I made it worse by running up a slip road and wasting a lot of time turning round and rejoining the track. With hindsight, I should have ridden straight over the grass and I could have got back onto the track much quicker. Anyway I fought my way back through to fourth place shattering the lap record on about four consecutive laps and would have caught the leaders if there had been just one more lap to go but as it was, I simply ran out of time.

My lead was down to just 13 points over Emmett (having been as much as 34 after Oulton) but I still wasn't panicking because I knew I had just made a slight rider error and we all make those from time to time.

Results: 2nd, 4th
Points: Hislop 246, Emmett 233, Rutter 212.5

Round 8: Knockhill, Fife, 7 July

Sean Emmett had been mouthing off to the press again before Knockhill saying how much he loved the track and how much I hated it but it was business as usual as I lined up in fifth place for the first race. I had been quickest throughout most of qualifying but then the rain interrupted things and I ended up on the second row of the grid.

The first race was a tough one but at least it was in the dry and I managed to win it proving that I can actually ride round Knockhill even though I don't like the place. But the second race was a disaster for me. I was confident of another win and was having a great dice with Rutter right up until the very last lap. The last corner at Knockhill is a really tight hairpin and I reckoned if I was leading into there I had the race won. I didn't dare look over my shoulder, I just put everything into defending my line and taking the corner as quickly as I could. Just as I made the entry apex into the corner and had let my fingers off the front brakes there was an almighty crunch and my world turned upside down. Rutter had gone into the corner way too fast and too desperately and he slammed into me and skittled me off my bike. What a bummer! I jumped straight back on to the Ducati and sprinted for the finish line taking a lowly seventh place at the flag when I should have had a win.

As soon as I got over the finish line I felt a lot of pain in my shoulder and thought 'Oh fuck, something's wrong here.' I continued on my slowing down lap and saw Rutter standing at the hairpin looking really apologetic – his hands were outstretched and his shoulders all hunched up as if to say 'Sorry mate, I feel really bad about that one.' I picked him up and gave him a lift back to the pits and he told me I could shoot him, hang him or kick him in the balls as punishment for taking me out. I was tempted but in the end I didn't bother because it was a racing accident and we have all made mistakes like that. Michael's a decent bloke too and he couldn't have been more apologetic.

I couldn't get my leathers off by myself because of the pain in my shoulder so I had to get help, then the surgeon at the track sat me down and gently pressed the sides of my shoulders and I almost fainted! It looked like my collarbone was definitely broken but I still drove myself back down to Liverpool to fly home because I wanted my own surgeon to look at it.

Emmett had finished second and third reducing my championship lead to just 11 points but at least there was a five-week break until the next race so I knew my shoulder would heal in time. Then I'd have to ride like hell again to make up for all the lost points.

Results: 1st, 7th
Points: Hislop 280, Emmett 269, Rutter 228.5

Round 9: Thruxton, Hampshire, 11 August

For once I thought I had a lucky break before Thruxton because Sean Emmett's IFC Ducati team folded when it ran out of cash and Sean was immediately signed up by my old Virgin Yamaha team. I thought it would take him time to adjust to the four-cylinder bike and even when he did, I didn't think he'd be as much of a threat on it as he was on the Ducati because the Yamaha R1 wasn't as well developed.

But if any circuit on the British calendar is suited

to a four-cylinder bike it's Thruxton, with all its flat-out straights and Sean actually had two great rides grabbing third in both races.

I started from ninth on the grid because I had messed up my Superpole lap and was second to Rutter in race one, which was a two-part event after being stopped because of rain. I actually led all the way in the second part but was too far back on aggregate time to catch Rutter. I thought I had the second race stitched up when Shaky Byrne completely surprised me on the finish line by sneaking past me and winning by a wheel. Fair play to him, I really wasn't expecting that, the sneaky little shit!

It was an emotional meeting for me because Kelly had finished with me again on the previous Monday and that was still very much on my mind over race weekend but I'll get to that in the next chapter.

Results: 2nd, 2nd
Points: Hislop 320, Emmett 301, Rutter 253.5

Round 10: Cadwell Park, Lincolnshire, 26 August

Cadwell Park may well have been the best meeting of my life as I completely dominated there setting pole position, winning both races and shattering the lap record.

I was sick of the way things had been going for me in the last few rounds of the championship and I'd decided I had to get my act together and demoralize everybody. I went quickest in every practice session and broke the lap record in four laps out of seven at one point during a race. I won both races by three seconds and Rutter and Byrne later told the press that they couldn't believe the pace I was riding at. Shaky said he was riding absolutely on the limit and I was still pulling away from him and Rutter said pretty much the same thing and that's exactly the effect I set out to achieve.

It was one of those days when everything was right; my attitude, the track, the bike, and on days like that I feel practically unbeatable. It was just what I needed to get my championship right back on course and because my points lead jumped up to 48 (Emmett struggled to fifth and sixth places), there was now a possibility I could wrap up the title in the second last round at Mallory Park. With another of my favourite tracks, Oulton Park, next on the agenda, I thought I was going to be unstoppable but fate always seems to have a little surprise in store for me.

Results: 1st, 1st

Points: Hislop 370, Emmett 322, Rutter 289.5

Round 11: Oulton Park, Cheshire, 1 September

The plan was to annihilate the opposition at Oulton just as I had at Cadwell and it was all working out until two laps from the end of the last race of the day when my bike died on me.

Emmett had crashed in practice and beaten himself up a bit so I really thought the championship was won there and then. He actually broke a couple of bones in his hand but never admitted it to anyone at the time thinking we would all prey on his weakness. That's standard practice amongst racers – never admit to your weaknesses.

So I set pole position yet again and won the first race with no problem from Shaky Byrne and in the second race I was leading and actually started looking round for the first time all year to see where everyone was. The TV commentator, Barry Nutley, thought I had a problem because I kept looking round but I was only looking for Rutter and Byrne.

Two laps from the end I thought, 'Right, I'll put a bit of effort in and break away from Reynolds and Plater,' who were with me but as I got to Island Bend my bike just went flat and died. I couldn't believe it; it was the first mechanical breakdown I had ever had with the MonsterMob team and it turned out to be a cam sensor failure. Unbeknown to me at the time, I would have been able to get the bike going again if I'd just switched the ignition off and on again but we only discovered that later when we checked the bike over. As it was, I could only sit by the side of the track and watch the end of the race. It was incredibly frustrating but fortunately I had enough of a points cushion to absorb the blow and Emmett had another bad weekend only managing ninth and sixth positions with his broken wrist, which was still a good effort considering.

Results: 1st, DNF
Points: Hislop 395, Emmett 339, Rutter 316.5

Round 12: Mallory Park, Leicestershire, 15 September

With a 56-point lead going into Mallory, all I had to do was finish in front of Sean Emmett to win the title. Instead, I had one of the worst weekends of my career and I still really don't know what went wrong.

Qualifying had gone quite well and I finished second to Rutter but I wasn't really bothered about him because he couldn't win the title anyway. Sean was only fifth on the grid and that was fine by me.

But something freaked me out that day and I'll probably never know what it was. Maybe the pressure did start getting to me but after seven seasons of bad luck, that was perhaps understandable – I just wanted the championship so badly.

I wasn't myself on race day morning that's for sure and I was worried about that stupid bloody Mickey Mouse hairpin. I once hit my knee off the wall at the inside of Mallory's hairpin and maybe that's stuck with me a bit; I just can't seem to get round that damned corner properly.

Emmett rode brilliantly in the first race, I'll have to give him that, but I struggled with a poor tyre and couldn't manage any better than sixth place, which was pathetic. But at least I had an excuse, which I really didn't have in the second leg. To this day I don't know what went wrong and it almost felt like there was someone else in charge of my body during that race – it's the only way I can explain it. Had my life depended on it, I still couldn't get round that hairpin any faster than I did and people were coming past me left, right and centre.

The only reason my team could think of was that I was using smaller brake discs than most riders because I find them lighter and more agile. But there's a lot of heavy braking involved at Mallory and maybe I should have run bigger discs – who knows?

I eventually finished a lowly fifth in race two and could have hanged myself in the truck after that; I was completely gutted. I stormed past my boss, Paul Bird, while making my way to the team truck and growled, 'I rode like a twat.' He agreed.

Soon afterwards I drove up the M6 in a foul mood and flew back home to the Isle of Man, still fuming at myself. I thought I was never going to win that bloody championship. But as soon as I picked up my boys from school on Monday all that shite was gone in an instant. They just lifted me up straight away and I forgot all about my racing troubles. The boys were due to come to Donington Park with me for the last round so I was pretty sure they would help me get through all the stresses and strains there. They've got to be worth five horsepower apiece, those little fellas!

On a brighter note, my MonsterMob team-mate Stuart Easton won the Supersport 600 championship at Mallory that weekend in his first season in that class. Good on him!

Results: 6th, 5th

Points: Hislop 416, Emmet 379, Rutter 357.5

Round 13: Donington Park, Leicestershire, 29 September

The final round. I had hoped many times that it wouldn't come down to this but it did and after my Mallory disaster I was determined to show everyone at Donington Park what Steve Hislop's made of.

It had always been my ambition to lap Donington faster than a Grand Prix bike because Troy Corser had done it once on a factory World Superbike Ducati so I knew it was possible. Problem was, I wasn't even on a WSB-spec machine, just a national level kitted bike. No matter, I thought I'd still give it a try.

In the Friday practice sessions I was a second and a half quicker than everyone else which is a pretty huge gap at this level of competition but I still wasn't happy with that. I set myself a target of getting into the 1min.31 seconds bracket. I stuck on a super-sticky qualifying tyre then went out and got a really clean lap with no one getting in my way. I put together one of my 'Hizzy computer laps' and by that I mean I was as cool, smooth, tidy, calculated and inch-perfect as I could be everywhere, as if a computer was in control of the bike. It felt like a smooth and rapid lap but not really any faster than the other good laps I'd done so I got a hell of a shock when I crossed the line and looked down at my on-board lap timer – it read 1min.31.45 seconds. No way! That was a full second quicker than I'd ever gone round Donington before. It meant that I had lapped the track faster than any man in the world including 500cc Grand Prix world champion, Valentino Rossi, whose best time was set on an almost priceless factory Honda V-five, which has about 50 horsepower more than my Ducati!

That really set the paddock and the press on fire; British Superbikes are not supposed to beat thorough-bred Grand Prix bikes whose riders gets paid millions of pounds for their skills. It was a great moment and I did another lap under Rossi's record during practice just to prove it was no fluke. For me, personally, it proved once again that I've always been worthy of a world championship ride but I still had a British title to win so I couldn't afford to dwell on lap times no matter how sensational. Anyway, lap records are only official if they're set during a race so my times didn't count.

Even if Sean Emmett won both races at Donington I knew I could still win the title by finishing ninth on each occasion. That sounds simple enough but the problem with bike racing is that you can crash out at any given moment and if you injure yourself it could all be over, even one corner from the finish line – it's been known to happen on many occasions. A bad tyre choice can handicap you, too, and if it had been wet I wouldn't have been too happy either. But as it was, the weekend was dry, so at least I didn't have to worry about rain although tyre choice and crashes were another matter.

I started the first race from pole position and, after the misery of Mallory Park, I decided I was going to blitz both races just to prove a point. But as soon as the race started it was obvious something was wrong. My bike was sliding around everywhere and I soon noticed that the other riders were having problems too; there was just no grip to be had despite the fact that it was bone dry.

The track had been awesome on Friday and again on Saturday so I couldn't understand why it was so slippery on race day. I blame it on fuel from a jet aircraft that was doing fly-pasts before the first race. It may sound daft but jet planes do burn off fuel and it falls as a vapour so, while you wouldn't see it, it could still make the track surface slippery.

Anyway, I led the race for a while before Sean Emmett came slithering under me at the Old Hairpin. His bike was sliding too and he looked pretty desperate, knowing he had to beat me at all costs to have any chance of the championship. Because my bike was sliding so badly also I gave up any ideas of winning the race and decided to just sit behind Sean, which was all I had to do to become champ anyway. It was too slippery to take risks for a win and Sean looked like he was on a bit of a kamikaze mission anyway. Sure enough, he eventually pushed too hard and was thrown over the high-side of his bike at the Esses as I was right behind him. I was lucky to avoid being scooped up by him but even if I had been I'd still have won the title because Sean then couldn't catch me on points. There were only 25 points up for grabs in the last leg and he would have needed 38 points to beat me.

I realized there and then that I was the new champion at last but I couldn't allow myself to think about it because I still had a race to finish. My team hung out a pit board saying, 'Position 1, 2002 – Emmett out,' (as if I hadn't seen him crash!) but it all felt incredibly hollow and not the way I was expecting to win at all. I thought I would have been over the moon but it was such an anti-climax initially. I knew I couldn't celebrate by winning the race because the leaders were too far gone and Glen Richards was too far behind me to be a threat so all I could do was ride round and wait for the finish which was really frustrating.

There was a bit of a celebration on the rostrum with the champagne and garlands and John Reynolds, the 2001 champion, gracefully handed over the number one plate to me, the new champion. But I still had another race to focus on so I didn't drink too much champagne and I certainly didn't have time to celebrate.

I went with a softer tyre in the second race and had good fun scrapping with Michael Rutter. However, he was on an even softer tyre and I couldn't match him for grip so he won the race and I had to settle for second place in the last race of the season, albeit after a great tooth-and-nail scrap that must have looked good for the spectators.

After the racing was over, the fact that I was the new British Superbike champion really started to sink in and it felt a whole lot better than it did at the moment when I first realized I had won it. All the traumas and heartaches of the last seven years, all the crashes and injuries, the hospital beds, the worry, the thousands of miles of travelling, the battles to motivate myself, the disappointments, the sackings – it had all been worth it. I had finally proved my worth as a short-circuit racer to match my already recognized abilities as a pure roads racer and no one will ever be able to take that away from me.

Just two years before I had been lying in a hospital bed with a broken neck thinking my career was over. But now, at 40 years old, I was riding better than ever and had beaten off all comers to win the British Superbike championship, the toughest domestic bike race series in the world.

It had not been an easy year and so many times it looked like things were slipping away from me. But I silenced my critics by coming back time and again to regain my grip on the crown and in the end I won it fair and square. I decided it was time to get drunk.

Before Donington, on the Isle of Man, when I was on my way from my house to the airport I passed the Fairie Bridge and shouted out, 'I'm not speaking to you little fuckers, I'm not going to ask for anything.' As I approached the same bridge on my way back home as the new British champion I couldn't help but feel smug when I told the fairies that I had won, that I had realized a lifetime's ambition – and I hadn't even needed their bloody help!

Results: 3rd, 2nd
Points: Hislop 452, Rutter 407.5, Emmett 379
2002 British Superbike champion

* * * * * *

After a great knees-up with my championship-winning MonsterMob team at Donington I flew back home to the Isle of Man to relax, feeling as if I had the weight of the world off my shoulders.

There were lots of interviews with the press and TV to be done. However I still managed to fit in a bit of helicopter flying before jetting off to Gran Canaria for a week's holiday with Kelly and the kids despite the fact that we had split up *again* after a brief period of living together.

I had met up with Kelly during the 2002 TT and we went out for dinner and had a good time and things went so well over the next two weeks that I proposed to her on the Friday night after the Senior TT. To my delight she said, 'Yes,' and I simply couldn't have been happier but, once again, it wasn't to last and just two months later it all fell apart again. The age gap has proved to be too much and Kelly simply wants different things from life than I do. We've pretty much accepted now that Kelly loves me like a brother but we're never going to be husband and wife so I'll just have to live with that.

Anyway, we remain close friends and we had a good holiday with me being completely oblivious to all the scheming and deal-making that was going on back in the UK. When I got home on a Friday night the phone rang and it was Paul Bird. My contract was up and I thought he was calling to start negotiations for 2003 but I was in for a shock. Some people had sent me texts when I was on holiday saying that they'd heard rumours that Paul was going to sign someone else instead of me for the following season. So I had sent him a text from Gran Canaria asking what was going on and he told me everything was cool and that we'd chat when I got home. Therefore I thought this phone call was going to be Paul making me an offer. He asked about my holiday and generally made some small talk until I finally asked him what was happening in 2003 and that's when he dropped the bombshell – my contract was not going to be renewed.

I couldn't believe it: less than two weeks ago I had won the British Superbike championship for his team and now I was no longer wanted! I can't think of any other British champion who's been treated like that. Paul said MonsterMob were going to double their sponsorship money if he signed a younger rider and I obviously didn't fit the bill. He also said he had a three-year project to go World Superbike racing but whatever his reasons the result for me was the same – I was out on my arse, British champion or not.

I think Paul was disappointed with some of my performances during 2002, particularly at Mallory Park, but I still delivered the title so what more could I do? Every championship campaign has its ups and downs and mine was no different but that didn't seem to matter to him.

I'd had a great couple of seasons with the team and everyone knows that I should have been champion in 2001 as well as 2002 but Paul's attitude changed towards me in 2002. We never had cross words or arguments but he was absolutely devastated when I didn't do well in a race and I think that got to him in the end. I think he saw a chink in the Hislop armour and he started believing the bad press I was getting when I had poor results. He had assured me throughout the season that we'd be racing again in 2003 but ultimately it wasn't to be. With hindsight, I think Paul must have had plans to get rid of me for quite a while – he wouldn't have just made up his mind two weeks after the championship was won.

I had a weekend to wonder what my next move was going to be and then on the Monday I had to go into hospital to have the plate that was put in after my Rockingham crash removed from my ankle. I couldn't use my mobile phone in hospital so I had to wait until Tuesday before I could start talking to other teams. Fortunately, every major team got in touch with me and at the time of writing this I'm awaiting a decision as to who I'll be riding for in 2003.

I know I'll get a ride with someone but it gets harder and harder facing each new winter not knowing if you've got a job for the following season. I hate that unemployed feeling and that's actually the hardest part about racing bikes for a living – there's just no security. When I was a mechanic I got paid every week and could plan my life around that but racing's not like that and I'd be lying if I said I didn't worry about where the next cheque is coming from.

That's the sad reality of a cruel sport and I don't know if I'd want my own two boys to have to go through what I've been through so I don't know if you'll ever see a Hizzy junior on a racing grid. Right now my boys are more interested in football than bikes and that's fine by me – I'd never force them on to bikes like some parents who want to live out their own dreams through their children. If they came to me and said they really wanted to go racing then I'd support them all the way but there are much safer livings to be made from playing football or golf if they're good enough at either sport.

I'll definitely be racing again in 2003 but after that I don't know. Racing has given me a life but as a sport it has changed beyond all recognition from when I started out. It used to be run by enthusiasts but now it's a business like any other and the people involved are ruthless and clinical so I don't enjoy being around them. Nowadays, a young rider can buy his way into a team by looking the part and bringing along trendy sponsors, so quite often the really talented riders don't get a look in and that's just not right.

Even if I was offered some kind of job in the paddock after I stop racing I don't think I would accept it because I don't want to be around the sort of people who run racing now. They're turning it into the money-spinning, cold-blooded business that F1 car racing has become and I'm not interested in being a part of that.

It's sad in a way that racing has turned me into a bit of a recluse too. I can't go out anywhere without people having a go at me for something I've said in the press or on TV or for something I've done and it really wears me out after a while. For example, I'll be having a meal in a restaurant and someone will come up and have a go because I said something about the

TT or about their favourite rider or whatever. It's got to the point where I hardly ever go out at all now because it's just not worth it. I've even been thrown out of pubs and clubs for no reason just so that the bouncers can tell their mates that they chucked Steve Hislop out the other night. It's pathetic.

So racing has been a mixed blessing for me; on the one hand it's allowed me to travel the world and ride exotic motorcycles and it's paid the bills and provided thrills beyond my wildest dreams. But on the other hand it's taught me just how ruthless and cruel people can be when there's money around, it's taken my brother and many friends from me and it's caused me more physical pain than I could ever have thought possible.

But if I had never thrown my leg over a racing bike I would never have lived; it's as simple as that. I could have avoided all the traumas by hiding under a car bonnet, beavering away as a mechanic and getting my monthly pay cheque to put towards a new conservatory and a holiday in the sun. But where's the fun in that? My life may have been filled with ups and downs, triumphs and tragedies, controversy and criticism but I wouldn't swap it for the world. And if the proverb's right and life begins at 40, I'd better start living. You ain't seen nothing yet.

17 The Final Lap

**'I can't walk away with a sad exit from
Rockingham. I'd like to have a good result
somewhere else then call it a day.'**

Steve Hislop wasn't unduly worried about being
dropped from his MonsterMob Ducati team at the end
of the 2002 season. In fact, as a man who quickly became bored with circumstances and routine, he was
quite excited about facing a new challenge again once
the initial shock had subsided.

While Steve hated the insecurity of not having a
job lined up to pay the bills, no one was in any doubt
that the reigning British Superbike champion would
find a new team before long. Few people, however,
thought a man on the wrong side of 40 would attract
the interest of a MotoGP world championship team
but Hizzy's racing career never did follow the obvious
path.

Having secured a highly-prized franchise to run
a team in the series again in 2003, the WCM (World
Championship Motorsport) squad found themselves

without riders as Gary McCoy had signed for Kawasaki while John Hopkins departed to join Suzuki. Unable to secure major sponsorship and factory machinery, the team had decided to build their own four-stroke Grand Prix machine for the coming season and the man that team boss Peter Clifford wanted to ride it was Steve Hislop.

There were many who queried whether 40-year-old Hislop was up for the challenge of a full world championship campaign but his Valentino Rossi-beating lap of Donington Park in the final round of the 2002 British championship proved beyond doubt that he at least still had the talent to challenge the best racers in the world; if he could only find the motivation required to sustain him over a long, arduous season.

Clifford asked his former GP rider Niall Mackenzie what he thought about signing Steve for the season and Mackenzie was quick to support the idea. 'Hizzy's lap of Donington rightfully gained him loads of publicity and convinced Peter that he was still a world class rider on a four-stroke machine. I'm sure he would have done a good job for Peter but I don't think the timing was right. You really need a three year plan in GPs and Steve would have been 41 when the season started so it was perhaps a bit too late for him.'

In the end, despite the sensation the story caused in the biking press, Steve was realistic enough not to be carried away by the flattery of the offer. 'The team didn't have a bike at that point and I didn't think they'd be able to build something competitive in such a short time frame so I wasn't very convinced from a machinery point of view.'

But for Steve there was another, and more important, reason for turning down the offer – his kids. 'It wouldn't have been easy travelling round the world and trying to look after my boys at the same time so that was a big factor for me and, to be honest, I like being at home between races so I don't think MotoGP would have been right for me at that stage in my career.'

While experienced GP campaigner Mackenzie may have expressed some concern over Hislop's age, he had no doubts that Hizzy was world championship material as far as riding skills were concerned but, as he explains, that was only part of the overall package required at world level and he believes Hizzy's attitude may have prevented him securing a Grand Prix ride years before. 'Steve said what he liked when he liked and while that made him such a character, teams and sponsors know what they want to hear from their riders and to get a Grand Prix ride you've got to play the game. Steve's record of inconsistency also worked against him. He was either setting the pace or was miles off it – there was no in between. But when he was on the pace he was awesome; completely flowing, smooth, accurate and right on the edge but able to control everything. He never looked like he was going to fall off.'

With the benefit of hindsight, turning down the WCM team proved to be a wise decision on Steve's behalf as their MotoGP bike was banned from the series for a number of races and suffered numerous technical difficulties.

His professional career may still have been up in the air in October of 2002 but Steve's private life was transformed around the same time when he met a 36-year-old private banker called Ally Greenwood. Having spent the last five months being single following his final estrangement from Kelly Bailey, Steve had almost convinced himself that he wasn't cut out for relationships. They had all failed in the past and, by his own admission, his defence barriers had gone up again.

After talking to all of the major British Superbike teams, Steve finally opted to return to the Virgin Yamaha squad he'd last raced for in 2000. He'd worked well with the team in the past and knew he could fit straight back in again but the big difference for 2003 was that he'd be riding a modified version of Yamaha's R1 road bike rather than the bona fide R7 racer he rode in 2000. Still, Hizzy felt the 1000cc four-cylinder machine would easily be a match for the dominant V-twin Ducatis since new rules for the coming season allowed them to produce more horsepower than before and, besides, Steve Plater had already shown the R1s were capable of winning races having taken two wins towards the end of the 2002 season.

After being dropped from the MonsterMob team so soon after taking the title, Steve was more motivated than ever for 2003 and he was never faster than when he had a point to prove. With a new girlfriend and a new deal signed for the 2003 season, Hizzy could not have been happier and he spent the remainder of the off-season enjoying the company of Ally, her daughter Shannon and his own two boys, Aaron and Connor.

After a winter of romance, Hislop felt refreshed, happy and ready to attack the new season on his Yamaha R1 but right from the word go he was plagued with problems. The Yamaha team had been due to test at Donington Park in the first week of February but when Steve flew in he found the circuit under two inches of snow, cancelling all hopes he had of trying out his new bike. But at that point he was still full of confidence, telling *Motor Cycle News* 'We've got another test booked at Snetterton on 19 March and then we're off to Spain. All I need is half a day to get used to the bike then I'll test some different parts and I'll be ready to race.'

But it wasn't to be so simple. Steve crashed during his first outing on the bike at Snetterton in Norfolk and suffered concussion. More importantly, he lost even more time from the team's already scant pre-season testing programme. 'It was a bit embarrassing really – I just ran into a corner too fast and had to take to the grass. But otherwise the bike felt good and I think I can be competitive on it and maybe even win the title on it.'

Hizzy crashed again in the team's final big test at Valencia in March. Having only crashed twice throughout the entire 2002 season, his record of two accidents before the new season even started did not bode well. This time, however, it wasn't Steve's fault;

he simply ran out of ground clearance when cornering which caused the bike's crank cases to touch down on the track and throw him off. Still, the team had enjoyed three full days of testing before the incident and Steve claimed he was finally comfortable with the bike and happy with the level of front end feel which was so crucial to his high corner-speed riding style.

There was to be just one more outing on the Yamaha before the season started and that was at an official BSB test day at Donington Park in March. For the first time Ally Greenwood got to see what Steve did for a living – and it wasn't altogether a pleasant experience. 'I have never felt so sick in all my life. I was standing alongside the pit wall and my whole body was shaking – and that was just practice. I couldn't walk away though and every time he came round the corner Id think 'Okay, he's made it safely round, that's one less lap to go.'

As the first race of the 2003 season finally got underway at Silverstone, Hizzy's initial pre-season confidence quickly waned. After scoring a win and a second place at the opening Silverstone round in 2002 on his Ducati, Steve could only manage disappointing eighth and fifth positions on the Yamaha this time around. He blamed brake problems for both results: 'I just couldn't stop the thing for the slower corners – it was skipping and juddering all over the place. I was lucky I didn't crash.'

But worse was to come at the Snetterton round in April where Hislop retired from both races saying the bike simply wouldn't handle. Although he had seemed happy with the chassis set-up during the Valencia test, now he couldn't get the Yamaha tuned in to run his trademark high corner-speeds. That Steve was no big fan of the Snetterton circuit didn't help matters but he certainly didn't do himself any favours within his team by abandoning both races. But that was true to form for Hizzy; if the bike wasn't performing as he felt it should be he simply wasn't prepared to risk his neck for anyone or anything, especially for a lacklustre midfield result.

Virgin Yamaha team boss, Rob McElnea, has his own take on why Steve failed to gel with the R1. 'Whenever you sign Hizzy you know there's going to be good times and bad times. I thought the good times would outweigh the bad in 2003 but I realized almost straight away that Steve wasn't clicking with the R1; he crashed twice in practice and that just wasn't like him so it was obvious he was struggling.'

'The Ducati is much more of a corner speed bike – like an overgrown 250cc bike – which suited Steve's style. The four-cylinder machines need to be stopped, turned, and sat up again onto the fat part of the tyre so the rider can get the power down early and that simply wasn't Steve's way of riding and I think he was just too old to adjust to it.

'We did some testing once the season had started and Hizzy was breaking lap records but on a race weekend his riding would deteriorate leading up to race day. I think in a race on the Yamaha he had to take more chances than he was comfortable with and more than he would have had to take on the Ducati.'

However justified Steve's reasons for abandoning those races were to him, they weren't good enough for McElnea who issued Hizzy with a written warning threatening to sack him if he didn't try harder. For some riders this would have been a major cause for concern but Steve was fairly nonchalant about the threat. 'I wasn't too worried because I've been sacked so many times anyway. One more wouldn't have made much difference. But I didn't just give up in those races like some people think. I was trying like hell but the bike was all over the place under braking and it was just really dangerous. It's not like I spat the dummy and ran off in a huff – I went straight back into the garage to debrief the mechanics to try and get the problem sorted for the next round.'

It appeared that McElnea's written warning did, however, have some effect because Hizzy was back on the podium at the following round at Thruxton with a second place in leg one which he followed up with fifth in race two and he was obviously a much happier man for it. 'I knew the Yamaha would be better suited to Thruxton because it's a fast circuit and I'd watched a video of Sean Emmett riding well on the same bike there the year before so I felt I could get a result.'

After struggling again with bike set up at Oulton Park, Hizzy still managed to bag another podium position in the first leg of the two-race meeting but only after Dean Ellison crashed out of third on the last lap, effectively gifting him the position. It wasn't

Steve's best result by any means but it was of great significance nonetheless as it turned out to be the last time he ever stood on a race podium.

Despite the fact that it was his home track, Hislop was never very fond of Knockhill in Scotland – at least on a Superbike. 'It's a nice track for a little 250' he admitted 'but it's just too tight and twisty for the big bikes.' Add to that sentiment the foulest weather conditions encountered in the season so far and it's easy to understand how Steve only managed a dire 13th place in the first leg (and was the last rider not to be lapped) before salvaging at least some pride with fifth in the second. Even so, he was lying in a lowly eighth place overall in the championship standings and realized the chances of retaining his title had all but disappeared.

A fifth and seventh at Brands Hatch were in keeping with Hizzy's poor form on the Yamaha and those who didn't know him wondered why he couldn't get closer to the front of the pack, even if his bike wasn't quite to his liking. After all, his younger and much more inexperienced team-mate Gary Mason was finding some form and proved the point by beating Hislop in both Brands races.

But those who really knew Steve were aware that he was mentally defeated and wasn't prepared to take chances on a bike which wouldn't do what he wanted it to do. Had he been 10 years younger, Steve might just have pushed that bit harder and taken more risks but having become totally disillusioned with the Yamaha he longed for his old thoroughbred racing Ducati which he could tailor so specifically to his needs.

Still, Steve was in good spirits – at least away from the racetrack – going into what would be his last ever meeting at Rockingham, the circuit which had so cruelly robbed him of the BSB title in 2001 when he crashed into a retaining wall and suffered injuries serious enough to put an end to his championship season.

No fan of the track itself and completely hacked off with the Yamaha R1, Hizzy turned in two of the worst performances of his career at Rockingham finishing in 10th and 11th places. It was no surprise to anyone when he parted company with the Yamaha team after the event following a sit-down with Rob McElnea who, analytical as ever, quickly measured up the reasons for Hizzy's dismal performances. 'I think Steve particularly struggled at Rockingham because he'd had a bad crash there before and because all the delays in practice (due to an organizational blunder over white lines being painted on the track) had unsettled him. It's also not the kind of fast, flowing circuit which he liked. After his results there I had to let him go; I've got to answer to Yamaha and my sponsors and the results just weren't good enough so we settled things as amicably as we could and went our separate ways.'

Hizzy himself was more relieved than anything else to be quit of the burden of riding the R1. 'I was glad to be out of the team because I just never felt comfortable with the bike so there was no point in going on. It was best for everyone if we just called it a day.'

One person who was sad to see Steve go was his Virgin Yamaha team-mate Gary Mason. The 24-year-old rider had said at the start of the season that he felt like Luke Skywalker being taught by Yoda in *Star Wars*, such was the difference in experience between the two riders. And even though their working relationship was brief, he felt he had learned at least a few tricks from the old master. 'I really, really liked Steve and even though he wasn't having a great season, he still pulled me aside and taught me so much about racing. He really brought me on in 2003 and said I could go all the way to the top and I desperately want to prove him right to show to everyone that he wasn't wasting his time on me.'

Unsure about whether he would race again in 2004, Hizzy was at least determined that he would not finish his career with such poor results. 'I can't walk away with a sad exit from Rockingham. I'd like to have a good result somewhere else then call it a day. At the end of the day I've had a great career but I wouldn't like to leave it the way it's finished.'

Privately, Steve wished he'd been sacked from Yamaha after the Snetterton round because ETI Ducati team boss, Alastair Flanagan, was keen to get Hizzy back on his title-winning Ducati which he himself was running in 2003 with John Crawford, albeit without much success. Had Hizzy been sacked instead of just receiving a written warning earlier in the year, he may have joined the ETI team in time to successfully defend his title but ultimately it was not to be. Steve did, however, call Flanagan soon after his sacking and was immediately offered a place in the team – on the condition that Sean Emmett approved. Emmett had been sacked from his Renegade Ducati team and was quickly signed up by Flanagan at the expense of Crawford who suddenly found himself without a ride. Due to contractual obligations which state that a rider must have access to two machines, it was Emmett's decision alone whether or not he would be prepared to sacrifice his spare bike by giving it to Hislop and, to his eternal credit, he called Steve personally and told him he could have the bike. Emmett may have fought tooth and nail with Hizzy for the 2002 title but the two remained good friends and his selfless gesture proved him to be a worthy sportsman.

Ally Greenwood knows better than anyone how important Steve's rides on the Ducati were going to be in influencing his career – or retirement. 'Steve was talking about retirement a lot but it all depended on how things went on the ETI Ducati. If he'd had great results on that in the last four races of the season he would probably have done another year; but only if he'd scored three or four wins. If he'd just managed a couple of podiums I think he would have retired. Steve was just trying to prove a point after his disappointing results on the Yamaha.'

Hislop sat out the Mondello Park round of the series because he didn't like the track and wouldn't have had time to test the ETI Ducati but he was amused at the comments made by his former team boss McElnea in *Motor Cycle News*. McElnea had referred to Hislop as an 'enthusiasm hoover' and pointed to Gary Mason's race-leading performance at Mondello as evidence that the team were functioning better without Steve's negative approach. Hizzy quietly made plans to get his own back at Oulton Park; plans that involved two grid girls pushing Dyson vacuum cleaners onto the grid in deference to McElnea's remarks!

Joking aside, the scene was well and truly set for Oulton Park: Hizzy was to be reunited with his beloved Ducati and would be making his comeback at his favourite UK track on 10 August. ETI team manager, Ian Simpson, knew Steve could deliver the goods – and would fit in perfectly with the squad's no-nonsense philosophy. 'It was going to be an absolute honour for the ETI team to have Hizzy riding for us. Steve was never one for all the corporate bullshit and after dinner speeches; he just wanted to race and that's what our team is all about. We're just a little tight-knit team nowhere near as big as Virgin Yamaha or Rizla Suzuki but that's the sort of set up Steve liked. I've no doubt that he'd have been flying at Oulton Park.'

Fast, open and undulating, Oulton was the closest thing to a pure road circuit that the BSB series had to offer and Hizzy loved it. Added to that was the accepted wisdom that a sacked Hizzy was a frighteningly fast Hizzy and few doubted that he would be out to prove to his former employers and any other detractors that he wasn't a spent force; that talent like his does not disappear overnight. It may have been too late in the season to have any hopes of retaining his number one plate but only a fool would have bet against Hizzy winning a race at Oulton Park. Then it happened.

Shortly after 11am on the morning of 30 July, 2003, the helicopter Steve Hislop was piloting crashed into remote moorland near Teviot Head in Scotland just six miles south west of his old stomping ground of Hawick. It exploded into a massive fireball killing Steve instantly. The world had lost a legend.

To anyone who had ever known Hizzy or watched him race it was, quite simply, incomprehensible. Fatalities amongst motorcycle racers are, unfortunately, all too common and 2003 had been as bleak a year as anyone in the sport could remember. First, popular racer and bike journalist Simon 'Ronnie' Smith had been killed in a road accident in January, and then the legendary Barry Sheene was taken from us by cancer in March. The following month, promising young racer Guy Farbrother was killed in a road accident at just 18 years of age and soon afterwards MotoGP superstar Daijiro Katoh lost his life in the opening round of the season at Suzuka. In June, the fastest ever man around the TT course, David Jefferies, was killed in practice for the 2003 event.

The bike racing world was numbed by the terrible losses it had already suffered but life had to go on. Racers kept racing, teams found other riders to replace those no longer around and the fans continued to turn up at circuits around the world because they all love the sport and they all know the risks.

Whichever way you choose to view it there is no escaping the fact that motorcycle racing is a very dangerous sport and, although safety standards have improved dramatically over the last 20 years, tragedies still do, and will continue to, happen on occasion. It is, quite simply, the nature of the beast. Riders sometimes pay the ultimate price to participate in their sport of choice and all of them are acutely aware that while motorcycle racing offers highs that few other sports can match, it can also provide lows that few other sports can equal.

But the terrible irony in Steve's case was that he was ready to retire from racing after more than 20 years of risking his life in one of the most dangerous sports on earth. He had scored an incredible 11 victories round the TT course, the most unforgiving racetrack in the world, at record speeds, and came away unscathed. He was ready to pack it all in after the 2003 season and dedicate his retirement to bringing up his beloved boys Aaron and Connor.

Sadly, it was never to be but it is of at least some comfort to those closest to Steve that he had come as close to finding true happiness in the last few months of his life as he had ever done, both in his personal life and in his relatively new-found passion for flying helicopters.

After so long racing bikes, no one was unduly worried about Steve's new hobby. He was, by all accounts, a very good pilot and it seemed a harmless way for him to get a buzz after he'd retired from racing. And who could deny him the pleasure when he had repeatedly stated that flying helicopters made him happier than anything else in the world with the exception of his family.

Yet the strangeness and cruelness of this world cannot be measured and on 30 July during what should have been a leisurely pleasure flight from his home town of Hawick down to High Wycombe in Buckinghamshire, the Robinson helicopter he was piloting fell from the sky and claimed the life of a man who had been a hero to thousands, a friend to hundreds, a father to two and a son to one incredibly brave woman who had already endured more suffering than any person should in a lifetime. Whatever way you looked at it, it was a tragedy.

Steve often visited Wycombe Air Park in Buckinghamshire where he was permitted to fly various helicopters belonging to friends. He would have dearly loved to have his own but couldn't justify spending upwards of £100,000 on a toy when he had two young boys to bring up. They always came first.

On Monday 28 July Hizzy borrowed the Robinson four-seater helicopter from a friend at Wycombe and flew around 300 miles north to Hawick in Scotland to visit Andrew Brodie. Brodie had been great friends with Steve ever since they were youngsters and the pair never lost touch even though Steve's commitment to his glittering career meant he couldn't spend much time back in his old neighbourhood. Andrew had been there for Steve from a very early age and he was there as a friend right to the end. He was the last person to see Steve Hislop alive.

'Steve had been talking about flying up to my place ever since he had started flying and when he came up for his grandmother's funeral in June he was standing in my garden looking at the lawn between my conservatory and hedge. He said 'I reckon I could land my helicopter in there you know' and I said 'Piss off, you're not landing a bloody helicopter in my garden.' So I ended up mowing a circle in the field behind the house and I mowed a little path to my garden wall and built a stile over it – it was mock red carpet treatment.'

'Anyway, on the Tuesday night (29 July) Steve took me, his ex-girlfriend Wendy Oliver and a good friend called Jock Hamilton up for a pleasure flight then Steve and I had a great night in my house doing what we did when we were boys – playing folk songs on my guitar and accordion. Steve loved his folk music and we churned out old favourites like *The Fields of France* and *The Fields of Athen Rye*. It was a great night, just like the old days and we sipped a couple of beers in the conservatory as the sun went down. I remember it being a beautiful summer's evening. At one point Steve spread out lots of maps on the floor to plan his route back to High Wycombe the next day and he pointed out all the places he would be flying over.

'On the morning of 30 July Steve came through from the spare room in his pants and T-shirt and went straight to the kitchen window to check out the weather. I distinctly remember him saying 'Look at that fucking weather – it's fucking shite.' Those were his exact words. It was a bit wet and misty but the forecast said the rain would clear from the west so I thought he'd be on his way by lunchtime.

'As I left to go to work at about nine in the morning he said 'I could still be here at dinner time with this weather. In fact I could still be here at fucking tea time.' So I said 'Well, what are we having for our tea then?' and he muttered something about fish and chips. We both walked through my utility room to my garage and I showed him how to shut the electric door from the inside after I'd left. I said 'I'll see you when I see you then' and he replied 'Aye, okay then.'

'My last image of Steve will never leave my mind. As I reversed out of my driveway he was silhouetted against the light from the garage window behind him, grinning and giving me the thumbs up. As he stood like that, the garage door came slowly down like a curtain falling and that was it: that was the last I ever saw of him.'

At approximately 11am, Steve finally left Brodie's house, apparently satisfied that the weather had cleared sufficiently to allow for a safe flight home. Despite his chosen profession, Steve Hislop was not a risk-taker; time and again he had shown he was a perfectionist and anyone who knew him would know that he would not have flown if the conditions were not right.

Shortly after 11am a local farmer, Walter Douglas, noticed a low-flying helicopter passing his farm at Carlenrig just off the A7 between Hawick and Langholm. Like anyone else casually observing a passing helicopter he thought nothing more of it and could never have imagined that the same aircraft would soon be lying in one of his own fields, a smouldering, burned-out shell.

The gentle valley in which the helicopter crashed was so remote and hidden from nearby roads that no one saw or heard anything of the massive fireball which occurred as the machine came down – the fireball which killed one of the most famous motorcycle racers of all time.

It wasn't until several hours later at about 4.30pm that Douglas himself discovered the wreckage while checking his livestock. The first thing he saw were the rotor blades lying on their own in the field but almost immediately afterwards he spotted the smoking wreckage of the Robinson R44 about 100 metres away – a sight which was so incongruous with his peaceful daily routine as to appear surreal. 'I was out on the hills checking my livestock and I spotted some wreckage by the river. I went to investigate and found a small helicopter. It was obvious the accident had happened quite a while beforehand and there was nothing much I could do to help anybody so I went straight back and reported it to the emergency services.'

Police logged Douglas's call at 4.50pm and 10 minutes later two officers from Lothian and Borders divisional headquarters in Hawick arrived at the scene. Upon surveying the scene, the officers immediately called for further assistance and were soon joined by fire engines and ambulances as the crash site was cordoned off and placed under 24 hour guard.

An ambulance later took Hislop's body to a mortuary in Edinburgh for a post-mortem while mountain rescue workers searched the remote area surrounding the crash site for further wreckage.

The Air Accidents Investigation Bureau (AAIB) was informed of the crash as a matter of routine and a three-man team left their base in Farnborough to drive overnight to the crash site, arriving in the early hours of Thursday morning. They were later joined by the Helicopter Manufacturers' European safety and technical investigator, Richard Sanford, who advised on the specifics of the Robinson R44 that Steve had been flying.

On Friday afternoon, two days after the crash, the helicopter wreckage was taken to Farnborough for forensic investigation and the AAIB announced that it could take four to six months before the exact cause of the accident was known. Without any eye witnesses to the accident and with very little left of the burned-out helicopter to analyse, it was immediately clear that this was going to be a difficult and prolonged case.

Predictably, rumours concerning the cause of the crash spread like wildfire as people scrambled to make at least some sense of what was a senseless tragedy. One of the most widely discussed theories was that military jets and a military Chinook helicopter were operating in the area and could have been involved in some manner. The downwash from a jet engine could easily be enough to destabilise a small helicopter but initial reports suggested that there were no jets in the area at the time of Hislop's accident. Others claimed the weather was poor and suggested that Steve should perhaps not have flown at all but Andrew Brodie insists conditions were dry with high cloud cover by mid-morning, around the time when Steve would have taken off. The only real fact known is that nothing will be certain until the AAIB publish their final report, whenever that may be.

One theory which angered those who knew Steve was the doubt expressed by some over his ability to fly the type of helicopter he was flying. Steve's close friend, fellow racer and fellow helicopter pilot Jim Moodie is just one well-qualified commentator who pours scorn on any such notion. Hislop had intended to fly up to Glasgow to visit Moodie on 29 July but when he called, Moodie told him he would be testing with his Valmoto Triumph team at Cadwell Park and would not be at home so the visit was cancelled. Moodie owns his own Robinson R44 – the same model of helicopter which Steve was flying at the time of his accident – and Hizzy had flown that too, very competently according to Moodie. 'What they said in the press about him not being experienced enough to fly that model was rubbish. I've been up with Steve and he was a very good pilot and had flown plenty of hours in the R44 – he had lots more hours in it in than the law required (the law required a minimum of five hours while Steve had racked up 22 hours in that specific model). Some people claimed the Robinson was too nervous and responsive for a pilot of Steve's experience but it's not at all. Steve was perfectly well qualified to fly that helicopter.'

Only time and extensive forensic analysis will reveal exactly what caused the crash and until that information has been published, further speculation is futile. But while it is important to know exactly what happened on Steve's last flight, it is of largely academic importance to those closest to him since the end result is the same: they have lost the man they loved and admired.

Mercifully, Aaron and Connor may comprehend little and remember little of the loss of their father; such is the resilience of young children. Ally was staying with a friend in Northern Ireland and hadn't heard from Steve all morning.

'That was unusual for us because we used to call and text all the time. I obviously couldn't call him because he was flying but when I got a text from Wendy Oliver asking if I'd heard from Steve I started to panic. I rang Mike Wilds, a helicopter instructor at Wycombe and a good friend of Steve's, to ask if he'd heard anything. He said he hadn't but told me not to worry.'

'My friend Maureen called the Scottish and Irish police but they didn't know anything. Then Mike called again and he spoke really quietly. He told me again there had been an incident but didn't come straight out with any details. It was only when I pushed him that he said 'The boy's no longer with us.'

Despite her own deep grief, Ally was a tower of strength for the one woman who had lost everything: Margaret Hislop, Steve's beloved mum. It is difficult to imagine one person having endured more grief than Margaret Hislop has with such dignity over the years. To lose her husband at such a young age (he was only 43 at the time of his death) was bad enough; to lose her 19-year-old son Garry just three years later was almost unthinkable and now, to lose her last remaining son just when he seemed at his happiest, would have been beyond the endurance of many a lesser woman.

Margaret had been holidaying in Ladron Bay in Devon with Steve's sons when the tragedy occurred. She could not be traced by police until the early hours of the morning since she was booked into a holiday camp under her partner's name of Hardy rather than her own name of Hislop.

It wasn't until the early hours of Thursday, 31 July, that police finally traced Margaret and George to deliver the news that every parent dreads and by that point the news had been leaked and broadcast with a shameful lack of respect for Steve's family. Steve had always considered his mother to be the strongest woman he had ever known because of the way she coped with the loss of Sandy and Garry. Margaret had shown a strength and dignity beyond belief during – and long after – those terrible times and had always been very close to Steve because of their shared loss. Now, unbelievably, Margaret Hislop was to be tested again in a way that no mother should ever have to be tested. Her only surviving son had been killed leaving her alone out of a once happy family of four.

Her grief at hearing the news of Steve's death can only be imagined but the only thing which kept

Margaret going was the false hope that the police had made a mistake. 'I remember I kept asking them if they were sure it was my Steven and they kept saying 'yes.' I simply couldn't believe that it had happened again.'

Knowing they would never sleep that night, Margaret and George left Devon around 2am and drove through the night back to their home in Denholm near Hawick with Steve's two boys sound asleep in the back of the car, still blissfully unaware of the tragedy which had struck.

Margaret Hislop is a resilient woman and, with the strong support of her tight-knit rural Scottish community and her partner George, she will surely pull through once again as she has done twice before in the face of huge adversity. Her memories of her most famous son, right to the end, are fond ones, made fonder still by the new-found contentment she noticed in Steve during the last months of his life.

'Steven came back to Hawick for his grandmother's funeral on 13 June and for some reason after the burial he wanted to go back up to look at the flowers. That wasn't like Steven so I was quite surprised but I went back up there with him. As he was standing at the graveside, I noticed for the first time that he looked really, really like his father Sandy. I don't know why but there was just something about him that day – he looked different.

'He stood in the cemetery and looked out over the hills and fields and started talking about his childhood. He was telling me that his brother Garry and him used to ride their bikes away over through the trees and that they knew they would be in trouble if their dad had ever found out because it was so far away.'

'Then he started to talk about his dad and he had never really talked about Sandy with me up till then. But that day he talked about them both so much and I'd just never heard him talk like that before. But he seemed so happy with his life and so at peace with himself. It's strange but there was just something different about him that day both in the way he looked and the way he was talking. All that time he was talking to me, Steven was standing on the very spot where he now lies.'

'The last time I ever saw my son was when I was taking his boys for a holiday in Devon. Steven brought Aaron and Connor over from the Isle of Man and George and I met them at a Travel Lodge at Burton-wood near Liverpool. George and I arrived after Steve and the boys and we could hear them all along the corridor playing daft games in their room. I could hear Steven shouting 'You're cheating, you wee monkey' and they sounded like they were having a great time. That night we had a meal and a few drinks and the boys decided to stay in the room with George and I. Steven said to them 'What? Are you leaving me to stay in that room all by myself?'

'After breakfast Steve got into his hire car because he was going down to Wycombe to fly his helicopter and we got in our car to drive to Devon. We followed him for about an hour on the motorway but then we

were due to branch off to go our own way leaving
Steven to go his. Just before we did, he drove right
up alongside our car and smiled and waved at his
boys. They waved back and that was the last we ever
saw of him.'

18 A Scottish Hero

'If I die young then I've still packed in more than most would do in two lifetimes.'

It is a sad fact of life that we do not always let people know how much they are loved and respected while they are still with us. But if ever a measure was needed to prove the high esteem in which Steve Hislop was held by his colleagues, friends, family, fellow motorcyclists and his local townsfolk, his funeral proved it beyond question.

Thousands of mourners descended on the small town of Hawick in the tranquil Scottish Borders on 7 August, 2003 to pay their final respects to Robert Steven Hislop. They had been gathering from all over the country since 7am to pay their respects in a town many had only heard of because Steve put it on the map.

The service took place at Teviot Parish Church at 12.30pm and every one of the 600 pews were taken up as the congregation listened to hear Hizzy's close friends Jim Davidson and Allan Duffus pay moving tributes to their fallen friend.

'When I think of Steve,' Duffus read, 'I think of a hero. He was a boy who dealt with the sudden loss of Sandy, his father, and he handled it like a hero. He also dealt with the tragic passing of his brother Garry at 19. Again, he handled it like a hero. He was a TT legend but he was more than that. He was a loving father to Aaron and Connor, son to Margaret, friend to most of the people here today and an inspiration to everyone.'

Davidson, a member of the comedy motorcycle stunt group The Purple Helmets which Steve occasionally performed with, provided a welcome relief from the sadness and tension with some heart-lifting tales of Steve's down-to-earth attitude and sense of humour. The following is an extract from the Eulogy penned by Davidson which he read out at the funeral service.

'I remember the time when Steve rang up to go out for a beer and offered to pick me up in his latest set of wheels. I couldn't believe my eyes when this thing appeared outside my house. It was an old Mazda pick-up. It did 20mpg on fuel and 10mpg on engine oil. The newest and most expensive thing on it was his personalised number plate! When I got in, there was cardboard holding the side window in place, and a piece of chewing gum on the dashboard from the previous owner. But at least it had air- conditioning – a huge hole in the floor! But Steve didn't care about material things or what other people thought. It was just a mode of transport to him.'

Davidson also explained his own personal theory

as to why Hizzy stopped racing on the Isle of Man TT circuit and once again, lightened the sombre atmosphere in a manner of which Steve would have fully approved.

'One Saturday afternoon in the depths of winter we'd just finished a mountain bike ride. It was freezing cold, it was dark, and we were soaked to the skin, and as some of you will know, Steve had poor circulation so he was suffering more than most. He was frozen to the bone so he hastily tied his bike onto his car-rack, then stripped all his wet riding clothes off, and drove home naked. His theory was that he would warm up quicker that way. Anyway, everything was going according to plan until he was rounding Windy Corner on the TT course. He casually glanced in his rear view mirror to see his mountain bike bouncing along the road behind him. Quick as a flash he stopped the car, reversed back along the road, and jumped out to retrieve the bike. Just as he was about to tie the bike back onto the car, he was caught in the full glare of an approaching vehicle's headlights. He later said 'I was stranded in the middle of the road like a startled rabbit and I couldn't think what to do so I just smiled and waved at the people in the car'. This must have been one of his scariest moments on the TT course. So the truth is that Steve was probably too embarrassed to ride at the TT ever again'.

As the hundreds who could find no place in the church listened to the service via speakers rigged up outside in the sweltering heat of an August day, the Reverend Neil R Combe aptly summed up Steve's attitude towards life. 'We live in a world where McDonald's is sued because it makes its coffee hot, where a jar of peanut butter has a label on it saying 'Warning – may contain nuts.' Someone like Steve opens our eyes to a bigger world, a world of exciting possibilities for those who are willing to take that calculated risk.'

The church may have been full to bursting but it was only when the hearse moved off towards Southdean cemetery that the sheer scale of the turnout could be witnessed by those who had been inside for the service. It was estimated that up to 1000 bikes followed the hearse through the streets of Hawick on Steve's last journey. The cortege took a full 10 minutes to pass through Hawick's narrow main street on the first leg of the 13 mile route to Hizzy's final resting place.

The only other time the sleepy little town had witnessed anything like it was way back in 1937 when more than 2000 people lined the streets to pay tribute to another motorcycle racing hero, Jimmy Guthrie. The six times TT winner had been an inspiration to the young Steve Hislop and he had always been proud of the fact that he'd met Guthrie's son in 1987.

Steve's mother Margaret was utterly amazed at the scale of the event and was truly humbled at the outpouring of affection and respect for her eldest son. 'I had no idea of the reaction there was going to be to Steven's death. I thought I was just burying my son so I told the undertakers that I wanted the service to be held in the small church in Denholm. He told me that it was never going to be big enough and that was when the wheels started turning in my mind. It was only then that I realized I wasn't just burying my son; that this was going to be something else. When the undertakers suggested having the service in Teviot Church because it was bigger and was next to a big car park where they could place speakers it really started to sink in.'

'The flowers and cards and tributes that started pouring in were just unbelievable. I couldn't believe how many there were; it was staggering and that helped so much in coming to terms with things, just knowing how much Steve was loved. But I could never have got through the whole thing without Steve's girl-friend Ally Greenwood. Ally, Wendy Oliver, Andrew Brodie, Jock Hamilton, Rae Oliver and my partner George. I wouldn't have been anywhere without them. George helped an awful lot as did all the villagers in Denholm and I just can't thank them all enough.'

'After the service I was asked if I minded all the motorcycles following the family cars and I said 'No, of course not' but I was thinking there would maybe be about 20 or 30 bikes. I had no idea what was going on outside the church. When we saw the bikes there were hundreds and hundreds of them. It was just unbelievable. Steven would have been so proud of such a send-off.'

It was a send-off which completely shattered the old stereotyped image of bikers as uncaring, disrespectful hooligans. Grown men in supposedly macho bike leathers wept openly as the hearse passed by the thousands of mourners who lined the streets. The spectacle prompted Chief Superintendent Watson

McAteer of Lothian and Borders Police to tell *Motor Cycle News* 'I've seen nothing like it in 34 years of policing. The dignity and respect shown towards Steve in people's behaviour was amazing. The respect in which he was held was shown in the number and quality of the people who were here today.'

Quality was the right word. Despite the remoteness of the location and the fact that the following day was the first day of practice for the Oulton Park round of the British Superbike championship, everyone connected with the series turned up to pay their last respects. Former rivals including Niall Mackenzie, Shane Byrne, Michael Rutter, Sean Emmett, Jim Moodie and Steve Plater respectfully attended as did Hizzy's former team bosses, Rob McElnea and Paul Bird, alongside many other famous faces from the sport Steve had dedicated his life to.

Ordinary fans, many wearing replicas of Hizzy's distinctive yellow racing helmet, also showed a quiet dignity and respect that was genuinely touching. As the cortege left Hawick for Southdean cemetery, few failed to miss the symbolic significance of the scene: Steve Hislop was leading a pack of pursuing motorcycles for one last time. He was at the front where he was accustomed to being – a winner to the very end. Leader of the pack.

Racing hero he may have been to countless thousands of fans but the floral wreath in the hearse simply reading 'Daddy' was a poignant reminder that Steve was also a loving father to two young boys who had idolized him and who would now have to grow up without a dad, something no young child should have to do.

Robert Steven Hislop was finally laid to rest in Southdean cemetery at 2.50pm alongside his brother Garry and his father Sandy. He was 41 years old. The stillness in the cemetery was overwhelming in the blistering temperatures. The only sounds which could be heard were the twittering of birds and the creaking of leather as hundreds of motorcyclists filed into the cemetery to see off their hero. Family friend Tim Douglas read this self-penned poem at Steve's graveside:

> Today, all the Border so sad is,
> Our summertime shaded with gloom,
> As we mind of two naughty wee laddies,
> As bright as the heather in bloom.
> Brave hearts, strong limbs and young faces,
> In days when the future was bright,
> The thrills and spills of great races,
> As fast as the falcon in flight.
>
> So skilful his hand on the throttle,
> Adrenalin flowing with ease,
> Hard work, dedication and bottle,
> That brought home 11 TTs.
> At home among friends or with strangers,
> For this was one hell of a man,
> Who mastered the worst of its dangers,
> And conquered the Isle of Man.

Our thoughts are with Margaret, his mother,
And two little laddies bereaved,
Who, when they grow up will discover,
The greatness their father achieved.
Fate strikes and its stroke is uneven,
What grief must a heart thole?
First Sandy, then Garry, now Steven,
Dull knives in a fond mother's soul.

On slabs made of marble or granite,
His name will be chiselled with pride,
And when folks in years to come scan it,
They will wonder at why Steven died.
Farewell to a brave Border callant,
In tune with his racing machine,
Who conquered the world with his talent,
And comes home to sleep in Southdean.

The funeral was only the start of the tributes to
Steve Hislop. Around the country, and indeed the
world, people were paying their respects in a variety
of ways, all trying desperately to come to terms with
the loss of their hero.

Flags at racetracks across the nation, including
Knockhill in Scotland, Oulton Park in England and
on the TT course on the Isle of Man, were lowered
to half mast. Internet message and chat boards were
inundated with moving tributes and messages of
condolence, and tributes were paid on various television channels including BBC Grandstand, Men and
Motors and Border News – Hizzy's local station both

when he lived in the Borders and on the Isle of Man.

But amongst the most moving tributes came at the Oulton Park round of the British Superbike championship immediately after Steve's funeral. Hizzy was, and in a certain sense always will be, the reigning BSB champion. Unable to defend his title, it will be his for eternity and his colleagues and fans did him proud over the Oulton Park weekend just as they had at his funeral.

Every rider taking part in the Superbike class wore a black armband in memory of Steve and also carried 'Hizzy Number 1' stickers on their bikes. The number one pit lane garage was allocated as a shrine to Steve and his 1992 TT-winning Norton was placed on display there with a single red rose resting on the fuel tank. Fans left countless floral tributes in the garage over the weekend and the crowd held aloft hundreds of Scottish Saltire flags simply proclaiming 'Hizzy.'

Before the start of the first Superbike race, Steve's Norton was wheeled out to sit at the front of the grid for a minute's silence in honour of the reigning British champion. Millions of television viewers around the country watched and reflected in silence upon the career of the man they'd become accustomed to seeing riding like the wind, fearless, skilful and courageous to the end. Only the hardest of hearts could have failed to be moved by the occasion.

A new chicane at the track was to be named after Hizzy (the owners of Knockhill have similar plans to name a corner in his memory) and, fittingly, his former team-mate and good friend, Stuart Easton, officially opened it by riding round it on Steve's white Norton.

Easton was nervous about the ceremony but deeply proud to be involved. 'I felt massively honoured when Steve's mum Margaret and his girlfriend Ally asked me if I would ride his TT-winning Norton round Oulton Park to officially open Hizzy's chicane – even though it was a scary experience. I'd never ridden a bike like that and I was really scared of dropping it because it's so special. It didn't help that it was pouring with rain and the bike had ancient cut slicks on it but I was really up for doing it and I managed to keep the bike upright. It really was a great honour.'

For Easton, Hizzy had been more than just a good friend; he had been an inspiration and a true mentor. 'I first met Hizzy at Knockhill in 1995, the year he won the BSB title. I was doing schoolboy motocross at the time but watching him inspired me to take up road racing. Steve helped me straight away with advice on bike set up and riding techniques and he also gave me little bits and bobs like knee sliders and stuff. Even though he was incredibly busy he always took time out to help me and I'll never forget that. Everything I learned from him I still make use of to this day and always will do.'

'Steve really taught me how to be more relaxed about my racing. He said I didn't need to eat lettuce leaves and spend my life down the gym and he taught me to relax before a race, saying that whatever was going to happen was going to happen and that worrying about it wouldn't change things. Now I can sit on the grid and look at other riders shifting from foot to foot and getting all wound up while I'm totally relaxed and that's all Steve's doing.'

'When he split from the MonsterMob team I missed his guidance and would sometimes sneak round to the Yamaha garage to ask him things. For example, I was having problems with my suspension at Thruxton in 2003 and asked my team-mate Shane Byrne for advice. He was having the same problems but couldn't really explain why so I asked Steve and he told me precisely what the bike was doing and how to fix it. I made the changes and they worked perfectly.'

'When Steve used to come past me in testing I would often abort my lap no matter how quickly I was going and just sit up on my bike to watch him for a couple of corners to try and learn something. He was inch-perfect and his lap times showed that; they were so consistent all day long when he was on it. He was incredibly smooth but so fast with it.'

'I'll remember Steve not only as a great racer but also as a great family man. All the advice he gave me will stay with me for the rest of my career. When I have a bad day I just think to myself 'Well, how would Hizzy deal with this?' and I can almost hear him saying 'Get yer bloody finger oot fella and get on with it.'

To ensure he will always be remembered, a Steve Hislop Memorial Fund was initiated soon after his death with the aim of raising the finances to commission two statues of him; one to be erected in Hawick (close to the statue of Hawick's other motorcycling legend Jimmy Guthrie) and the other to be placed at an as-yet undesignated spot on the Isle of Man where Steve not only made his name but lived happily for the last 12 years of his life.

Many events were held to raise the necessary money including a fund-raising night on the Isle of Man, a motorcycle ride-out in the Scottish Borders, a memorial track day at Cadwell Park and an evening auction event in Kelso near Hawick to name but a few. Countless fans who were unable to attend any of these events sent cheques to the fund along with notes of condolence to Steve's family. It is probably fair to say that Steve would have been stunned by the reaction of so many people to his passing for he truly didn't realize just how much he was loved and respected.

Another permanent memorial to Hizzy will be housed in the Duchess room of Drumlanrig Towers in Main Street, Hawick. Steve's trophies, helmets and leathers as well as his first 125cc race bike will be housed there from March 2004 alongside other mementoes from his glittering career. The Summerland leisure complex on the Isle of Man is also hoping to have a Hizzy room displaying memorabilia in the not-too-distant future.

But the best mementoes of Steve Hislop are not trophies, helmets or leathers, they are memories; memories not only of a loving father and devoted son, but of one of the greatest motorcycle racers who ever lived. Results don't always tell the full story of a rider's career and this was never truer than in Steve's case. His career CV lacks only one thing and that is a world championship title, yet few doubt that Steve was easily capable of beating the best in the world on his day as he proved by setting pole position at the Donington Park World Superbike round in 2001 and by lapping the same circuit faster than four-times world champion Valentino Rossi the following year.

So why was he never a world champion? Why did the ultimate accolade escape such a talented rider? It is the last great unanswered question about Steve's life and it seems that everyone has their own opinion on the subject which, when taken together, seem to converge on the same salient points. Hizzy's good friend Jim Moodie offers up his own theory: 'Steve was definitely good enough to have been a world champion. In fact, I'd say that he was the most talented rider never to have been a world champion. There's a lot of people who have been world champions who were never as good as him and there's been a lot of talk about why he never got that break but I don't think it had anything to do with him speaking his mind like most people think – I've always spoken my own mind and it's never done me any harm in getting rides. I think it was more to do with his temperament; he was either in the mood to race or he wasn't and I could tell straight away, either on the phone or in person, if he was in the mood to win. If he was all animated and talking at 100 miles an hour then I knew he was going to win because when he was excited and wound up like that he was practically unbeatable. During qualifying for the 2001 World Superbike round at Donington I told Niall Mackenzie (who was commentating on the event) that Hizzy was going to get pole after talking to him and sure enough he did. But if he was down in the mouth and not saying much I knew he wasn't going to be anywhere.'

As a multiple Isle of Man TT winner himself, Moodie also knows what it takes to win round the most demanding racetrack in the world and he is still in awe as he remembers Hislop's ability round that track. 'Steve was the most awesome racer I ever saw round the TT course – bar none. He just had the complete package of track knowledge, smoothness and speed. It was incredible to watch him round there.'

Hizzy's fierce rival from his British Superbike days, John Reynolds, was equally in awe of Steve's ability at the TT having witnessed it at close quarters. 'I remember racing in my only ever TT in 1989. I entered Barregarrow which is a very fast downhill section where the bike's suspension bottoms out and as far as I was concerned I was going flat out until Stevie came past me like I was standing still. Sparks flew off his bike as the suspension bottomed out and he shot off into the distance towards Kirkmichael with the bike shaking its head all over the place. I thought there and then that if that's what you have to do to win a TT then it's not for me.'

Rob McElnea may have been forced to let Hizzy go from his Virgin Yamaha team in 2003 but few people recognized Steve's talents as acutely as he did. 'I first worked closely with Steve in 1998 when I managed him and Niall Mackenzie in the Cadbury's Boost Yamaha team and it was obvious that his talent then was just so untapped and wasted. He was already 37 years old and pretty much not going to go anywhere else other than the British championship and I could see that was such a great shame. I got lucky enough to race in Grands Prix as did Niall Mackenzie, and Carl Fogarty went World Superbike racing and won four world titles but Hizzy was probably better than all of us; he was definitely better than I was. He was a natural rider and if he'd had the opportunities that Niall, Carl and I had I think it would have been a different case.'

'The guy was totally, 100 per cent committed once he knew where he stood with the bike and the track and the settings. If things were right he rode on pure confidence and could ride perfect laps time after time, way more than the rest of us could ever do. Most riders manage one or two near-perfect laps during a race weekend but Steve could churn them out all day long when he wanted to. He was focused to the point of being mad.'

'There's no question that Steve could have gone a lot further than he did. He certainly had the riding ability but unfortunately it's not just about that. To be a world champion you've got to take the knocks and still be able to perform; you've got to say the right things and do every part of the job that's expected of you. Steve hated all that corporate stuff – he only wanted to ride the bike but you just can't do that any more. Maybe 20 years ago he could have gotten away with it but not now. It's a shame because I really believe he could have been a world champion.'

Michael Rutter, another of Steve's former BSB rivals shares the same sentiment. 'He was the fastest bloke in the world. On his day no one could beat him. Anyone will tell you that; the bloke was so fast, so bang-on line, he just didn't put a foot wrong.'

And Ian Simpson, who would have been Hizzy's team manager had Steve lived long enough to take on the ETI Ducati ride, is yet another believer that Hislop's career potential was never quite fulfilled. As an old friend, he also respected Hizzy's down-to-earth approach to life. 'I knew Steve when he was still working as a mechanic and I was a van driver. He later became a superstar in everyone else's eyes but never in his own. He was one of the best in the world on his day – nobody could touch him. He was absolutely something special. The only reason he never got a chance at world level is that he was just too temperamental. One day he'd be half a lap in front of everybody else and the next weekend he'd be nowhere. I don't know why that was and I don't even think Steve knew why that was. I suppose it's just human nature – nobody's perfect.'

'In my opinion Steve was the best racer ever round the TT without doubt. Nobody could touch him round there and, having thought about it, I think I know why now. Basically, he could go to any short circuit race and within five minutes of the first session he'd be about five seconds quicker than anyone else. Other riders had to work up to speed but Steve's ability to ride a bike fast round those first few corners without any warm-up time was amazing and that worked so well on the pure road circuits like the Isle of Man. At the TT you don't get many practice laps so you're just riding the course as you see it and Steve could do that better than anyone else. He had an uncanny ability to judge racing lines, weather conditions, what the bike was capable of and just to judge how fast he could go under any given circumstances.'

'But that had its downsides too as far as concentration went. Steve would always be fast in Friday practice but by Saturday or Sunday it was almost like he was bored. If you do 150 laps a day of a circuit over two or three days it's easy to see how some people would get bored; again it's just human nature. I think sometimes you can do too much racing and while some riders never seem to suffer from that I think Steve did. It's like any job though; if you do it too much you get sick of it.'

'But that's of no importance now. All that matters is that two young boys have lost their dad and a mother has lost her son. Anyone who knew Steve even a little bit knows what a big softy he was and how much he loved his kids. His death was a real tragedy.'

A corporate hat may never have sat comfortably upon Steve Hislop's head but he would have made a great mentor for younger racers, such was his eagerness to help them avoid the pitfalls that he was all too aware he'd fallen into himself. Almost every rider in the BSB paddock will testify to having been helped by Hizzy at some stage. Shane Byrne, the man who succeeded Steve as BSB champion in 2003 is just one of them. He told TV's *Men & Motors* programme: 'When

I first moved onto a Superbike in 1999 Steve was so helpful to me. He used to make a point of coming over to see how I was getting on because he was on the same bike as me so he'd run through what gearing he was using and suggest different tyres to try. He was just an absolutely spot-on bloke and I always said I'd love to have him as a team-mate and I believe he said the same sort of thing about me.'

Hizzy's titanic battle with his team-mate and fellow Scotsman Niall Mackenzie in 1998 provided one of the most intense and thrilling BSB seasons ever witnessed. The pair fought out a war of words in the press and a war of attrition on the racetrack but all differences were immediately forgotten when Mackenzie heard the dreadful news of Steve's death. 'When Steve died it completely changed the way I thought about him. He irritated me at racetracks but with hindsight I realize it was only because he was pushing me so hard on the track and I didn't like that because I was so used to winning. I just wish he was here to irritate me now. The saddest thing is that Steve never realized how much respect other riders had for him. Everyone looked up to him as a rider but he just wasn't aware of it. He definitely had enough pace and talent to win a world championship but unfortunately that didn't happen.'

There can be no greater accolade than the respect of your peers and it is clear that Hizzy had the full respect and admiration of every last one of his racing colleagues even if, as Mackenzie suggests, Steve himself never quite realized it. But he would have been even more stunned to hear of the illustrious company with which he was posthumously compared to.

Whilst celebrating the life and achievements of Steve Hislop at his funeral, the Reverend Neil R Combe compared Hizzy with two of Scotland's greatest heroes – Robert the Bruce and William Wallace. Highbrow historians may have frowned at the comparison with a modern motorcycle racer but anyone who ever had the privilege to know Steve or to watch him race would not disagree with Combe's sentiment. Motorcycle racing may only be a sport rather than a matter of national importance but the qualities needed to compete at Steve's level were the same as those required by the heroes of antiquity; intelligence, fearlessness, skill and courage.

Many times Steve came back from horrific injuries to continue the fight against his rivals; he simply refused to lie down, roll over or give up. Muscling a fearsome 190mph motorcycle around the TT course takes as much courage as facing any enemy in battle and Steve repeatedly proved that he was better than any opponent in the world at his chosen, and dangerous, profession. His natural skill on a bike combined with his lightning fast reactions and keen intelligence made him a fearsome opponent on any track and on any machine. He may have been accused of surrendering on occasion but it is only wise men who know when a battle cannot be won. If there was ever a fighting chance of victory, then Steve fought like a man possessed, with a passion and determination which will never be known or experienced by most of us.

In motorcycle racing as in battle, the risks are high and lives are inevitably lost. Steve's skill on a motorcycle ensured he never became another racing casualty. Instead he was taken from us in a tragic accident during a leisurely pleasure trip. After spending years cheating death at frightening speeds on some of the most powerful racing motorcycles in the world, the manner of his death was the greatest of ironies.

But it has been said that as long as a person lives on in the memories of others then he will never truly die. There can be no doubt that countless thousands will pass on tales of Steve Hislop's achievements to new generations ensuring that his life's work and his character will be remembered forever. Whatever the opinion of crusty academics, Hizzy rightfully deserved to be compared to two of Scotland's greatest ever warriors. He was a true Scottish hero.

From his friend and mentor, Wullie Simpson, Steve picked up the phrase 'We're all going to die if we live long enough.' It may sound morbid but it is a stark truth and Steve had a realistic enough grasp on life not only to live by the expression but to read into the humour and irony of it. He fully accepted the risks of his chosen profession and refused to be intimidated by them even when motorcycle racing claimed the life of his younger brother Garry. Likewise, Hizzy accepted the risks involved in flying helicopters and was never happier than when he was at the controls of an aircraft. 'It's like riding a motorcycle in the sky' he once said, beaming at the thought of it even when he was standing on terra firma.

It is true that everybody dies but it is equally true that not everyone really lives. In his own words, Robert Steven Hislop packed more into his 41 years than most people would in two lifetimes so no one should grieve for a life that was wasted. Hizzy lived in the fast lane from a very early age, not just when he was racing a motorcycle at phenomenal speeds but in every aspect of his life. He enjoyed countless triumphs and endured incredible heartache in almost equal measures and always with the greatest dignity – a trait he must have learned from his mother Margaret.

Steve's parting quote for the first edition of this book was 'You ain't seen nothing yet' and it's a quote which has become strangely prophetic. If there is life after death, we can all rest assured that Steve Hislop will be living it to the full – just as he always did.

Career Results

1979

Venue/Race	Class	Place
Croft	125cc	21st, DNF
Ouston	125cc	11th

1980

Croft	125cc	18th
Beveridge Park	125cc	6th
Croft	125cc	13th, 12th
Mallory Park	125cc	9th
East Fortune	125cc	2nd
Knockhill	125cc	5th, 3rd, 4th
Knockhill	125cc	4th
East Fortune	125cc	3rd

1981

Knockhill	125cc	6th, 9th
Knockhill	125cc	10th, 9th
East Fortune	125cc	6th, 11th

1982

Note: Steve did not compete this season.

1983

Venue/Race	Class	Place
Knockhill	125cc	2nd
	350cc	6th
Manx GP (Newcomers)	350cc	2nd
Manx GP (Lightweight)	350cc	11th
East Fortune	125cc	6th

1984

Knockhill	350cc	5th, 5th
Manx GP	Junior	DNF
	Senior	5th

1985

East Fortune	350cc	2nd, 2nd
Isle of Man TT	F1	21st
	Classic	18th
	750 Prod	10th
East Fortune	350cc	3rd
Pembrey	250cc	2nd
	350cc	2nd
	1000cc	3rd, 4th, 2nd

1986

Snetterton	350cc	6th, 9th
Thruxton	F2	9th
Mallory Park	F2	9th
Oliver's Mount	350cc	3rd, 3rd, 6th
Isle of Man TT	Junior	9th
	F2	6th
	Prod B	11th

Venue/Race	Class	Place
Ulster GP	F2	3rd
Donington Park	F2	18th, 5th
Oliver's Mount	F2	1st
Donington Park	350cc	DNF
Cadwell Park	350cc	5th
Oulton Park	350cc	DNF
Oliver's Mount	350cc	2nd
	F2	1st
Silverstone	F2	1st
Cadwell Park	F2	1st

TT F2 British championship: 3rd
TT F2 world championship: 5th

1987

Donington Park	350cc	12th
Thruxton	350cc	10th
	F2	5th
Oliver's Mount	350cc	2nd, 1st
Snetterton	F2	10th
North West 200	350cc	1st
Isle of Man TT	F2	1st
	Prod D	5th
Mallory Park	250cc	2nd
Donington Park	250cc	6th
Cadwell Park	250cc	3rd
Knockhill	250cc	3rd
Knockhill	350cc	1st, 12th
Snetterton	250cc	4th
Cadwell Park	250cc	16th
Ulster Grand Prix	350cc	4th

Venue/Race	Class	Place
Cadwell Park	350cc	1st
	F2	2nd
	250cc	8th
Oliver's Mount	350cc	1st
	F2	2nd
	1000cc	8th, 1st
Donington Park	350cc	4th
	F2	2nd
Jurby	350cc	2nd, 4th, 1st, 1st
Brands Hatch	250cc	5th
	F2	4th

Star UK 350cc championship: =7th
Star UK TTF2 championship: 5th
TT F2 world championship: 4th

1988

Brands Hatch	350cc	3rd
Donington Park	350cc	5th
	600 Prod	9th
	750 Prod	10th
	1300 Prod	16th
Thruxton	350cc	2nd, 1st
Snetterton	350cc	1st, 1st
	F2	1st
Brands Hatch	350cc	6th
Mallory Park	350cc	2nd
	1300 Prod	16th
North West 200	750cc	4th
Isle of Man TT	Prod B	1st

Venue/Race	Class	Place
	Prod C	3rd
	Senior	2nd
	Junior	24th
Knockhill	TTF1	4th
	600 Prod	5th
	Superstock	2nd
	Seniorstock	7th
Snetterton	350cc	5th
Snetterton	600 Prod	7th
Snetterton	750cc	2nd, 4th
Mallory Park	TTF1	6th
	350cc	2nd
	750cc	4th
Ulster GP	TTF1	2nd
	750cc	3rd
Cadwell Park	350cc	3rd
	Superstock	6th
Donington Park	F1	7th, 2nd
Knockhill	250cc	2nd
	750cc	1st, 2nd
Thruxton	350cc	6th
Mallory Park	TTF1	5th
	Superstock	1st
	600cc	5th
Donington Park	TTF1	6th
Kirkistown	250cc	6th, 5th
	750cc	2nd
Knockhill	250cc	1st, 1st
	1000cc	3rd, 2nd, 2nd

Venue/Race	Class	Place
Cadwell Park	TTF1	10th
Fuji	F1	10th

TTF1 British championship: 10th
Superstock championship: 3rd

1989

Venue/Race	Class	Place
Jarama	Euro 250	16th
Brands Hatch	250cc	2nd
Donington Park	250cc	1st, 4th
	750cc	11th, 9th
	WSB	DNF, 4th
Zolder	Euro 250	4th
Hungaroring	WSB	19th, DNF
Donington Park	Superbike	5th
	TTF1	4th
North West 200	350cc	5th
	600cc	2nd
	750cc	1st, 1st
Isle of Man TT	F1*	1st
	Senior	1st
Isle of Man TT	600cc	1st
	Prod 750	3rd
Donington	TTF1	5th, 3rd
Assen	TTF1*	11th
Vila Real	TTF1*	1st
Kouvola	TTF1*	2nd
Donington Park	Superbike	4th, 3rd
Ulster GP	TTF1*	1st
	750cc	2nd
Thruxton	Superbike	5th

Venue/Race	Class	Place
	TTF1	7th
Donington Park	Euro 250	19th
	Superbike	3rd
Brands Hatch	250cc	6th
	Superbike	8th
	TTF1	5th
Cadwell Park	250cc	3rd
	TTF1	4th
	750cc	3rd
Donington Park	TTF1	5th
	Superbike	6th, 8th
Mondello Park	250cc	5th, 4th
	750cc	6th
Brands Hatch	250cc	5th
	TTF1	7th
	Superbike	6th
Knockhill	250cc	1st, 2nd
	750cc	3rd, 5th, 3rd
Macau GP	1000cc	3rd

* = TTF1 world championship: 2nd
TTF1 British championship: 7th
TTF1 Supercup championship: 9th
Superbike Supercup championship: 8th

1990

Jerez	E250	2nd
Donington Park	250cc	3rd
Hungaroring	E250	20th
Hockenheim	E250	25th
Snetterton	250cc	2nd

Venue/Race	Class	Place
Isle of Man TT	F1	9th
	Junior	2nd
Isle of Man TT	SS400	6th
Donington Park	250cc	2nd
Cadwell Park	250cc	3rd
Pembrey	250cc	3rd
Knockhill	250cc	1st
Donington Park	750cc	3rd, 4th
Ulster GP	250cc	2nd
	750cc	1st, 16th
Thruxton	250cc	5th
Mallory Park	250cc	5th
Oulton Park	250cc	2nd
	750cc	5th, 2nd
Donington Park	250cc	4th
Lydden	250cc	3rd
	750cc	1st
Knockhill	250cc	1st, 2nd
	1000cc	3rd, 5th, 3rd
Brands Hatch	750cc	14th, 7th
Macau GP	1000cc	2nd, 1st
British 250cc champion		

1991

Daytona	1000cc	10th
Donington Park	E250	2nd
Le Mans	WEC	4th
Jarama	E250	3rd
Rijeka	E250	6th
Salzburgring	E250	6th

Venue/Race	Class	Place
Isle of Man TT	SS400	2nd
	SS600	1st
	F1	1st
	Senior	1st
Cadwell Park	250cc	10th
Spa-Francorchamps	WEC	2nd
Magny-Cours	GP250	25th
Suzuka 8 Hours	WEC	3rd
Donington Park	GP250	DNF
Oulton Park	250cc	4th
Mallory Park	250cc	5th
Bol D'Or	WEC	7th
Kirkistown	250cc	2nd, 5th
Macau GP	1000cc	12th, 9th

World Endurance championship: 5th
European 250cc championship: 4th
British 250cc championship: 10th

1992

Oulton Park	1000cc	9th, 7th
Donington Park	1000cc	6th
Brands Hatch	1000cc	2nd
Shah Alam	1000cc	1st, 2nd
Isle of Man TT	SS600	2nd
	Junior	2nd
	F1	2nd
	Senior	1st
Spa-Francorchamps	WEC	2nd
Johor	WSB	12th, DNF
Shah Alam	1000cc	2nd/DNF

Venue/Race	Class	Place
Johor	1000cc	2nd/DNF
Bol D'Or	WEC	1st
Brands Hatch	1000cc	11th, 6th, 7th, DNF

World Endurance championship: =6th
Malaysian Superbike championship: 3rd

1993

Venue/Race	Class	Place
Brands Hatch	1000cc	2nd
Knockhill	TTSB	5th, 4th
Mallory Park	TTSB	2nd, 2nd
Snetterton	TTSB	2nd, 2nd
Oulton Park	S/CUP	6th, 2nd
Donington Park	TTSB	1st, DNF
Donington Park	S/CUP	3rd, DNF
Brands Hatch	750cc	2nd, 2nd
Snetterton	S/CUP	2nd, 2nd
Donington Park	TTSB	1st, DNF
Cadwell Park	TTSB	7th, 7th
Oulton Park	TTSB	4th, 2nd
Brands Hatch	TTSB	DNF, DNF
Mallory Park	S/CUP	3rd, DNF
Donington Park	WSB	12th
Kirkistown	750cc	1st, 2nd, 2nd
Knockhill	750cc	4th
Brands Hatch	TTSB	3rd, 1st
Venue/Race	Class	Place
Macau GP	750cc	1st, 3rd
Sentul	750cc	1st, 3rd

Supercup Superbike championship: 6th
TT Superbike championship: 3rd

1994

Venue/Race	Class	Place
Donington Park	S/CUP	4th, 5th
Snetterton	S/CUP	2nd, DNF
Isle of Man TT	F1	1st
	Senior	1st
Knockhill	S/CUP	4th, 4th
Donington Park	750cc	2nd
Pembrey	S/CUP	DNF, DNS
Cadwell Park	S/CUP	11th, 3rd
Oulton Park	S/CUP	DNF, 5th
Brands Hatch	S/CUP	6th, DNF
Macau GP	750cc	1st, 3rd

TT Superbike championship: 10th

1995

Mallory Park	750cc	4th, 2nd
Donington Park	BSB	4th, 3rd
Mallory Park	BSB	2nd, 2nd
Oulton Park	BSB	2nd, 1st
Brands Hatch	750cc	2nd, 2nd
Misano	WSB	20th, 15th
Oulton	750cc	3rd, 1st
Snetterton	BSB	4th, 1st
Knockhill	BSB	1st, 2nd
Suzuka	WEC	14th
Brands Hatch	WSB	8th, 9th
Cadwell Park	BSB	1st, 1st
Brands Hatch	BSB	1st, 1st
Assen	WSB	11th, DNF
Bishopscourt	1000cc	1st, 1st, 1st

British Superbike champion
International Shell Oils Trophy: 2nd

1996

Venue/Race	Class	Place
Donington Park	BSB	2nd, DNF
Thruxton	BSB	6th, 6th
Oulton Park	BSB	DNF, 5th
Snetterton	BSB	10th, 9th
Brands Hatch	BSB	DNS, DNS
Knockhill	BSB	3rd, 3rd
Cadwell Park	BSB	3rd, 5th
Mallory Park	BSB	2nd, 3rd
Bol D'Or	WEC	11th
Brands Hatch	BSB	DNF, 7th
Donington Park	BSB	4th, 3rd

BSB championship: 5th

1997

Donington Park	BSB	3rd, DNF
Oulton Park	BSB	DNF, 4th
Snetterton	BSB	13th, DNF
Brands Hatch	BSB	11th, 7th
Thruxton	BSB	12th, 18th
Oulton Park	BSB	DNS, DNS
Mallory Park	BSB	3rd, 2nd
Knockhill	BSB	2nd, 4th
Cadwell Park	BSB	DNF, 12th
Brands Hatch	BSB	8th, 7th
Bol D'Or	WEC	3rd
Donington Park	BSB	8th, DNF

Venue/Race	Class	Place
Bishopscourt	1000cc	1st, 2nd
BSB championship: 9th		

1998

Brands Hatch	BSB	7th, 2nd
Donington Park	WSB	10th, 9th
Oulton Park	BSB	9th, 1st
Thruxton	BSB	3rd, 2nd
Snetterton	BSB	1st, 3rd
Donington Park	BSB	1st, 2nd
Oulton Park	BSB	3rd, 3rd
Brands Hatch	WSB	8th, 11th
Knockhill	BSB	DNF, 2nd
Mallory Park	BSB	6th, 7th
Cadwell Park	BSB	DNS
Silverstone	BSB	DNS
Brands Hatch	BSB	1st, 5th
Donington Park	BSB	11th, DNF
BSB championship: 3rd		

* Steve missed the Cadwell and Silverstone rounds through injury.

1999

Brands Hatch	BSB	8th, 6th
Thruxton	BSB	4th, 4th
Le Mans 24 Hour	WEC	1st
Oulton Park	BSB	7th, 10th
Donington Park	WSB	8th, 9th
Snetterton	BSB	5th, 5th
Donington Park	BSB	DNF, 9th

Venue/Race	Class	Place
Silverstone	BSB	8th, 10th
Spa-Francorchamps	WEC	DNF
Oulton Park	BSB	DNS, DNS
Knockhill	BSB	DNS, DNS
Mallory Park	BSB	DNS, DNS
Cadwell Park	BSB	5th, 4th
Bol D'Or	WEC	7th
Brands Hatch	BSB	4th, 6th
Donington Park	BSB	4th, 5th
Kirkistown	1000cc	1st, 1st, 1st

BSB championship: 9th

* Steve was sacked from his Kawasaki ride mid-season and missed three rounds before signing for Yamaha.

2000

Venue/Race	Class	Place
Brands Hatch	BSB	3rd, 2nd
Donington Park	BSB	DNF, 4th
Thruxton	BSB	5th, 2nd
Donington Park	WSB	12th, DNF
Oulton Park	BSB	5th, 5th
Snetterton	BSB	8th, 10th
Silverstone	BSB	7th, 3rd
Oulton Park	BSB	3rd, 5th
Brands Hatch	WSB	DNF/DNS

BSB championship: 7th

* Steve broke his neck in the Brands Hatch WSB round and missed the rest of the season.

2001

Venue/Race	Class	Place
Donington Park	BSB	2nd, 4th
Silverstone	BSB	2nd, 1st
Snetterton	BSB	2nd, 2nd
Oulton Park	BSB	1st, 1st
Donington Park	WSB	3rd, DNF
Brands Hatch	BSB	1st, 1st
Thruxton	BSB	1st, 6th
Oulton Park	BSB	1st, 1st
Knockhill	BSB	3rd, 2nd
Cadwell Park	BSB	1st, 1st
Brands Hatch	BSB	1st, 2nd
Mallory Park	BSB	3rd, 1st
Rockingham	BSB	DNF, DNS
Donington Park	BSB	DNS, DNS

BSB championship: 2nd

2002

Silverstone	BSB	2nd, 1st
Brands Hatch	BSB	1st, 1st
Donington Park	BSB	3rd, 6th
Oulton Park	BSB	1st, 2nd
Snetterton	BSB	4th, 2nd
Brands Hatch	BSB	12th, 2nd
Rockingham	BSB	2nd, 4th
Knockhill	BSB	1st, 7th
Thruxton	BSB	2nd, 2nd
Cadwell Park	BSB	1st, 1st
Oulton Park	BSB	1st, DNF

Venue/Race	Class	Place
Mallory Park	BSB	6th, 5th
Donington Park	BSB	3rd, 2nd
British Superbike champion		

2003

Silverstone	BSB	8th, 5th
Snetterton	BSB	DNF, DNF
Thruxton	BSB	2nd, 5th
Oulton Park	BSB	3rd, 5th
Knockhill	BSB	13th, 5th
Brands Hatch	BSB	5th, 7th
Rockingham	BSB	10th, 11th

* Rockingham was Steve's last race. He was lying 8th in the British Superbike championship at the time of his fatal helicopter crash.

KEY TO ABBREVIATIONS

BSB = British Superbike championship
WSB = World Superbike championship
WEC = World Endurance championship
GP = Grand Prix
TTSB = TT Superbike championship
TTF1 = TT Formula 1
F1 = Formula 1
F2 = Formula 2
Prod = Production Class
SS = Super Sport
S/CUP = Supercup 750cc British championship

E250 = European 250cc championship
DNS = Did not start
DNF = Did not finish

Index